SLOW T

D0864551

Northun

Local, characterful guides to Britain's special places

Gemma Hall

EDITION 1
Bradt Travel Guides Ltd, UK
The Globe Pequot Press Inc, USA

Bradt

Northumberland

Northumberland is where holiday makers come to get away from it all. Enjoy wide, empty beaches framed by medieval castles, heather moors, Roman ruins and wildlife islands.

1 Take a gentle riverside walk to Thrum Mill. 2 The silky sands of Druridge Bay. 3 Black grouse, merlin and otters can be spotted in the North Pennines AONB. 4 You'll find a variety of off-road cycling trails around Kielder Water. 5 Blanchland's 18th-century sandstone houses.

H ATHEY/S

VK

MARTIN ROGERS/NP

GEMMA HALL

DAVE HEAD/S

IN SEARCH OF SOLITUDE

Northumberland National Park is sparsely populated and offers walkers miles of lonesome walks in the Cheviot Hills and North Pennines.

GEMMA HALL

JASON FRIEND PHOTOGRAPHY LTD/A

ALSTON
—TO—
HEXHAM MILES 23
PENRITH 19
BRAMPTON 20
MIDDLETON 22
STANHOPE

VK

1 If you look closely, you'll spot prehistoric cup and ring rock art on many stones in the Simonside Hills. 2 View of the South Tyne River from Lambley Viaduct. 3 Cycle across hills and moors and hours of solitude will await you. 4 Kielder Water and its surrounding heather moorland. 5 Winshield Crags on the Hadrian's Wall Path. 6 Northumberland is the last stronghold for the native red squirrel. 7 Take a dip in Harthope's icy plungepool in the Cheviot Hills.

IAN FOSTER/HBDT

GEMMA HALL

RICK THORNTON/VK

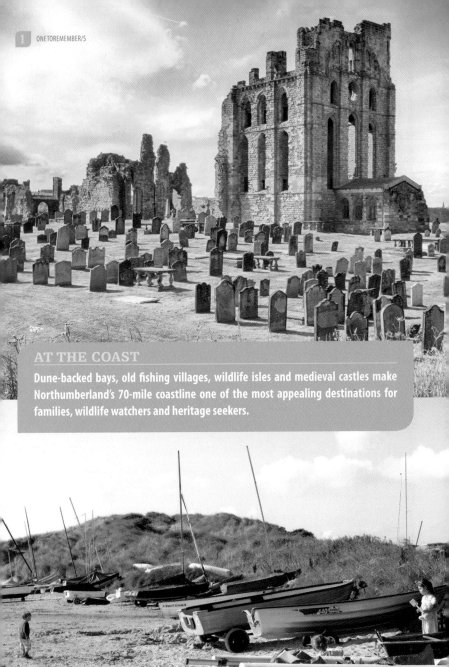

AT THE COAST

Dune-backed bays, old fishing villages, wildlife isles and medieval castles make Northumberland's 70-mile coastline one of the most appealing destinations for families, wildlife watchers and heritage seekers.

CHRIS MATTISON/A

1 The towering ruins of Tynemouth Priory. 2 Playing among the boats on Newton Haven beach. 3 Craster's harbour is a popular stopping point for walkers on the Coast Path. 4 Traditional fishing cobles are seen in a number of coastal villages. 5 The busy working port in the fishing town of Seahouses. 6 The local term for a curlew is a 'whaup'. 7 Alnmouth is one of the most distinctive places on the Northumberland coast.

GEMMA HALL
DENNIS JACOBSEN/S
GEMMA HALL
GAIL JOHNSON/S

GEMMA HALL

NEWCASTLE & GATESHEAD

Newcastle's Georgian architecture and Gateshead's nationally renowned arts scene make Tyneside an obvious stopping point for visitors heading into Northumberland.

1 Old meets new at Newcastle's quayside. 2 The interior of Newcastle's Central Arcade dates back to the early 1900s. 3 *The Angel of the North* is an icon of the North East.

GEMMA HALL

VIKTOR KOVALENKO/S

AUTHOR

Gemma Hall (⊘ www.gemmahall.co.uk) is a freelance travel, nature and outdoors writer from the North East who began her career in journalism writing for *BBC Wildlife* magazine. She also works for many other outdoor and heritage titles and, alongside writing and her professional photography work, she co-ordinates conservation projects in the UK and abroad. Her family live in Newcastle and Northumberland and she has extensively explored the coast and hills on many sailing, cycling, birdwatching and camping trips. A keen walker, she's hiked many long-distance trails including Hadrian's Wall Path, St Cuthbert's Way and the Northumberland coast path. Gemma has worked for the National Trust, the Royal Society for the Protection of Birds (RSPB), Trust for Conservation Volunteers (TCV) and is a Fellow of the Royal Geographical Society.

AUTHOR'S STORY

'I like it cold' wrote W H Auden, the 'Pennine Poet'. His words strike a chord with me, having grown up in Newcastle and having studied at the universities of Edinburgh and Lund, Sweden. Sunny, cool and wild – that's my kind of place. Northumberland is often all of those things.

In revisiting old haunts as well as places I knew less well for this update, I often reported home that I'd walked for half a day in the Cheviot Hills, over a Pennine Moor or along one of my favourite remote beaches (Ross Back Sands, for example) and only encountered the odd person and occasionally no-one at all. There really are few places in England where you can wander alone in the countryside like this and it's undoubtedly one of the county's greatest draws.

Northumberland is wild in another sense, too, and I'm also fascinated by those buildings that evoke the rough, lawless centuries during invasions from the north and at the height of clan warfare in the 16th and early 17th centuries: the shattered bastle houses of Redesdale, fortified manor houses in the Tyne Valley, and Northumberland's medieval castles. The buildings that deeply affect me, though, are the uniform rows of Victorian red-brick terraces you see across Tyneside and in a number of Northumbrian towns and villages. When the East Coast Main Line train nears Newcastle and before the Tyne Bridge comes into view, they are the first buildings that tell me I'm home.

Reprinted February 2016
First edition published March 2015
Bradt Travel Guides Ltd
IDC House, The Vale, Chalfont St Peter, Bucks SL9 9RZ, England
www.bradtguides.com
Print edition published in the USA by The Globe Pequot Press Inc,
PO Box 480, Guilford, Connecticut 06437-0480

Text copyright © 2015 Gemma Hall
Maps copyright © 2015 Bradt Travel Guides Ltd includes map data © OpenStreetMap
contributors
Photographs copyright © 2015 Individual photographers (see below)
Project Managers: Anna Moores & Katie Wilding
Series design: Pepi Bluck, Perfect Picture
Cover research: Pepi Bluck, Perfect Picture

The author and publisher have made every effort to ensure the accuracy of the information
in this book at the time of going to press. However, they cannot accept any responsibility
for any loss, injury or inconvenience resulting from the use of information contained in this
guide. All rights reserved. No part of this publication may be reproduced, stored in a retrieval
system, or transmitted in any form or by any means, electronic, mechanical, photocopying,
recording or otherwise without the prior consent of the publisher. Requests for permission
should be addressed to Bradt Travel Guides Ltd in the UK (print and digital editions), or to The
Globe Pequot Press Inc in North and South America (print edition only).

ISBN: 978 1 84162 866 0
e-ISBN: 978 1 78477 121 8 (e-pub)
e-ISBN: 978 1 78477 221 5 (mobi)

British Library Cataloguing in Publication Data
A catalogue record for this book is available from the British Library

Photographs
© individual photographers credited beside images & also those from image libraries
credited as follows: Alamy.com (A), Berwick Food Festival (BFF), Dreamstime.com (D),
English Heritage (EH), Haydon Bridge Development Trust (HBDT), Hay Farm Heavy Horse
Centre (HFHHC), Northern Experience Images/www.northernexperienceimages.co.uk (NEI),
North Pennines AONB (NP), RSPB, Shutterstock.com (S), SuperStock.com (SS), Visit Britain
(VB), Visit Kielder (VK), Visit Northumberland (VN)

Front cover Bamburgh Castle (Henk Meijer/A)
Title page Puffins on Coquet Island (Paul Morrison/RSPB)
Back cover Hadrian's Wall (Joe Cornish/VB)

Maps David McCutcheon FBCart.S and Liezel Bohdanowicz

Typeset from the author's disc by Pepi Bluck
Production managed by Jellyfish Print Solutions; printed in the UK
Digital conversion by www.dataworks.co.in

ACKNOWLEDGEMENTS

The predecessor to this book would never have happened if I hadn't got chatting to Rachel Fielding from Bradt at a travel show. For her enthusiasm for a guide to Northumberland and commissioning me to write the first edition and update this one, I am very thankful. The team at Bradt did a superb job of pulling this guide together but particular gratitude must be paid to sharp-eyed Katie Wilding and the ever-upbeat, patient and unflappable Anna Moores.

Many people provided insight on Northumberland's heritage and its natural history which I must acknowledge. They include Katrina Porteous, Geoff Heslop, Ian Tait and Martin Kitching, experts at English Heritage, the National Trust, and rangers at Northumberland National Park and the North Pennines Area of Outstanding Natural Beauty.

My thanks also to friends and family in the north for all your suggestions, corrections and nuggets of information; to my husband, Owen, for his encouragement; and to sunny Farne for accompanying me on research trips and not complaining too much.

DEDICATION

This book is dedicated to my Dad for instilling a love for the outdoors, tolerance for bad weather and not letting me perish (only just!) in the North Sea as a child. And to the ever-supportive Mezza – this second edition is definitely for you.

FEEDBACK REQUEST & UPDATES WEBSITE

At Bradt Travel Guides we're aware that guidebooks start to go out of date on the day they're published – and that you, our readers, are out there in the field doing research of your own. You'll find out before us when a fine new family-run hotel opens or a favourite restaurant changes hands and goes downhill. So why not write and tell us about your experiences? Contact us on ☏ 01753 893444 or ✉ info@bradtguides.com. We will forward emails to the author who may post updates on the Bradt website at ⬥ www.bradtupdates.com/northumberland. Alternatively, you can add a review of the book to ⬥ www.bradtguides.com or Amazon.

SUGGESTED PLACES TO BASE YOURSELF

These places make ideal starting points for exploring localities the Slow way.

NORTH SEA

NORTHUMBERLAND COAST AONB

SCOTLAND

BAMBURGH pages 81–5
Village on the Heritage Coast with a magnificent castle and long sweep of sand. Nearby are Lindisfarne and the Farne Islands.

SEAHOUSES pages 77–9
Touristy fishing village and departure point for trips to the Farne Islands; popular with families.

ALNWICK pages 51–60
Medieval castle and renowned gardens in a prosperous market town between the coast and national park.

WOOLER pages 233–4
Market town and popular gateway to the Cheviot Hills.

ROTHBURY pages 239–43
Handsome town in the national park and excellent base for trips into the Cheviot Hills and Coquetdale.

CHAPTER 2 page 38

CHAPTER 6 page 210

FARNE ISLANDS

LINDISFARNE (HOLY ISLAND)

Berwick-upon-Tweed

Tweed

Wooler

CHEVIOT HILLS

COLLEGE VALLEY

HARTHOPE VALLEY

BREAMISH VALLEY

Ingram

Alwinton

COQUETDALE

Bamburgh

Seahouses

Craster

Alnwick

Alnmouth

Warkworth

Rothbury

A1

B6341

A697

A68

N

0   5 miles

0   10 km

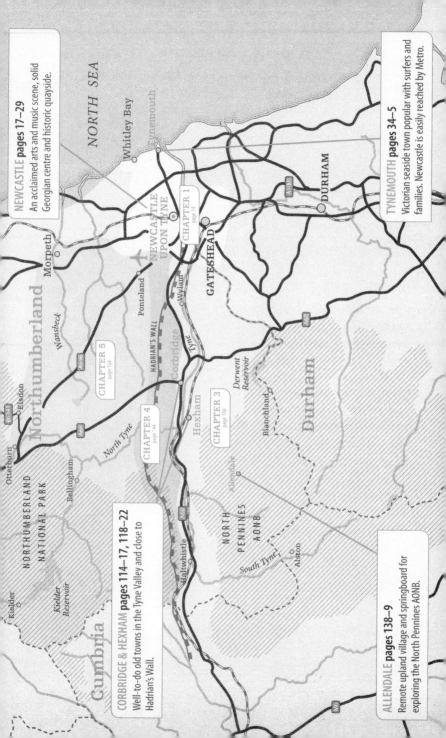

NORTH SEA

NEWCASTLE pages 17–29
An acclaimed arts and music scene, solid Georgian centre and historic quayside.

TYNEMOUTH pages 34–5
Victorian seaside town popular with surfers and families. Newcastle is easily reached by Metro.

CORBRIDGE & HEXHAM pages 114–17, 118–22
Well-to-do old towns in the Tyne Valley and close to Hadrian's Wall.

ALLENDALE pages 138–9
Remote upland village and springboard for exploring the North Pennines AONB.

Whitley Bay

Tynemouth

NEWCASTLE UPON TYNE

GATESHEAD

CHAPTER 1
page 14

DURHAM

A1(M)

A68

Morpeth

Ponteland

Wylam

Corbridge

Tyne

Hexham

CHAPTER 3
page 100

Derwent Reservoir

Blanchland

Durham

Northumberland

Wansbeck

A696

HADRIAN'S WALL

CHAPTER 5
page 164

North Tyne

A68

Elsdon

B6341

Otterburn

Bellingham

CHAPTER 4
page 144

Allendale

NORTH PENNINES AONB

A686

South Tyne

Alston

Haltwhistle

A69

NORTHUMBERLAND NATIONAL PARK

Kielder

Kielder Reservoir

Cumbria

CONTENTS

NORTHUMBERLAND ONLINE

For additional online content, photos, accommodation reviews and more on Northumberland,
visit ⌖ www.bradtguides.com/northumberland.

NORTHUMBERLAND

A comprehensive and independent guide to Northumberland seemed to be missing on the travel shelves of bookshops labelled 'North' before the first edition of this book was published in 2012. I hope this fully updated guide continues to fill that gap and offer something a little different in its approach. It's far-reaching in its scope: from the Tyne to the Tweed and encompassing Newcastle and its hinterlands; the bays, islands and fortresses along the coast; Hadrian's Wall; the Cheviot Hills and the North Pennine fringes. There's a strong leaning towards places with heritage appeal, adventures on foot and by bicycle, the lesser-known and the outdoors.

But what about that word 'Slow'? It's a deliberate nod to the Slow Food and Slow Tourism movements and you'll find this book embraces a similar ethos in its celebration of local distinctiveness, vernacular architecture, regional flavours and simple pleasures. It encourages visitors to seek out the unobvious, explore footpaths, railway trails, byways and B-roads – and linger awhile.

I spent a year researching and writing the first edition of this guide and another six months updating it, which involved revisiting my favourite spots and picking through the hills and coastline in search of the hidden and unsung corners of Northumberland. Friends, relatives and contacts provided tips and suggestions, but many of the curious and more unusual places peppered in these pages were gleaned by cycling the back roads, chatting to locals, driving along unclassified lanes, going for a wander and, most of all, having a nosey around.

Some places may be too obscure, unconventional or out of the way to tempt many visitors, but even if you don't seek them out, I hope you enjoy reading about them. Sometimes it's nice just to know that attractions like the Cement Menagerie in Branxton and Prudhoe's manmade chalk grasslands exist; and to imagine as you read these words that Rapper sword dancers are practising upstairs in Byker's Cumberland Arms, a Northumbrian piper is playing a centuries-old ballad in Morpeth Chantry, and the primeval stone faces depicting the Green Man in Old Bewick's church are gnashing their teeth at worshippers as they have done for hundreds of years.

NORTHUMBERLAND

There are six areas in which Northumberland excels: castles, heather moorland, industrial heritage, Roman architecture, sandy beaches and solitude. I can think of many more (prehistoric rock art, bridges, salmon rivers, railways, upland birds, waterfalls, Georgian architecture and fishing villages) but those are the six that really stand out.

Regarding solitude: a glance at a night sky map of England shows that the northeastern shank of the country is sparsely inhabited and supremely bleak in places. From the Cheviot Hills to the Pennine moors; through England's largest forest and across the empty beaches of Ross Back Sands and Druridge Bay; over the rugged hills of Redesdale and the wild Whin Sill escarpment where the Roman emperor Hadrian built his wall – miles and miles of raw upland and coastal scenery beneath the most star-filled skies you will see anywhere.

Here you can hunker down in the dunes or walk all day through the heather and see only a handful of people; pitch a tent undisturbed on the fells; experience a private viewing of a hen harrier skydancing; take the plunge butt-naked in a Cheviot waterfall; and get up early and see Hadrian's Wall ribboned across the hills without another rambler in sight.

The poet W H Auden, who dearly loved the North East's fells, isolation and climate, wrote in an article for *House and Garden* in 1947: 'the North of England was the Never-Never Land of my dreams . . . the wildly exciting frontier where the alien south ends and the north, my world, begins.' That sense of escape and wildness is undoubtedly the region's greatest appeal.

SAVOURING THE TASTES OF NORTHUMBERLAND

In updating this guide I was struck by how many restaurants, pubs and food stores have got behind the organic and local food revival experienced elsewhere in the country in recent times. Many menus in good restaurants and cafés often state the provenance of ingredients; pubs serving regional ales are now too numerous to list; and I found plenty of B&B and hotel owners taking pride in serving local foods such as kippers from Craster (so much so that I almost stopped remarking on this in my reviews). Northumberland boasts many of the best salmon and trout rivers in England, extensive game moors and working fishing communities, so it makes sense.

For those self-catering, you'll find thriving farmers' markets in most large towns, excellent fishmongers and/or smokeries at North Shields Fish Quay, Craster and Seahouses, and farm shops like Vallum and Blagdon near Ponteland.

THE SLOW MINDSET

Hilary Bradt, Founder, Bradt Travel Guides

We shall not cease from exploration
And the end of all our exploring
Will be to arrive where we started
And know the place for the first time.

T S Eliot, 'Little Gidding', *Four Quartets*

This series evolved, slowly, from a Bradt editorial meeting when we started to explore ideas for guides to our favourite country – Great Britain. We wanted to get away from the usual 'top sights' formula and encourage our authors to bring out the nuances and local differences that make up a sense of place – such things as food, building styles, nature, geology, or local people and what makes them tick. Our aim was to create a series that celebrates the present, focusing on sustainable tourism, rather than taking a nostalgic wallow in the past.

So without our realising it at the time, we had defined 'Slow Travel', or at least our concept of it. For the beauty of the Slow movement is that there is no fixed definition; we adapt the philosophy to fit our individual needs and aspirations. Thus Carl Honoré, author of *In Praise of Slow*, writes: 'The Slow Movement is a cultural revolution against the notion that faster is always better. It's not about doing everything at a snail's pace, it's about seeking to do everything at the right speed. Savouring the hours and minutes rather than just counting them. Doing everything as well as possible, instead of as fast as possible. It's about quality over quantity in everything from work to food to parenting.' And travel.

So take time to explore. Don't rush it, get to know an area – and the people who live there – and you'll be as delighted as the authors by what you find.

Dishes unique to the North East include sandwiches made with stottie bread (flat, spongy and slightly sweet) that are fairly easy to find in take-away shops and cafés, and, occasionally featuring on bistro menus, pan haggerty (a filling potato and onion side dish) and singin' hinny (a kind of scone that 'sings' as it hits the bubbling butter on a griddle pan).

NORTHERN WARMTH & WIT

Southerners often remark that those in the north – and particularly Geordies – are 'really friendly' and 'have a great sense of humour' (as well as a few less complimentary things). I've always been sceptical of such well-meaning words, partly because I suspect they've never been to the Bigg Market after Newcastle United have just lost to Sunderland, and also because there is a tendency for those in the south to romanticise the north as a back-of-beyond region where uncouth pinched folk in hard towns make humour out of their meagre share of the cake.

Certainly, Geordies like banter, but more so than a Cockney? And whenever I experience an act of kindness – the lady in a South Shields car park the other day who gave me 80p when I asked if she could change a tenner ('diven't be daft, pet,' she said with a wave of her hand when I protested) or the bus driver who got out of his cabin to give a passenger directions on the pavement – I remind myself this could happen anywhere in the country. I suppose the only difference is that it doesn't surprise me in the North East.

But, if there's one example of spontaneous humour that could only have occurred in the North East, it's the time a group of locals celebrating the Magpies reaching the FA Cup Final in 1998 made a replica Newcastle United football shirt large enough to fit the newly erected *Angel of the North*. They got up at dawn to hoist the giant top over the 65-foot sculpture using fishing lines, ropes and catapults, and in doing so they showed that, not only do Geordies worship football and have a fondness of ridiculing anything highbrow, they also love a bit of mischief.

HOW THIS BOOK IS ARRANGED
ACCOMMODATION

On the **accommodation** front, I've been very choosy: this is not a review of all of the best places to stay in the region but a hand-picked selection of some of the special B&Bs, campsites, bunkhouses and small hotels I came across while researching this book. They were selected on the basis of how comfortable and clean they were with a preference for interesting or historic buildings, 'green' credentials and use of local produce. No prices are stated (they change so frequently and often according to availability) so instead I've given an idea of how they compare to others in the area. As a guide, I took £75 for a double room to be about average.

All accommodation is listed at the back of the guide (page 271) and referenced throughout the book under the heading for the area in which they are located, with hotels, B&Bs and self-catering options being indicated by 🏠 and campsites indicated by ⛺. Go to ⬧ www. bradtguides.com/northumberlandsleeps for further details and my reviews of each place listed.

PUBLIC TRANSPORT

An overview of **public transport** options is provided at the beginning of each chapter, but, like the cuts in tourist information facilities, many bus routes are being discontinued so you should check timetables before setting off.

MAPS

The **numbered points** on the map at the beginning of each chapter correspond to the numbered headings in the text. They are mostly larger settlements (not necessarily the most interesting places to visit) with attractions and smaller places nearby listed in the text under their own (unnumbered) headings.

You'll find a 🚶 symbol on these maps to indicate that there is a walk in that area. I've also included sketch maps for these walks where I've found it necessary, but have always suggested which OS map to use for a more detailed look at the route.

FOLLOW BRADT

For the latest news, special offers and competitions, subscribe to the Bradt newsletter via the website ⬧ www.bradtguides.com and follow Bradt on:

🅕 www.facebook.com/BradtTravelGuides   🅣 @BradtGuides

🅘 @bradtguides   🅟 www.pinterest.com/bradtguides

ATTENTION WILDLIFE ENTHUSIASTS

For more on British wildlife, check out Bradt's *52 Wildlife Weekends*. Go to ⬙ www. bradtguides.com and key in 52WW40 at the checkout for your 40% discount.

ACCESSIBILITY

If you see a ♿ symbol, the place listed has step-free access, an entrance wide enough for a wheelchair and, if it's a place to eat, a disabled toilet. Most larger attractions in Northumberland have very good wheelchair access including the likes of The Alnwick Gardens and Kielder Forest and Water. Particular mention should be made of the National Trust for showing how, with a little imagination, historic attractions can be made accessible to those with disabilities and particularly for those who cannot walk. Bravo too to Bellingham's Carriage Tea Room (page 182) with its ingenious narrow wheelchair that allows disabled diners to access a table inside the old train.

OPENING TIMES

Under places, I've listed contact information where it seemed useful and listed non-standard opening times. 'Daily' means Monday to Sunday from around 09.00/10.00 to 16.00/17.00. Opening times change from year to year so it's always best to call and check.

SLOW NORTHUMBERLAND ONLINE

Slow travel is about getting under the skin of a place and making time for the detail of a location, whether historical, descriptive or simply anecdotal. Sadly, the economics of guidebook publishing mean that there are inevitable restrictions on what we can fit in a book. Therefore, we have included additional information online for those who wish to delve further into Northumberland's story. Throughout this guide you will see the following symbol ✋ which signifies that there is more information on a particular subject online.

IMPARTIALITY

Reviews in this guide are totally independent. The accommodation providers, attractions, museums, restaurants and tour companies were selected on the quality of their services, and no business paid to receive a mention in this guide.

NOT-SO-OBVIOUS NORTHUMBERLAND

Here's my Wild Card list of 12 unsung or lesser-known places and attractions in Northumberland, Newcastle and Gateshead, some of which are simply under-visited because they are out of the way or require a map and bit of detective work to find. They are all described (with directions) in this book. In no special order, they are:

1 **Ross Back Sands**: a remote three-mile stretch of beach that's wonderfully empty, even in high summer (pages 85–6).

2 **The Cement Menagerie (Branxton)**: one of the most curious informal museums you will find anywhere. Housed in the back garden of an ordinary house in a hilltop village are full-sized concrete animals and figures (page 264).

3 **Literary & Philosophical Society (Newcastle)**: library open to the public with much historic appeal and just a short stroll from Central Station (page 25).

4 **Preston Tower**: Northumberland's Wild West past is revealed inside this superbly preserved pele tower a few miles inland from Seahouses (pages 74–5).

5 **Lindisfarne's beaches**: better known for its monastic heritage and castle, most visitors never make it to the north of the island which is fringed by a string of pristine and gloriously empty beaches (pages 87–93).

6 **Routin Lynn waterfall (Doddington)**: you'll need a map to find this little-known gem of a fall and nearby prehistoric rock art (page 255).

7 **Isaac's Tea Trail**: the least known of all the long-distance footpaths in Northumberland takes in some of the most beautiful river, woodland and moorland scenery in the North Pennines (page 104).

8 **Tarset Valley (Kielder/Redesdale)**: unsung valley with woods inhabited by red squirrels, upland flower meadows and some superbly well-preserved bastle houses (page 176).

9 **The Bagpipe Museum (Morpeth)**: a wonderful little museum where visitors are sometimes treated to the soft notes of the Northumbrian pipes (pages 195–6).

10 **Dunston Staiths (Gateshead quayside)**: the largest timber structure in the UK and a striking reminder of the coal industry that fuelled the growth of Tyneside in the 19th century (pages 30–1).

11 **Football Hole (Newton-by-the-Sea)**: a small, seldom visited sandy bay just over the dunes from some of Northumberland's better-known beaches (page 73).

12 **Blyth's lighthouse**: curious for its location in the back lane of a residential street (page 44).

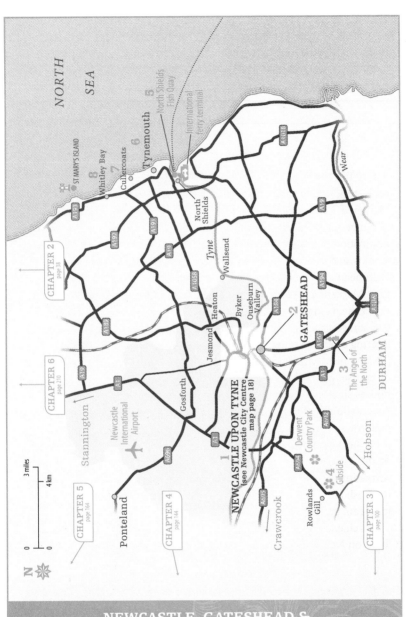

N

3 miles
0
4 km
0

NORTH

SEA

CHAPTER 2
page 38

CHAPTER 6
page 210

CHAPTER 5
page 164

CHAPTER 4
page 144

CHAPTER 3
page 100

ST MARY'S ISLAND

Whitley Bay   8

Cullercoats   7

Tynemouth   6

North Shields Fish Quay   5

International ferry terminal

North Shields

Wallsend

Tyne

Byker

Heaton

Ouseburn Valley

Jesmond

Gosforth

Newcastle International Airport

Stannington

Ponteland

Crawcrook

Rowlands Gill

Gibside   4

Derwent Country Park

Hobson

GATESHEAD   2

The Angel of the North   3

DURHAM

Wear

NEWCASTLE UPON TYNE
(see Newcastle City Centre map page 18)   1

A193

A191

A191

A19

A189

A19

A696

A1

A1058

A184

A167

A1

A694

A692

A195

A1(M)

A194

A19

A1(M)

NEWCASTLE, GATESHEAD &
THE NORTH TYNESIDE COAST

14

1
NEWCASTLE, GATESHEAD & THE NORTH TYNESIDE COAST

Before the 1990s and *The Angel of the North*, **Tyneside** was famed for coal, steel, shipbuilding, fanatical football supporters, Newcastle's Bigg Market drinking area and scantily dressed girls. Since the cessation of heavy industry, however, the region has been reinvented as an arts destination. Factories have been demolished or converted into galleries, studios and loft-style apartments; high-profile arts centres now front Gateshead's once rundown waterfront, and the Diamond Strip is the new Bigg Market (that alone tells you almost everything you need to know about the regional economy). Newcastle United football fans though are still some of the most loyal of any club, and revellers have not taken to wearing coats in winter. The last two things are unlikely to change.

Many historic buildings and relics from past centuries remain intact, of course, particularly on the quayside where 300-year-old merchant houses sit alongside modern glass-clad buildings. And in the centre of **Newcastle**, elegant Georgian avenues radiate from Grey's Monument in long rows of some of the finest neo-classical buildings in England.

In the Victorian era, seaside resorts developed around the mouth of the Tyne at places like **Whitley Bay** and **Tynemouth**, providing a recreational space for Tynesiders to escape the city smoke and take in the fresh air. Then, as now, locals enjoy a walk along the promenade, an ice cream on the seafront or a dip in the sea.

This chapter takes in the highlights of a visit to Tyneside with particular focus on Newcastle's city centre and its historic architecture.

GETTING AROUND

The **Metro** system links Newcastle, Gateshead, Sunderland, the north and south Tyneside coasts, Central Station and Newcastle International Airport (25 minutes from Newcastle city centre). In Newcastle, the most useful stop

i TOURIST INFORMATION

Newcastle Gateshead Visitor Information Centre Central Arcade, Newcastle NE1 5BQ (near Monument) ✆ 0191 277 8000 ⌖ www.newcastlegateshead.com ⊙ daily ♿
North Shields Tourist Information Centre Unit 18, Royal Quays Outlet Shopping, Hayhole Rd, North Shields NE29 6DW (near the ferry terminal) ✆ 0191 200 5895 ⊙ daily ♿
Whitley Bay Tourist Information Centre York Rd, Whitley Bay NE26 1AB ✆ 0191 643 5395 ⊙ Mon–Sat ♿

for the city centre is Monument, with Haymarket and Central Station close by. **QuayLink Q1** services Gateshead's quayside from Newcastle Central Station and Gateshead's central bus and Metro terminus. **Q2** shuttles between Newcastle's quayside and the city centre (Monument).

A recommended, cheap taxi company in Newcastle is **Blueline Taxis** (✆ 0191 262 6666).

An open-top city **sightseeing bus** (✆ 0191 228 8900 ⌖ www.city-sightseeing.com ⊙ early Apr–end Oct, daily, & weekends in autumn) operates a few times a day. Tickets allow you to hop on and off over a 24-hour period. Download a timetable from the website which also includes a list of stops.

WALKING & CYCLING

Newcastle city centre is compact and is best explored on foot (there are few cycle paths and you can't ride along the main pedestrian shopping streets). Alongside the **river** and **seafront** are long promenades, perfect for strollers (and cyclists).

Heading upriver on **Hadrian's Cycleway** from **Newcastle to Wylam** the landscape becomes increasingly green and makes for a lovely afternoon's ride (page 112).

You can also cycle from **Newcastle to Tynemouth** on an almost completely car-free route by following the **Coast to Coast** ('C2C')

✋ TRAVELLING WITH CHILDREN?

If you're travelling as a family and want suggestions of free things to do in Newcastle and on the coast, find my top tips at ⌖ www.bradtguides.com/newcastlewithchildren.

markers. The **Coast and Castle** long-distance route to Edinburgh is described on page 41.

CYCLE HIRE & REPAIRS

Cullercoats Bike & Kayak 1A Norma Crescent, Whitley Bay NE26 2PD ✆ 0191 251 9412
🖰 www.cullercoatsbikekayak.co.uk
The Cycle Hub Quayside, Newcastle NE6 1BU ✆ 0191 276 7250 🖰 www.thecyclehub.org
⊙ daily ♿ including café.
Edinburgh Bicycle Cooperative 5–7 Union Rd (top of Shields Rd), Byker NE6 1EH ✆ 0191
265 8619
Tyne Cycles 19–20 Rydyerd St, North Shields NE29 6PR ✆ 0191 259 2266

1 NEWCASTLE
For numbered points within Newcastle, see map page 18.

1 GRAINGER TOWN

As for the curve of Grey Street, I shall never forget seeing it to perfection, traffic-less on a misty Sunday morning. Not even Regent Street, even old Regent Street London, can compare with that descending subtle curve.

Poet and architectural historian, John Betjeman speaking at the Literary and Philosophical Society in Newcastle, 1948

Grey's Monument marks the retail centre of Newcastle – and the heart of the city's celebrated Grainger Town where there are more Georgian buildings than anywhere outside London and Bath. The most distinguished 400 yards of beautifully dressed sandstone in Newcastle is found on **Grey Street** – a wide neo-classical boulevard that falls steeply away from Lord Grey's fluted column towards the River Tyne.

Clustered around Monument are the main shopping centres and streets and many of the city's key attractions including the **Theatre Royal** (Grey St ✆ 0191 244 2500 🖰 www.theatreroyal.co.uk ♿), the regional home of the Royal Shakespeare Company, and the restored Art Deco **Tyneside Cinema** (10 Pilgrim St, NE1 6QG ✆ 0845 217 9909 🖰 www.tynesidecinema.co.uk; bar & coffee lounges; ♿) which began life as a news theatre in 1937. With an interior dating to the early 1900s is the **Central Arcade** (50 yards downhill from Monument on the right-hand side) – an exquisite Edwardian shopping centre decorated with mosaics and fine Burmantoft's tiles. The **tourist information centre** (page 16) is in the arcade. A short stroll from Monument in the direction of Central Station is the **Grainger Market** – a wonderful Victorian covered market. Those with a keen eye for relics will appreciate stalls including an original **Marks & Spencer's Penny Bazaar**, still with its original 1895 frontage and decorative glass windows.

The **Laing Art Gallery** (New Bridge St, NE1 8AG ✆ 0191 232 7734 ◌ www.twmuseums.org.uk/laing ◷ Tue–Sun (opens on Sun at 14.00) & bank holidays; free admission; café; ♿) is housed near the library. A good number of works by pre-Raphaelite and Impressionist artists hang here as well as a couple of excellent exhibitions showcasing works by 19th-century regional artists, many of which depict local scenes.

¶¶ FOOD & DRINK

Grainger Town is not short of cafés, restaurants and bars; some of the best are detailed below. If you're just after a quick bite to eat and a coffee, try (with your discerning eye) some of the new places in the Grainger Market such as **La Petite Crêperie** (run by two French chaps), and **Pumphrey's** which has been trading since 1750 and sells coffees to takeaway.

Bacchus 42–8 High Bridge, NE1 6BX ✆ 0191 261 1008 ♿. A regular winner of the CAMRA Tyneside Pub of the Year in recent years.

Café Royal 8 Nelson St, NE1 5AW ✆ 0191 231 3000 ♿. All croissants and pastries at this elegant café in the heart of Grainger Town are made in the on-site bakery. Typical lunch menu items include fishcakes, posh burgers and soups. The coffees are consistently strong and well made.

dAt bAr 11 Market St, NE1 6JN ✆ 0191 244 2513 ♿. A huge selection of bottled and cask beers and really good burgers and sourdough pizzas draw in a cool crowd of 30-something pub-goers.

Panis High Bridge, NE1 6BX ✆ 0191 232 4366 ♿. A firm favourite with many locals is this lively, youthful Italian bar and restaurant. Excellent seafood, meat, salad and pasta dishes, all very reasonably priced (a lasagne or ciabatta stuffed with parma ham, mozzarella, tomatoes and rocket (at lunchtime) costs under £4.50).

Tyneside Coffee Rooms 10 Pilgrim St, NE1 6QG ✆ 0845 217 9909. An old favourite with Tynesiders housed on the top floor of a restored Art Deco cinema, where film buffs mingle with students and elderly folk. It's changed very little over the decades and serves delightfully unsophisticated dishes (sandwiches, fishcakes and even good old scrambled egg on toast).

2 HISTORIC QUAYSIDE: THE CLOSE, SANDGATE & SIDE

There is something surprising in the sight of the Tyne, with its busy traffic, its fleet of keels and steam-tugs, coal-ships, and merchant vessels from the north of Europe . . . The banks are for the most part high and steep, rough and bare, or patched with ragged grass; pantiled cottages dot the slopes, or crowd the levels and hollows, and here and there dormer windows appear that look as if imported ready made from Holland.

Victorian view of the quayside from Walter White's *Northumberland, and the Border,* 1859

A wander along Newcastle's medieval roads and alleys reveals the city of past centuries when wealthy merchants lived by the Tyne and the riverside was a wall of masts and rigging.

Overshadowed by the towering legs of the High Level Bridge and screened by Customs House and the Guildhall are some of the oldest buildings on Tyneside, dating from the 16th to 18th centuries when the city was rapidly expanding and this was the commercial centre. The architecture of **Sandgate** and the **Close** evoke days when sailing ships and wherries lined the quayside, merchants occupied the now crooked timber and brick buildings set back from the river, and boatmen called 'keelmen' transported coal along the Tyne to waiting ships.

"The most striking of all the merchant houses and warehouses is the wide Tudor-looking building on the corner of the Side, Bessie Surtees's House."

One of the oldest buildings on the Close is the mid 16th-century timber-framed **Cooperage** (where barrels were made) beyond the Swing Bridge; but the most striking of all the merchant houses and warehouses is the wide Tudor-looking building on the corner of the Side, **Bessie Surtees's House** (✆ 0191 269 1200 ☉ Mon–Fri; English Heritage). It has an equally impressive Jacobean interior with extensive wood panelling and ornate plasterwork, and is named after a girl who eloped in 1772 with a man who would later become Lord Chancellor. Around the corner on **Side**, the long-established **Side Gallery** (✆ 0191 232 2208 ⊘ www.amber-online.com ☉ Tue–Sun (on Thu until 19.00); free admission) showcases a range of documentary photography and houses a small **independent cinema** (♿) with screenings on Thursday evenings.

Hidden quayside: back streets & alleys

Narrow passageways and streets called '**chares**' (possible Anglo-Saxon origins from 'cerre' meaning a bend or turning) connect the waterfront with the medieval markets near the cathedral and castle. They are full of surprises: the sudden appearance of the medieval town walls, a concealed Georgian church, and an archway through the castle wall. **Hanover Street** – a long lane to the west of the Copthorn Hotel linking the Close with Forth Street – still has its smooth granite tracks on the uphill side of the road from the days when horses pulled carts around these parts.

Dog Leap Steps off the Side, **Long Stairs** next to the Cooperage and **Castle Steps** opposite the Swing Bridge, are still used by pedestrians. The latter passageway climbs steeply to the Castle Keep in 107 steps, passing the crumbling masonry of the castle, a well and continuing under an archway through the old castle wall. Once there were small shops selling old clothes and clogs here.

At the top of **Broad Chare** (next to the Law Courts) and just past a bonded warehouse that is now the **Live Theatre** (✆ 0191 232 1232 ◌ www.live.org.uk; plays, music, comedy & workshops ♿), an archway leads to a medieval courtyard and one of the most fascinating historic buildings on the quayside: **Trinity House** (✆ 0191 232 8226; visits by appointment). It was originally a charitable guild formed by seafarers to support mariners in the city. Highlights inside include a wooden chapel dating to 1505 and an 18th-century Banqueting Hall. On the hill above Broad Chare, reached by climbing **Dog Bank**, is the oval-shaped **All Saints Church** (page 24).

Quayside Market
Between the Tyne Bridge & Millennium Bridge NE1 3DE ☉ Sun

Historical records of a market on the quayside go back to 1736. Today it's held on Sundays and is very busy with families. Pick up original artworks, secondhand books, jewellery, handmade beauty products, artisan breads and chocolates, and locally produced food.

Bridges over the Tyne

Seven bridges link Newcastle with Gateshead. **Gateshead's Millennium Bridge** is the newest (2001), flashiest and one of the greatest contemporary pieces of architecture on Tyneside which tilts to allow boats to pass underneath.

Upriver is the green **Tyne Bridge**, which defines Newcastle more than any other building or structure. At the time of opening in 1928 it was the largest single-span bridge in Britain, and was designed by architects in Middlesbrough (the same company that built the Sydney Harbour Bridge that opened a few years later but was designed prior to the Tyne Bridge).

Joining the quayside promenades either side of the Tyne is the **Swing Bridge** – the eye-catching red and white wrought-iron bridge that pivots on a central point to allow ships to pass (a rare occurrence these days). It's driven by hydraulic engines and was engineered by Victorian industrialist, William Armstrong.

Robert Stephenson's combined road and rail crossing, the **High Level Bridge**, marches across the Tyne at 120 feet above the water. Known as 'Lang Legs' after it opened in 1849, its cream, wrought-iron frame is best appreciated from the pedestrian walkways, which are encased by arches across its entire 450-yard length.

Next is the **Queen Elizabeth II Metro Bridge** (painted brilliant blue), then the **King Edward VII Rail Bridge** and finally the **Redheugh Bridge**, a lofty concrete crossing with a pedestrian footway that is as windswept as standing on the top of the highest hill.

¶¶ FOOD & DRINK

Newcastle's waterfront is not short of bars and places to eat. For Michelin-standard dining, try the five-course tasting menu at the **House of Tides** (28–30 The Close, NE1 3RF ✆ 0191 230 3720 ♿). Not quite in the same league but less expensive is **Café 21** (Trinity Gardens, NE1 2HH ✆ 0191 222 0755 ♿), which has been one of the premier places to dine in Newcastle for some years, and **Six** over the river at the BALTIC Centre for Contemporary Art (page 30).

The Bridge Tavern 7 Akenside Hill, NE1 3UF ✆ 0191 261 9966 ♿. Cool microbrewery with an outside terrace directly under the Tyne Bridge. The food is equally good – lots to fill carnivores (rabbit and leek pie, steak with bone marrow butter and chips, game faggots; all reasonably priced) – and rather special bar snacks (pig's head croquettes, Lindisfarne Oysters).

Broad Chare 25 Broad Chare, NE1 3DQ ✆ 0191 211 2144 ♿. Relaxed pub serving local beers and good British dishes made with some local ingredients like Lindisfarne Oysters.

Crown Posada 31 The Side, NE1 3JE ✆ 0191 232 1269. This wonderful step-back-in-time real ale pub has bags of character with its wood-panelled interior, stained glass and music that's played from a gramophone.

3 MEDIEVAL NEWCASTLE & CHINATOWN

In four things Newcastle excels: walls, gates, towers, and turrets.
William Gray, historian, 1649

Within bowshot of the **Castle Keep** is Newcastle's medieval quarter characterised by winding streets and alleys that lead in one direction to the quayside and in the other to the markets around the cathedral. Cloth Market, Flesh Market, Groat Market and the Bigg Market (bigg was a type of barley) evoke a sense of what this area must have once looked (and smelled) like.

Newcastle gets its name from a 'new' timber castle built in 1080 by the son of William the Conqueror on the site of the old Roman fort, Pons Aelius. The wooden fortress was replaced a century later in stone and it is this later Norman building (well, its keep, mid 13th-century gateway and barbican at least) that still stand to this day. Inside, the Castle Keep (Castle Garth & St Nicholas's St, NE1 1RQ ✆ 0191 232 7938

HA'WAY THE LADS

Strawberry Pl, NE1 4ST ✐ 0844 372 1892 ⌖ www.nufc.co.uk

Geordies, if you haven't noticed, are obsessed with football. For fans not at the St James's Park stadium on a Saturday afternoon, there's no sound quite as joyous as the roar when Newcastle score. It's so loud in fact that as I write this from over two miles away, I can hear the cheers (two goals for Newcastle so far).

At no time are passions stirred more than when the players – known as the 'Magpies' on account of their black and white shirts – are playing Sunderland. Rivalry between the two teams goes back a long time and you'll quite often hear Geordies using the pejorative term 'Mackem' to describe not just Sunderland supporters, but anyone from Wearside. Its origins don't go back that far – perhaps only to the 1980s – and are thought to stem from the dockyards: Sunderland shipbuilders would make the boats and the Geordies would fit them out, hence mack'em and tack'em (make them and take them).

Book tours of St James's Park by calling the number above. Otherwise, for a glimpse of fans in the arena (you can't see the pitch), take the lift to the roof of Eldon Square car park (the concrete spiral car park at the back of Marks & Spencer).

⌖ www.castlekeepnewcastle.org.uk ⊙ Mon–Sat & Sun afternoons) is a labyrinth of stone staircases which leads into many chambers including the Great Hall and up to the roof where you gain a stupendous view of Newcastle's bridges. Downstairs, in a small **museum**, cabinets contain many curious objects discovered during excavations.

By the mid 14th century, Newcastle was enclosed by a stonking **town wall** that formed a protective two-mile loop around its perimeter with towers, gateways and turrets along its length. It was 25 feet high and seven feet thick and was said to 'far passith all the waulls of the cities of England and most of the cities of Europe'. The **West Walls** near Stowell Street in **Chinatown** is the most substantial length of the barricade remaining, with four towers and standing to full height.

Just within the protective boundary of the West Walls is the restored 13th-century **Blackfriars** cloisters (now workshops and a restaurant) on Monk Street. The cloisters' walkway is no longer covered but the building as a whole is worth seeking out and you can still see the outline of where the church once stood.

One of the oldest working Victorian theatres in the world, the **Tyne Theatre** (✐ 0191 243 1171 ⌖ www.millvolvotynetheatre.co.uk);

THREE CHURCHES

All Saints Church (Pilgrim St, NE1 3UF – best reached by climbing the King St stairs from the end of Queen St; open only to worshippers on Sun) is one of Newcastle's great Georgian treasures. A tremendously tall steeple and Grecian-styled portico hide its unusual oval body, a characteristic shared by just a handful of other churches in England.

Compared to many of England's other cathedrals **St Nicholas's** (St Nicholas's St, NE1 1PF ✐ 0191 232 1939) is neither stupendously impressive nor particularly elegant (with the exception of the steeple) mainly because it originated as a 15th-century parish church. However, it bears some curious features including a small square of medieval coloured glass depicting the Virgin Mary breastfeeding Jesus. The tower once contained a navigational lantern that helped guide mariners along the river.

St Andrew's Church near Chinatown (Newgate St, NE1 5SS ✐ 0191 222 0259 ☉ Mon–Fri until 15.00) is clearly very ancient (parts of which were constructed in the 12th century) and even contains a stretch of the old town wall running through the churchyard, and stone slab roofing. Here lies Charles Avison ('England's Mozart') who lived in Newcastle and died in 1770, as well as 15 women executed in 1650 for witchcraft.

stages mainly family shows and comedy as well as music performances by the likes of Rufus Wainwright, Ray Davies and Slade. It faces Westgate Road and houses its original stage machinery which was discovered hidden behind a screen in the 1970s. The sumptuous auditorium dates from 1867.

⟦⟧ FOOD & DRINK

Blackfriars Restaurant Friars St, NE1 4XN ✐ 0191 261 5945. Some of the best hearty, traditional British (and Northumbrian) dishes you will find in Newcastle served in the 13th-century surroundings of a Dominican monastery or outside in the cloister gardens.

Settle Down Café 61–2 Thornton St, NE1 4AW ✐ 0191 222 0187. Artsy (read: a bit shabby) café with mismatched furniture serving wholesome, inexpensive light lunches (soup, sandwiches and good veggie options).

Tea Sutra 1st floor, 2 Leazes Park Rd, NE1 4PF ✐ 07575 010173. What you might call 'alternative' with floor cushions (very 'Zen'), world music and the smell of nourishing homemade soup. Best of all is the tea. If you think different tea varieties should be served in different types of pots, like the sound of a menu offering 100 teas and expect your green tea served exactly at 80°C, then you'll love it here.

4 CENTRAL STATION & AROUND

🏠 **Sleeperz Hotel** (page 271), **Roomzzz** (page 271)

The area around Newcastle's much-admired Victorian station is not somewhere many visitors spend much time but there are a couple of really interesting buildings open to the public, and a great museum.

The **Literary & Philosophical Society** (23 Westgate Rd, NE1 1SE ✆ 0191 232 0192 🖥 www.litandphil.org.uk ⊙ Mon–Thu until 19.00 (on Tue until 20.00), Fri until 17.00 & Sat until 13.00; free admission) library is a little known gem a short stroll from Central Station. Bookshelves extend almost to the dome glass skylights and oak chairs and tables, wooden coat stands and antique clocks evoke a bygone era. Politics and religion were the only topics banned when this society was founded in 1793 as a 'conversation club'. Over the years, many distinguished engineers, historians and writers have lectured here including Joseph Swan on 20 October 1880 during which he demonstrated the electric light making this the first public building to be lit by electricity in the world. The tradition of public lectures continues today (see the society's website for upcoming talks).

Next door to the 'Lit and Phil' is the **Mining Institute** (Westgate Rd, NE1 1SE ✆ 0191 233 2459 🖥 www.mininginstitute.org.uk ⊙ Mon–Fri 10.00–17.00; free admission ♿ possible but phone in advance to arrange), which was founded when mines operated all over the North East in the 19th century. The **Neville Hall Library** has an outstanding interior with tiers of stained-glass windows, a lofty central atrium and superb wood panelling and fittings, and contains journals, geological surveys and books on engineering, geology and mining.

The **Discovery Museum** (Blandford Sq, NE1 4JA ✆ 0191 232 6789 🖥 www.twmuseums.org.uk/discovery ⊙ Mon–Fri 10.00–16.00, Sat–Sun 11.00–16.00; free admission ♿) is one of

"The Discovery Museum is one of the most engaging and well-visited museums on Tyneside."

the most engaging and well-visited museums on Tyneside, devoted mainly to the region's industrial and maritime heritage, and is conveniently found a ten-minute walk from Central Station. Dominating the interior is the 115-foot-long *Turbinia* – the first ship to be powered by steam in the world – which was launched into the Tyne at Wallsend in 1894. Displays are not just related to science, however, and you'll find rooms devoted to various aspects of Newcastle's social and cultural history including

NEWCASTLE, GATESHEAD & THE NORTH TYNESIDE COAST

the excellent Toon Times exhibition showcasing an extensive display of Newcastle United memorabilia. For young children, a water-based installation themed around activities on the River Tyne provides lots of fun (waterproof aprons provided).

¶¶ FOOD & DRINK

Central Station stands close to a clutch of pubs and cafés, some of the best of which are squeezed into **Pink Lane** opposite the station entrance. They include **The Forth** (✆ 0191 232 6478), a popular pub and restaurant (more the latter these days) and the **Jazz Café** (✆ 0191 222 9882 ♿) which has been a venue for live jazz for years (if you're local and haven't visited for a while, you'll find it's had a refurb since the old chap with the beard died a few years ago, and the food is much improved). For a caffeine kick, head straight to **Pink Lane Coffee**, a little retro café in the street's elbow. The **Centurion Bar** (✆ 0191 261 6611 ♿) within Central Station has a couple of real ales and serves average coffees, breakfasts and lunches but the real reason you should come here is for the interior which is every bit as sumptuous as you'd hope of a Victorian first-class passenger lounge.

For a lively food, drink and music event the **Boiler Shop Steamer food festival** (Robert Stephenson Centre, Sussex St, NE1 3PD – round the back of Central Station ⊘ www.theboilershopsteamer.com) is held on the first Friday and Saturday of every month in the cavernous 19th-century factory where Robert Stephenson's *Rocket* railway engine was created.

5 HAYMARKET, THE CIVIC CENTRE & THE UNIVERSITIES

🏠 **Jesmond Dene House** (page 272)

Haymarket Metro station at the top of Northumberland Street marks the end of the main shopping area. You have left the classical streets of Grainger Town and are now in a more modern space by the Civic Centre and Newcastle and Northumbria universities, albeit one with an imposing Victorian church and a scattering of old buildings.

Both universities have art galleries worth visiting. Exhibitions change regularly at Newcastle's **Hatton Gallery** (✆ 0191 222 6059 ⊘ www.twmuseums.org.uk/hatton ⊙ Mon–Sat ♿ entrance on King's Walk) with contemporary solo artists and university students showcasing their work. Northumbria's long-established **University Gallery** (✆ 0191 227 4424 ⊘ www.northumbria.ac.uk/universitygallery ⊙ Mon–Sat ♿), in the corner of St Mary's Place, puts on contemporary exhibitions (mainly painting, sculpture and photography) by national and international artists.

Northern Stage (✆ 0191 230 5151 ⌖ www.northernstage.co.uk), in the grounds of Newcastle University, is a well-known production theatre. Nearby is the Great North Museum (Barras Bridge, NE2 4PT ✆ 0191 208 6765 ⌖ www.twmuseums.org.uk/greatnorthmuseum ⊙ daily; free admission ♿) housing an impressive collection of stuffed animals, Roman finds and indigenous ceremonial costumes.

Standing between the two universities is the Scandinavian-influenced **Civic Centre** (Barras Bridge (close to Haymarket Metro station), NE1 8QH ✆ 0191 277 7222; tours cost just a few pounds & must be booked in advance), a much under visited and underappreciated modern building. Externally, the most striking feature of the office block, designed in 1950, is the square **tower** crowned with seahorses, but get in closer and you'll find **sculptures** including five steel swans (said to represent the Nordic countries) and an **auditorium** on stilts surrounded by a modern interpretation of a medieval moat.

The fantastically well-preserved interior will make Danish design aficionados weep. The architect is said to have travelled all over Europe sourcing the finest marbles for the corridors, landings and staircases; woods for the ceilings, screens and banisters; and slates for the walls. Upstairs in the **committee rooms**, walls are decorated in red silk and orange leather; the rosewood chairs, tables and sideboards are the work of Danish furniture maker, Arne Vodder. The Council Chamber is superbly unchanged, still with its original 149 green leather chairs.

¶¶ FOOD & DRINK

Flat Caps 13 Ridley Pl, NE1 8JQ ✆ 0191 232 7836. Hidden away in the basement of a shop selling healing crystals is this snug, 'I know a little place . . .' kind of a place. The interior is nothing special but the coffees are (it's run by an award-winning barista).

Quilliam Brothers 1 Eldon Pl, NE1 7RD ✆ 0191 261 4861 ⊙ Mon–Sat 10.00–midnight. A superior teahouse with a student/artsy vibe run by three brothers. Some 60 varieties of teas in caddies line the shelves behind the counter waiting to be sampled with a slice of cake, a stottie sandwich, soup or a full English breakfast.

6 OUSEBURN VALLEY

🏠 **Hotel du Vin** (page 271), **Malmaison** (page 271)

Stepney Bank/Lime St, Quayside East, NE1 2NP ✆ 0191 261 6596 ⌖ www.ouseburntrust.org.uk

A concealed tributary of the River Tyne flows under the giant brick archways of Byker Bridge, a mile east of Newcastle city centre and where there were once lead works, lime kilns, flour mills, iron foundries, glassworks and potteries at different times over the last 500 years. It remained a ramshackle sort of a place with garages, a boat maker's factory and scrap yards until the late 1990s. One by one these have been converted into cultural venues, recording studios and artist workshops, and the whole area named the Ouseburn Valley. Despite gentrification, the Ouseburn remains a laid-back, unpretentious place that is still agreeably scruffy round the edges. Regulars like it that way.

On sunny weekends, young and old lounge outside on the 'village' green between the Cluny pub and the delightfully higgledy-piggledy **city farm** (Ouseburn Rd, off Lime St, NE1 2PA ✆ 0191 232 3698 ⏚ www.bykerbridge.org.uk/farm ☉ daily ♿). Horses from nearby Stepney Bank Stables trot by and a steady stream of families wander in and out of the **Seven Stories** exhibition centre (30 Lime St, NE1 2PQ ✆ 0845 271 0777 ⏚ www.sevenstories.org.uk ☉ daily ♿) which is devoted to children's literature and has an excellent bookshop.

Unbeknown to casual visitors is a subterranean tunnel that runs right across Newcastle. The **Victorian Tunnel** (✆ 0191 261 6596; booking

OUSEBURN VALLEY PUBS

Four great pubs with a lively independent and folk music scene centre around the Ouseburn. The **Cluny** (36 Lime St, NE1 2PQ ✆ 0191 230 4474 ♿) pub and club attracts a young-ish crowd and especially known for hosting fairly big name bands and up and coming artists. **The Tyne** bar (Maling St, NE6 1LP ✆ 0191 265 2550) is another youthful pub with a vibrant live music scene. A bit of a walk away but offering an unbeatable view of the River Tyne is **The Free Trade Inn** (St Lawrence Rd, off Walker Rd, NE6 1A6 ✆ 0191 265 5764). It's a scruffy little drinking hole popular with students, artists and university lecturers and the selection of ales is good. The beer garden is soaked in sunshine on summer evenings. Attracting a similar crowd is **The Cumberland Arms** (James Place St, NE6 1LD ✆ 0191 265 1725), another much-loved shabby pub with wooden furniture, open fires and a range of local drinks. The Cumberland is best visited on a balmy summer's evening when you can sit outside in the sun with a pint of cider, or on cold nights in winter when the fires are roaring, the windows are steamed up and the fiddle players are really going for it. On Wednesday evenings, Rapper sword dancers practise in the upstairs room and will allow you to watch if you ask. ♨ See ⏚ www.bradtguides.com/rappersworddancing for more on this traditional sword dance.

essential &) was opened in 1835 and designed for wagons to carry coal underground from a colliery near the Town Moor to the quayside, rather than through the streets. During World War II it served as an air-raid shelter. A 700-yard length of the narrow tunnel, which has an entrance on Lime Street, is open to the public via one- or two-hour guided tours – which are highly recommended.

A five-minute walk from the main Ouseburn Valley hub is the **Biscuit Factory** (Stoddart St, NE2 1AN ℘ 0191 261 1103 ℰ www.thebiscuitfactory. com ☉ daily from 10.00, opens 11.00 on Sun &) – which claims to be the UK's largest independent commercial art gallery. It has a reputation for quality, range and affordability, and sells jewellery, sculptures and paintings, as well as large works by international and local artists.

¶¶ FOOD & DRINK

New independent cafés are popping up all the time in the **Ouseburn Valley**. They include **The Tower Café** on Stepney Road, a tiny Caribbean eatery on the roadside with deckchairs from where you can take in the Reggae beats over a jerk chicken sandwich and mint tea, and **The Cookhouse** on Ouse Street (by the Victoria Tunnel), an imaginative chic little café housed in two shipping containers with a regularly changing food menu and committed to sourcing local produce. **Ernest** (Stepney Rd ℘ 0191 260 5216) is a café and bar known for its music, cool clientele and for serving good food from breakfast to 21.00.

Artisan The Biscuit Factory, Stoddart St, NE2 1AN ℘ 0191 260 5411 &. Modern art gallery restaurant with a very good reputation for its seasonal British menu. Northumbrian lamb, beef and game, and fish straight off the boats at North Shields.

The Bake 98 Byker Bank, NE6 1LA ℘ 0191 228 9000 ☉ daily, 12.00–midnight. Great bring-your-own Lebanese restaurant (mezze, kebabs, biryani, wraps and so on).

2 GATESHEAD

Traditionally the smaller, less glamorous cousin of Newcastle on the south side of the River Tyne, Gateshead has attracted national attention in recent decades for its daring contemporary architecture and arts venues – and made Newcastle sit up and take notice. Rejuvenating Gateshead's quayside began with the success of *The Angel of the North* on a hill outside of the town. Following Gormley's masterpiece, the forward-thinking council embarked on a major redevelopment of the riverfront which put Gateshead on the arts map of Britain, though Newcastle often gets the credit.

Gateshead's centre lacks the Victorian architecture and stately streets of Newcastle but it does have the odd historic building and attraction worth seeking out, including the **Shipley Art Gallery** (opposite) and **Saltwell Park** (Saltwell Rd South, NE9 5AX) a wonderfully restored 19th-century public parkland and garden. Further afield, the National Trust's **Gibside** (page 32) is one of the finest Georgian landscaped gardens in England and makes for a popular day out.

GATESHEAD QUAYS

South Shore Rd ⊘ www.gateshead-quays.com; QuayLink bus Q1 from Gateshead Metro station or take Q2 (or walk) from Newcastle's Monument to the quayside & cross the Millennium Bridge on foot

Gateshead's quayside is now a major culture and leisure attraction sharing similarities with cities like Bilbao in Spain that also underwent arts-led regeneration works in the 1990s. Our Guggenheim equivalent is **The Sage Gateshead Music Centre** (⊘ 0191 443 4661 ⊘ www.thesagegateshead.org ⊘) – an organic-shaped building wrapped in steel on a bank above the Tyne. Sir Norman Foster's masterpiece has completely transformed the quaysides of both Gateshead and Newcastle.

Inside the Sage, it's airy, bright and voluminous and there's a well-placed café with views of the Tyne Bridge and Newcastle's waterfront. If you come to a concert here you'll be able to appreciate the much-praised acoustics in the timber halls. Many big names and up and coming folk, indie and world music stars perform at the Sage; it's also the permanent home of Folkworks, the North East's traditional music organisation, as well as the Royal Northern Sinfonia orchestra.

The **BALTIC Centre for Contemporary Art** (⊘ 0191 478 1810 ⊘ www.balticmill.com ☉ daily; free admission ⊘) started life in the mid 20th century as a flour mill. Over the years, there have been some superb exhibitions here, including the Turner Prize in 2011 and a couple of shows by the North's favourite contemporary artists, Antony Gormley and Anish Kapoor. It's worth going in just for the views of the Tyne from the top floors.

Just over a mile upriver from the Sage, **Dunston Coal Staiths** is another relic from Tyneside's industrial era. The late 19th-century pier-like structure, said to be the largest wooden construction in Europe, once enabled wagons loaded with Durham coal to transport their contents directly onto ships moored along its side. The staiths ceased operating in the 1980s but it remains largely intact.

At the time of writing there was no public access (this may change once the structure is restored) but it is easily viewed from the promenade or railway bridge (when crossing the river by train, look upriver, away from the Tyne Bridge).

SHIPLEY ART GALLERY
Prince Consort Rd, NE8 4JB ✆ 0191 477 1495 ⊘ www.twmuseums.org.uk/shipley-art-gallery ⊙ Mon–Sat ♿

There's always an eclectic display of art at the Shipley – crafts, fine art, contemporary film installations and so on, but it's particularly known for its craft shows and permanent collection of pottery and glass. The UK's most comprehensive collection of Sowerby's and Davidson's glassware is held here. Past exhibitions have included portraiture from the 17th century to the present, chair design through the ages and a display of African bead work. At the back of the gallery hangs one of the most cherished North East paintings, *The Blaydon Races* – a lively depiction across a large canvas of the popular 19th-century event. The song of the same name is a well-loved Geordie anthem.

3 THE ANGEL OF THE NORTH
Signposted off the A1 south of Gateshead, also reached from the Durham Road; parking on site; **The Angel Bus** (Go North East services 21 ⊘ www.simplygo.com) runs daily at least every 10mins from Eldon Square Bus Station in Newcastle (& a few other stops in the city centre) or Gateshead Interchange

Boasting a wingspan the breadth of a jumbo jet was something of a PR disaster when the then largest sculpture in Britain was unveiled in 1998. *The Angel of the North* was much criticised by locals who thought the 65-foot sculpture did indeed look like a plane and not the elegant, feminine form perhaps some had hoped for. Many residents hated the sculpture – really hated it – and wanted it taken down; others ridiculed it, including, quite memorably, a group of football fans in 1998 (page 10), but locals have come to love Antony Gormley's rusty red masterpiece.

The prominent hillock on which it stands was once a colliery and the mining history of the site – and the region – is very much reflected in the colour, steel fabric and form (undeniably masculine). It's said to be one of the most viewed pieces of public art in Britain, situated as it is by the A1 and in sight of the London to Edinburgh railway line. Other memorable sculptures around Gateshead include Sally Matthews's life-size metal goats below the blue Metro Bridge and *Cone* by Andy Goldsworthy (west of the High Level Bridge).

4 GIBSIDE

Near Rowlands Gill, Gateshead NE16 6BG ✐ 01207 541820; ☉ parkland & tea rooms open daily (check website for chapel opening times); music events & concerts in summer; farmers' market & 'pub' (below); ♿ National Trust

Once you set foot in this Georgian parkland on the outskirts of Gateshead, you'll feel as cut off from the 21st century as you would on any remote National Trust estate. The grounds have all the grandeur you would expect of an 18th-century landscaped garden with eye-catching monuments, wooded walkways, classical architecture and open vistas. A stroll from the **Palladian chapel** along a half-mile tree-lined **avenue** to the 140-foot **Column to Liberty** is wonderfully romantic, especially in autumn when the intensity of light and colour is spectacular. The ruins of an **orangery** and **Jacobean hall** lie halfway between the two.

Don't leave before visiting the recently restored **walled kitchen garden** dating to 1734. You can buy vegetables grown here at the regular **farmers' market** on the first and third Saturday of every month. On Friday evenings throughout the year (and Saturdays in summer) the café becomes a '**pub**' and the walled garden a beer garden where you can soak up the last rays of sunshine or cosy up beside log fire braziers with a pint of Wylam Brewery's finest ale.

🚶 If you want to walk to Gibside from Tyneside, directions can be found on ✐ www.bradtguides.com/gibsidewalk.

⫪ FOOD & DRINK

Both the **BALTIC Centre for Contemporary Art** and the **Sage** music centre have cafés, bars and restaurants with fabulous views of the river and Newcastle's quayside. Menus vary in price, as does the ambience: for example, the ground floor at the BALTIC (with outdoor seating) is more of a bistro whereas right at the top is **Six** (Gateshead NE8 3BA ✐ 0191 440 4948 ♿) – a fabulous restaurant with lofty views of the Millennium and Tyne bridges serving modern British/European dishes. Gateshead's town centre offers nothing in the way of a good dining experience but there are a couple of places worth considering in the nearby countryside, including the café and pub at the National Trust's **Gibside** (above) and the very well-regarded **Feathers Inn** at Hedley-on-the-Hill (NE43 7SW ✐ 01661 843607).

THE COAST: NORTH SHIELDS TO WHITLEY BAY

Pleasure beaches at Tynemouth, Cullercoats and Whitley Bay became hugely popular during the 19th century when train travel made the seaside resorts accessible to ordinary people. Tyneside's coast is still easily reached by public transport with Metro stations at all the sandy beaches plus North Shields. The journey by Metro from Newcastle City Centre to Tynemouth for example takes just 20 minutes. You can also cycle to the coast from Newcastle (page 41).

5 NORTH SHIELDS FISH QUAY

It's a lively scene when the fishermen are landing their catch: crates of fish being passed from the boats to the harbour wall, engines throbbing, seabirds swarming behind the trawlers as they travel up the Tyne, and the incessant cry of herring gulls announcing the start of another fishing day.

Even at quiet times, the Fish Quay is an appealing place to wander around with the old Victorian Customs House and Shipping Office buildings, open yards where rows of girls once stood over barrels filleting herring, fish shops, and eateries on the riverfront.

"It's a lively scene when the fishermen are landing their catch: crates of fish being passed from the boats to the harbour wall, engines throbbing, seabirds swarming…"

The area's fishing heritage goes back some 800 years since the monastery at Tynemouth developed fishermen's huts (shielings, hence North *Shields*) on the banks of the river. **High Lights** and **Low Lights** are the two navigational white towers built in 1802 to warn mariners of the dangerous Black Middens Rocks at Tynemouth, scene of numerous shipwrecks. Climb up the bank to High Lights for an expansive view of the Tyne or walk along the promenade (♿ suitable for wheelchairs) to Tynemouth in about 15–20 minutes.

FOOD & DRINK

The Fish Quay is gaining a reputation for its seafood restaurants – not just fish and chip take-aways – and you'll find a string of good places to dine including **Irvins Brasserie** (Union Quay ✆ 0191 296 3238 ⊙ Wed–Sun ♿) and **David Kennedy's Food Social** (50 Bell St, NE30 1HF ✆ 0191 296 6168 ⊙ Tue–Sun & bank holidays).

6 TYNEMOUTH

♠ Martineau House (page 272), **Number 61** (page 272)

The striking ruins of Tynemouth's 11th-century priory stand on a commanding rocky cape keeping watch over the North Sea and mouth of the River Tyne. The attractive **town centre** with all its cafés, bars, craft and antiques shops kneels behind, and stretched along the seafront are the grand Victorian houses for which Tynemouth is celebrated.

There are three **beaches** within a short walk from the town centre. **Longsands** is the largest expanse of sand and is popular with families and surfers. Those wanting to take to the waves can hire surf boards or take lessons with the **Tynemouth Surf Company** (Grand Parade, NE30 4JH ✐ 0191 258 2496 ⌂ www.tynemouthsurf.co.uk).

A vibrant **flea market** (Station Terrace, NE30 4RE ⌂ www.tynemouth-market.com ☉ Sat & Sun 09.00–16.00 ⅅ) is housed in Tynemouth's sumptuous Victorian train station (now the Metro station) – surely one of the most ornamental stations of its era anywhere in England. It's worth coming here even when the market is not on, just to see the huge amount of decorative ironwork in the canopies and pillars. The original covered timber bridge arches steeply over the railway from where you gain a near bird's-eye view of the market stalls – easily over 100 – selling bric-a-brac, restored vintage telephones, old records, books, jewellery, crafts, antiques and regional foods. On the third Saturday of the month, the station also hosts a **farmers' market**.

Tynemouth priory, castle & battery

Pier Rd, NE30 4BZ ✐ 0191 257 1090 ☉ early Mar–end Oct, daily; weekends only in winter ⅅ except the gun battery; English Heritage

Built in 1090 on the site of an earlier Anglican monastery that had been destroyed by invading Danes, the current building survives remarkably well considering its position and age. Up close, the sandstone has been heavily worn away by the elements, and the faces of headstones have formed strange patterns. Though gaunt, the priory is still impressive displaying soaring lancet window arches, a wealth of elaborate stone carvings and a 15th-century **chapel** with its rib vaulted ceiling and 33 roof bosses. Elsewhere are a ruined medieval gatehouse (**Tynemouth Castle**) and a **World War II battery**, complete with gun emplacements and store rooms containing the original mechanisms for transporting ammunition to the guns above.

Tynemouth Volunteer
Life Brigade Watch House Museum

Spanish Battery, between Tynemouth & North Shields, NE30 4DD; easily walked from
Tynemouth Priory ✆ 0191 257 2059 ⟁ www.tvlb.org ⊙ Tue–Sat 10.00–15.00 & Sun
10.00–12.00; free admission (but donations appreciated)

This is a special museum that deserves to be better known. Packed inside
the striking 1887 blue, white and yellow wooden building (being restored
at the time of writing) is a hoard of artefacts amassed over the years that
it has operated as volunteer-manned station: bells, clocks, old black and
white photographs, a breeches buoy and several ship's figureheads. An
old wooden lifeboat is installed at the back of the building.

▮▮ FOOD & DRINK

Tynemouth's **Front Street** has many cafés, coffee shops and bars and a couple of good
places for lunch including **Dil & the Bear** (also for cakes) and **Allard's Lounge** (✆ 0191
447 3252), a café and wine bar which looks more like the latter but trading mainly in
gourmet sandwiches, seafood tapas and posh burgers. For coffee (especially a mocha),
Gareth James's chocolaterie (✆ 0191 257 7799) on the corner of Percy Park Road is
good; don't leave without trying their Earl Grey truffle. Afternoon teas are served in the
quiet drawing room of the **Grand Hotel** (✆ 0191 293 6666) on Grand Parade. **Crusoe's**
(Longsands Beach ✆ 0191 296 4152 ♿) is an extremely popular café right on the beach.

7 CULLERCOATS

🏠 **Southcliff Apartments** (page 272)

Very familiar indeed is the figure of the Cullercoats fishwife,
as, clad in blue serge jacket, short petticoats with ample skirts,
large apron and black straw bonnet she trudges along with a
heavy creel of fish on her shoulders, calling, in shrill and not
unmusical tones of voice 'Buy fee-s-ch.'

W W Tomlinson *Comprehensive Guide to Northumberland*, 1888

A mile north along the seafront from Tynemouth, this former fishing
village faces the sea above a quiet sandy cove where Sunday strollers
take in the salty air from the clifftop promenade and braver children –
their legs and arms pink with the cold – jump off the little pier. This bay
formed the backdrop to many paintings by the **Cullercoats Colony** of
artists who captured the lives of local people here from around 1870 to
1920: men returning from sea in their wooden boats, women mending
nets, collecting seaweed and carrying baskets of fish and scenes similar

to those observed by the Victorian travel writer Tomlinson in the excerpt above. A small number of these atmospheric paintings hang in the Laing Art Gallery in Newcastle including John Charlton's well-known 1910 masterpiece, *The Women*, which depicts the rescue of the *Lovely Nellie* ship that ran aground on New Year's Day in 1861 near St Mary's Lighthouse. A storm prevented the Cullercoats lifeboat reaching the stricken vessel so it was pulled overland for two miles to where it could be launched. Everyone was saved except for the cabin boy. The focus in the painting is on the strong local women, shirts rolled up, heaving the boat in lashing rain alongside men and boys.

The old lifeboat station is still operational, but much has changed in the village: many buildings were razed in the latter half of the 20th century, and where Tomlinson counted some 40 fishing boats in his 1888 guide; today just a few cobles are moored in the bay.

For visitors, there's not much in the way of attractions but you could hire a kayak from the friendly **Cullercoats Bike & Kayak centre** (1A Norma Crescent, NE26 2PD 0191 251 9412 www.cullercoatsbikekayak.co.uk) and head along the coast to St Mary's Lighthouse. You'll see plenty of birdlife and perhaps bottlenose dolphins.

ᵭ FOOD & DRINK

The Snug café at the Cullercoats Bike & Kayak centre (see above) is open to everyone. True to its name, it is warm and welcoming and offers a small selection of healthy soups, salads and sandwiches. **Beaches and Cream** (1 Victoria Crescent 0191 251 4718) is a popular, period-fashioned coffee house and fancy ice cream parlour opposite the promenade.

8 WHITLEY BAY

The sharp bite of the saline waters at Whitley Bay is of the utmost value in all cases of debility, and especially to the jaded business man.
Guidebook to Whitley Bay, 1909

Once the Blackpool of the North, Whitley Bay's popularity as a seaside resort began to wane in the latter half of the 20th century; today the words 'faded grandeur' come to mind but things are looking up for Whitley. The fine sea-facing Victorian buildings are being renovated (though some have been tragically demolished in recent times) and the landmark **Spanish City** pleasure hall – an eye-catching Edwardian building with a huge white dome and two towers – is undergoing a major revamp. The two dancing girls on either tower (one plays the cymbals, the other a tambourine) were restored to their copper-green best in 2010. When built in 1910 with a theatre and roof gardens it had the largest dome in the UK after St Paul's Cathedral in London.

From Spanish City to St Mary's Lighthouse, a wide grassy bank separates the **promenade** (♿ accessible the whole way) from the road and town, making a stroll along the seafront very pleasant indeed. You can also walk on the **beach** of course – a long expanse of beige sand that meets the black reefs of **St Mary's Island** (great for rockpooling and birdwatching) at its northern end.

St Mary's Lighthouse

Whitley Bay NE26 4RS ℰ 0191 200 8650 ⊙ May–Sep, daily, then weekends & school holidays only through the winter (subject to tides)

St Mary's Lighthouse first shone her beam across the North Sea on 31 August 1898 and for the next 86 years the white beacon helped keep mariners away from the dangerous rocks off the coast of Whitley Bay until it was decommissioned in 1984. A short causeway links the mainland with the lighthouse isle. Visitors can climb to the top of St Mary's by way of 137 steps up a dizzying spiral staircase and enjoy the expansive view at the top: from Blyth to the mouth of the Tyne.

¶ FOOD & DRINK

Fish and chip shops, cafés and inexpensive Italian restaurants are fairly plentiful in Whitley Bay's town centre, along the seafront and around Spanish City. For a coffee with a sea view, head to the **Links Art Gallery and café** (Dukes Walk, NE26 1TP ℰ 0191 447 5534) on Whitley Bay's promenade. With more space and a fetching vintage interior is the **Rendezvous Café** next door (ℰ 0191 252 5548).

Discover more...

Download our **Newcastle Upon Tyne** e-city guide to learn more about the North East's most vibrant city. Available from **www.bradtguides.com**

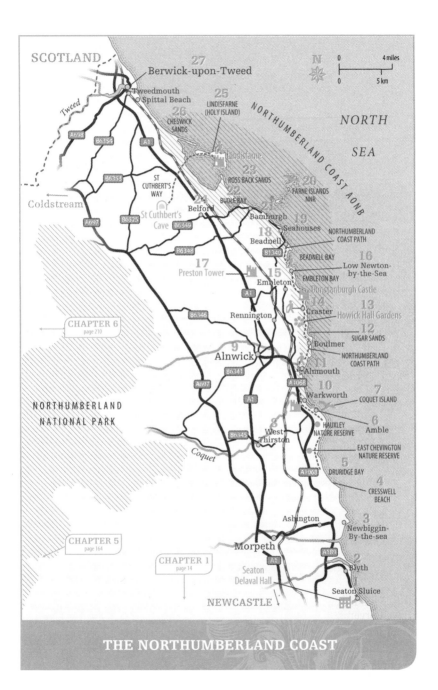

THE NORTHUMBERLAND COAST

SCOTLAND

Berwick-upon-Tweed

27

Tweedmouth
Spittal Beach

26 CHESWICK SANDS

25 LINDISFARNE (HOLY ISLAND)

Lindisfarne

NORTHUMBERLAND COAST AONB

NORTH SEA

Coldstream

ST CUTHBERT'S WAY

St Cuthbert's Cave

24 Belford

23 ROSS BACK SANDS

22 BUDLE BAY

Bamburgh

21 20 FARNE ISLANDS NNR

19 Seahouses

NORTHUMBERLAND COAST PATH

18 Beadnell

BEADNELL BAY

16 Low Newton-by-the-Sea

17 Preston Tower

15 Embleton

EMBLETON BAY

Dunstanburgh Castle

14 Craster

13 Howick Hall Gardens

Rennington

12 SUGAR SANDS

Boulmer

NORTHUMBERLAND COAST PATH

9 Alnwick

11 Alnmouth

10 Warkworth

7 COQUET ISLAND

6 Amble

NORTHUMBERLAND NATIONAL PARK

8 West Thirston

HAUXLEY NATURE RESERVE

EAST CHEVINGTON NATURE RESERVE

Coquet

5 DRURIDGE BAY

4 CRESSWELL BEACH

Ashington

3 Newbiggin-By-the-sea

CHAPTER 6 page 210

CHAPTER 5 page 164

Morpeth

CHAPTER 1 page 14

Seaton Delaval Hall

2 Blyth

Seaton Sluice

NEWCASTLE

N

0 4 miles
0 5 km

2
THE NORTHUMBERLAND COAST

'There's nothing like the Northumberland coast, is there?' said a cheerful angler passing me as I walked towards Dunstanburgh Castle one sunny morning in August. Anyone who makes a trip along the dune-backed shores between the outskirts of Tyneside and Berwick-upon-Tweed will know what he means. Where else in England can you walk along a pristine sandy beach on a summer's day and meet only a handful of people? The Northumberland coast is like this for much of its 70 miles.

Besides beaches, you'll find old fishing villages, offshore islands and a string of arresting castles. Nowhere are these landscape features more conspicuous than between Warkworth and Berwick-upon-Tweed, the Northumberland Coast Area of Outstanding Natural Beauty (AONB), also known as the **Heritage Coast**. Here you'll find most of the best bathing beaches, the Farne Islands National Nature Reserve, Lindisfarne Priory and all the castles.

"Where else in England can you walk along a pristine sandy beach and meet only a handful of people?"

But, don't overlook the **south Northumberland coast**. Some of the longest and most silky sands are at Cresswell and Druridge Bay. Birdwatchers, walkers and anyone looking for some of the best fish and chips in Northumberland should come here. North Tyneside's coastal strip between North Shields and Whitley Bay is covered in *Chapter 1*.

GETTING AROUND

If using public transport to access the Heritage Coast, you'll have to be well organised as buses (page 40) are not particularly frequent (except for services to Alnwick) and the **train stations** (Berwick, Alnmouth and Chathill) are set back at least a few miles from the shore. A combination of bicycle and train is a good way to get around if you don't have a car.

i TOURIST INFORMATION

Alnwick Market Pl, NE66 1TN ✎ 01665 511333 ☺ Easter–Nov, daily; Mon–Sat at other times of the year ♿

Amble Queen St, NE65 0DQ ✎ 01665 712313 ☺ Easter–early Nov, daily (on Sun 10.00–14.00) ♿

Berwick-upon-Tweed 106 Marygate, TD15 1BN ✎ 01289 301780 ☺ end Mar–early Nov, daily (on Sun until 15.00); Mon–Sat during winter ♿

Craster Car park behind the harbour, NE66 3TW ✎ 01665 576007 ☺ Apr–end Oct, daily; Nov–Easter weekends only ♿

Seahouses Seafield car park, Seafield Rd, NE68 7SW ✎ 01665 720884 ☺ end Mar–early Nov, daily ♿

BUS

Getting to the **south Northumberland coast** is relatively easy, with several buses an hour from Newcastle (below). You can also reach Cresswell Beach from Blyth (1) and Newbiggin and Woodhorn from Morpeth (35 and 35A). For details of these services and those to Blyth listed below, go to ✎ www.arrivabus.co.uk.

The **north Northumberland Heritage Coast** is not as well serviced and there are only three buses of use, listed below. Also see ✎ www. northumberland.gov.uk.

Newcastle–Blyth via Whitley Bay & Seaton Sluice (308) Several times an hour Monday to Saturday and twice hourly on Sunday.

Newcastle–Blyth via Seaton Sluice & Seaton Deleval Hall (X4) Couple of times an hour Monday to Saturday and once an hour on Sunday.

Newcastle–Berwick via Alnwick & the Heritage Coast (Warkworth, Alnmouth, Craster, Embleton, High Newton, Beadnell, Seahouses and Bamburgh) (X18) Around six services Monday to Saturday and fewer on Sunday. Travelsure buses also run a service a few times a day on Monday and Saturday between Alnwick and Belford (418) that stops at places on the Heritage Coast and connects with the X15 and X18.

Newcastle–Berwick via Alnwick & Beal (for Lindisfarne) (X15) Hourly service Monday to Saturday; around five services on Sunday. This is a faster service to Alnwick than the X18. For Lindisfarne, change to the 477 at Beal.

Berwick–Lindisfarne (Holy Island) via Beal (477) Two return journeys Monday to Saturday in summer (times vary depending on the tides) and only a couple of times a week at other times of the year. For Newcastle, change at Beal for the X15.

CYCLING

The popular **Coast and Castles** route from Newcastle to Edinburgh (some 200 miles) runs the length of Northumberland's coastline for much of the way to Berwick. At the border you turn inland and trace the Tweed for the final leg to Edinburgh. The whole route is manageable on a touring bike and covered by **National Cycle Network (NCN) Route 1**, though you can stay by the sea from Berwick to Edinburgh by transferring to **NCN Route 76**.

For **bike hire**, pick up and drop-off services and bike and baggage transfers, contact **Pedal Power** (page 147).

WALKING

Linear walks along Northumberland's beaches are unbeatable and well marked thanks to the 64-mile **Northumberland Coast Path** from Cresswell to Berwick-upon-Tweed. The long-distance path is easily walkable in six days with few challenges.

Another long-distance route is **St Cuthbert's Way** which takes in the best of Northumberland's hill and coastal scenery on the 62½-mile journey from Melrose in Scotland across the Cheviot Hills to Lindisfarne. There is a tremendous view of the coast once you reach the Kyloe Hills and this final nine-mile leg from Holborn (parking at Holborn Grange) to Lindisfarne makes for a superb linear day hike (book a taxi for the return).

Generally, the scenery inland is flat and really not in the same league, so mostly you're confined to the coast itself. If you want to vary linear **day walks**, you're best off along the beach on the outward journey and taking headland or dune paths (or vice versa) on the return. You can do this for much of the way between Dunstanburgh Castle and Beadnell, for example. Also, see the Craster to Howick circular route on pages 71–2.

Recommended half-day routes are Newton-by-the-Sea to Craster (page 74), Beadnell or Seahouses; Bamburgh to Budle Bay; and the Lindisfarne round-island walk (pages 92–3). Druridge Bay, Alnmouth Bay, Ross Back Sands and Cheswick Sands are the ultimate beaches for a lonesome windswept walk.

HORSERIDING

Horseriders trotting through the surf at Bamburgh, Lindisfarne and Newton-by-the-Sea are an enviable sight. If you want to join them (experienced riders only) contact **Slate Hall Riding Centre** at Seahouses

(South Lane, NE68 7UL ✆ 01665 720320 ⌨ www.slatehallridingcentre.
com) or **Kimmerston Riding Centre** in Wooler (NE71 6JH ✆ 01668
216283 ⌨ www.kimmerston.com) who go to Lindisfarne regularly in
summer. A two-hour beach ride with either company costs in the region
of £50.

TAXIS
A2B Taxis Berwick & Lindisfarne ✆ 07732 520385
Croft Cabs Belford ✆ 01668 213639, 07803 496278
Hunters Taxis Seahouses ✆ 01665 720400
Knights Taxis near Alnmouth ✆ 01665 714555, 07760 751667
Yellow Taxi Alnwick ✆ 01665 541250

THE SOUTH NORTHUMBERLAND COAST

Between Seaton Sluice and the mouth of the River Coquet at Amble,
the coastline offers glimpses of what makes Northumberland's shores
so renowned: vast stretches of soft sands, high dunes and old seaside
towns. Though the sands are interrupted now and then by places that
hold little appeal to tourists, beaches like at Cresswell and Druridge Bay,
known well to locals and Tynesiders, are very attractive to families and
walkers. The industrial past of the south Northumberland coast reveals
itself at Blyth and Ashington. To learn more about the mining history
in these parts, a tour of the engaging Woodhorn Museum (pages 45–6)
near Ashington is highly recommended.

1 SEATON SLUICE
The main reason you are likely to come here is to visit Seaton Delaval
Hall (opposite), a Baroque mansion which has far outlived the coal and
glass industries on its doorstep. The settlement gets its name from the
sluice gates in the harbour designed by one of the Delavals to keep the
inlet clear of silt on each tide. This improved the export of salt, coal and
glass – as did enlarging the harbour by blasting through the cliff. The
colliery and the six 18th-century glassworks cones that used to frame
the skyline, however, are long gone. In 1862, 204 men and boys died at
the nearby Hartley coal pit when the mine shaft caved in, imprisoning
them underground.

Seaton Delaval Hall

The Avenue, NE26 4QR ✐ 0191 237 9100 ⊙ variable opening times so call or check the website; café; National Trust

Seaton Delaval Hall has become one of the region's most visited historic properties, celebrated for its formal gardens and exterior by Sir John Vanbrugh (the most famous country house architect in England during the early 1700s), who died a few years before the mansion – one of his greatest – was completed in 1730.

A fire destroyed the interior of the central block in 1822 (the heat was so intense that the roof leading was said to have 'poured down like water') and the **great hall** and saloon remain gutted, but you gain a strong sense of how grand and lavish the entrance must have been before the disaster. Armless busts and statues line the walls and a wrought-iron balcony frames the first-floor landing. Either side of the portico are the **stables** (east wing) and **kitchen** (west wing). To the rear of the central block, the south portico opens with an expansive view of countryside. Walk around the side to reach the beautiful **gardens**: formal hedging, roses, herbaceous borders and a magnificent weeping ash planted at the time the manor was built. Children tend to make a beeline for the natural climbing structures in the **woodland play area**.

The only furnished part of the house today is the **west wing** which was later used by the family. One of the highlights is a row of exquisitely embroidered early 18th-century chairs. Portraits on a nearby wall include that of the only male heir of Sir John Delaval who died before his father. Apparently the young man was already a sickly creature when he was kicked in the genitals by a maid whom he had assaulted. He never recovered from his injuries. The boy is buried in the church at Doddington in Lincolnshire which was painted black for some 25 years after his death.

Near the hall is the Norman **Church of Our Lady** on the edge of the National Trust estate. It dates to 1102 and was for 700 years the private chapel of the Delaval family. It's unusual in having two Norman arches spanning the interior.

You can **walk** from the coast to Seaton Delaval Hall in 15 minutes along the A190, but if you have the time, I recommend the longer 2½-mile riverside route from Seaton Sluice (start from below the Melton Constable pub). You'll need ❄ OS Explorer map 316. The first leg of the walk follows the river through Holywell Dene where trees crowd the water meadows; the second half is across fields with Seaton Delaval's obelisk coming into view through a parting in the trees. You'll pass the aforementioned 12th-century church before reaching the hall. Return to Seaton Sluice by bus X4 (bus stop right outside the hall) or walk the short distance (15 minutes) to Seaton Sluice along the main road (quick enough and on pavement).

2 BLYTH

From Seaton Sluice, a thick belt of dunes criss-crossed by sandy trails and a paved path leads to Blyth. Though its town centre is quite rundown, there's one historic street worth seeking out. Look for the house on Bath Terrace with a prominent stone porch and the word 'BATHS' inscribed above which dates to the early 19th century when the building was converted to a bath house. As attractive as the street is, it's actually the rear of Bath Terrace that is of most interest. Have you ever seen a **lighthouse** in a back lane? Neither had I. Standing some 60 feet tall, the lean white beacon (now decommissioned) looks completely out of place as if the terrace has been built around it. Interestingly, the striking tower and setting caught the eye of painter, L S Lowry who made a sketch of the building. The lower half of High Light (which once communicated with Low Light at the harbour) was built in 1788; the tiers above were added in the Victorian era.

"Colourful beach huts face the sea and a World War I and II battery stand prominently in the dunes. The pale pink and grey observation towers and gun emplacements are a striking feature and children seem to enjoy running around them."

Blyth's **South Beach** – a popular bay with dog walkers and families – is pleasant enough. Here, colourful beach huts face the sea and a World War I and II **battery** stand prominently in the dunes. The pale pink and grey observation towers and gun emplacements are a striking feature of the seascape and, though you can't enter the buildings, children seem to enjoy running around them. North of Blyth is **Cambois Bay** – another desolate expanse of sand popular with locals.

♯ FOOD & DRINK

Coastline Fish and Chips South Beach, Links Rd, Blyth NE24 3PL ✆ 01670 797428
☺ Mon–Sat. Fish and chips and ice cream parlour just behind the beach.

3 NEWBIGGIN-BY-THE-SEA

When I last visited this former seaside resort, a wicked northeasterly was blasting the promenade where I watched a woman and her dog both walking sideways to the wind. It wouldn't be unfair to describe Newbiggin as a rather pinched-looking place, but that shouldn't stop those with an interest in maritime heritage from paying a visit. Below the 14th-century **St Bartholomew Church** is the wonderful **Maritime Centre** (Church Point, NE64 6DB 01670 811951 www.newbigginmaritimecentre. org.uk daily in summer, closed Mon in winter; sea-facing café;), which tells the story of the fishing and coal-mining heritage along this stretch of the coast. The main attractions are the *Girl Anne* coble and the *Mary Joicey* lifeboat.

A short way along the promenade, between a fleet of tractors and a fine collection of fishing cobles, is the **RNLI (Royal National Lifeboat Institution) lifeboat station**, the oldest working station in the UK, established in 1851. On Sundays you can see the modern lifeboat and artefacts collected over the last 160-odd years. Every recorded incident in the lifeboat station's history is detailed on the blackboards lining the walls. Before the first tractor pulled the lifeboat to the sea in 1949, an army of women volunteers assisted the crew. The services of the legendary women lifeboat launchers of Newbiggin were utilised fairly recently when the old *Mary Joicey* lifeboat was brought to the Maritime Centre, and elderly ladies, children, mums and UGG boot-wearing teenagers came out to pull the boat to its final resting place.

Woodhorn Museum

Ashington NE63 9YF 01670 528080 www.experiencewoodhorn.com daily during school holidays; Wed–Sun at other times; free admission but a small charge for parking; café;

A few miles inland is the best surviving example of a late 19th-century northern colliery, complete with winding houses, yards and pit-pony stables. Without the miners, horses, smoke and clatter of machinery and wagons, it's hard to get a true sense of what it was like here before the colliery closed in the 1980s but the excellent visitor centre and approachable stewards, some of whom are former miners, bring that side of the colliery to life.

An indoor exhibition takes you forward in time from the height of coal mining through to the strikes and closures in the late 20th century. The museum also provides insight into the domestic life of miners and

THE PITMEN PAINTERS

Here I found an outlet for other things than earning my living. There is a feeling of being my own boss for a change and with it comes a sense of freedom.

Harry Wilson, founder member of the Ashington Group, quoted at the Woodhorn Museum

The story of how a group of coal miners from Ashington became painters is an unlikely one, hence its appeal (and success as a theatre production that made it to Broadway and the West End of London in recent years). In 1934, a group of miners hired a lecturer from Durham University to teach them about art appreciation. Instead, they learned to paint and were encouraged to capture their surroundings on canvas. They did this for 50 years to much acclaim while continuing to work in the colliery.

Their unsentimental paintings depict men working underground, domestic life, the close communities in which they lived and their leisure activities (growing leeks, dog racing, bowling, pigeon-keeping and so on). A superb collection of their paintings is on permanent display in the Woodhorn Museum near Ashington (pages 45–6).

their pastimes. Nowhere is this more vividly represented than in the **Ashington Group gallery** with its collection of artworks by the Pitmen Painters (see box, above). Outside the gallery is a display of old miners' banners (rousing socialist slogans and images of a better future).

Close to the museum, the **QEII Country Park** is a large lake (once the largest spoil heap in Europe) with picnic tables and a lakeside trail; a narrow-gauge railway line runs for a few hundred yards from Woodhorn Museum at weekends.

4 CRESSWELL BEACH

Day trippers from Tyneside love Cresswell because it's easily accessible from the coast road and the first family-friendly beach you come to in Northumberland that offers a traditional 'trip to the seaside' experience. Picture a soft sandy bay, high dunes and a great ice cream shop that also sells buckets and spades. The village itself is not remarkable though it does shelter the ruins of a 14th-century **pele tower** (facing the ice cream shop across the large green).

Cresswell's brackish lake (north of the village) fringed by reeds is a **nature reserve** and known stopping-off point for migrant birds in autumn and winter. Look out for pink-footed geese and snow buntings.

¶¶ FOOD & DRINK

Pick up sandwiches and teas from the **Drift Café** (NE61 5LA ☺ daily) on the main coast road heading north out of Cresswell. **Cresswell Ices** (NE61 5LA ☺ Apr–end Oct, & Feb school holidays) in the middle of the village has been around for years. The owner makes her own ice cream.

5 DRURIDGE BAY

Northumberland's most desolate beach is a sweeping expanse of sand that extends for six wind-whipped miles from Cresswell to just south of Amble. The shore is sheltered somewhat by high dunes, but it's hard to completely escape the bracing winds. Perhaps this explains in part why Druridge Bay is not the most popular bucket-and-spade beach. You'll easily find a spot to yourself where the nearest family is several hundred yards away. Walkers will love it here.

Behind the dunes is a broken chain of (sheltered) lagoons fringed by reedbeds and farmland that attract large numbers of wildfowl in winter. They are linked by the coast path which takes a varied route along the beach, tracks and grassy dunes.

The wetland **nature reserves** which were reclaimed from old coal mines attract rare migrants, as well as over wintering species, including pink-footed geese, bitterns, short-eared owls and whooper swans.

Within the **Druridge Bay Country Park** (access from Red Row) is the family-friendly **Ladyburn Lake** (NE61 5BX ✐ 01670 760968 ☺ weekends & school holidays, daily ♿) where there's a **visitor centre**, café and large picnic area. Watersports courses (and canoe hire) are on offer during the summer months. If you have your own canoe, windsurfing board or sailing boat, you need to purchase a permit from the visitor centre to use the lake (April to October only). From here you can also access the beach or walk around its perimeter (♿ a surfaced path around the south shore is wheelchair accessible).

East Chevington Nature Reserve

Nestled behind Druridge Bay's dunes is a wetland reserve managed by the Northumberland Wildlife Trust and a very good place to watch birds on the coast. The reedbeds, woodlands, rough grasslands and dunes are usually reached from Hadston via Druridge Bay Country Park though there is also a lane from Red Row. You can walk around the whole reserve on soft ground but there's one substantial stretch along the aforementioned paved lane. You'll see a good variety of species, particularly in autumn and winter when large flocks of waders and geese descend on the grasslands and pools. Splinter paths lead to the beach and bird hides (I've spotted reed buntings and reed warblers here in summer and I once saw a bittern clamber out of the reedbeds in a rare burst of extroversion; they are not uncommon in winter when the UK's population expands with European bitterns).

Hauxley Nature Reserve

At the northern end of Druridge Bay is this Northumberland Wildlife Trust reserve which is reached by walking along the dunes (♀ NU285023) or by road from Low Hauxley. Viewing hides overlook a secluded lake (once an open cast coal mine) where wildfowl and gulls gather throughout the year (four species of terns visit in summer). Don't overlook areas of scrub woodland and meadows or the area around the visitor centre where there's a thriving population of tree sparrows (like a house sparrow but with dark patches on either cheek). Close by are the fossilised remains of two tree trunks (on the other side of the fence by the car park) said to be about 250 million years old.

Hauxley Haven & Amble Links

The dune-backed sands between Low Hauxley and Amble tend to get overlooked by those travelling along the coast, but not by birdwatchers and locals who appreciate a lonesome stroll with a view of Coquet Island and the promise of excellent fish and chips and ice cream on reaching Amble (below). Children may also enjoy the rock pools along the way. From the vantage point of the dunes, you might see puffins, eider ducks and gannets out at sea and wading birds on the shore.

6 AMBLE

The tourist board describes this busy work a day town (once an important coal exporting port) at the mouth of the River Coquet as a 'retro-chic seaside town'. If they mean it's being gentrified, that sounds about right to me. Indeed, the town seems to get smarter every time I visit and in recent years a couple of chi-chi eateries have appeared near the harbour (see opposite). No doubt the fishing tackle shops will become art galleries in years to come and the eye-catching old coble boats currently parked in a back lane by the harbour may sadly go out of service.

COBLE BOATS

The traditional wooden fishing boat peculiar to the North East was for a long time a familiar sight all the way along the Northumbrian and Yorkshire coasts. Painted bright colours and with broad sides, a high bow and a characteristic flat bottom (easy for hauling up the North East's sandy beaches), cobles have operated out of fishing villages and ports for many hundreds of years. Some say the design originates from Viking boats.

You still see a scattering of cobles in Cullercoats, Newbiggin-by-the-Sea, Amble, Boulmer, Craster and North Shields, but most were abandoned or scrapped during the collapse of the North Sea fishing industry in the 20th century. There are probably only around 40 left, a very small number of which are the original sailing type. The most famous coble belonged to Grace Darling and is now housed in her namesake museum in Bamburgh (page 82).

Amble's tangle of streets is hard to navigate, but just keep heading eastwards and you'll soon meet the **harbour** with its long pier, and the town's rocky shore. The **tourist information centre** is in the town square (page 40). Four or five fishing boats and a small number of traditional coble boats moor in the harbour, and at low tide, below the old timber staiths on the north side of the harbour, the rib cages of a couple of wrecked ships poke through the sands.

Warkworth's castle rises prominently to the northwest; below are the seemingly unreachable white sands of Alnmouth Bay backed by high dunes. If touring the coast northwards, this should be your next stop. You can actually **walk** to Warkworth from Amble along the coast path which follows a fairly busy road although the path itself hugs the Coquet and is really quite pleasant, particularly where the riverbanks become leafier on entering Warkworth.

¶¶ FOOD & DRINK

Amble boasts a couple of upmarket restaurants, including **The Old Boat House** (Leazes St, NE65 0AA ☎ 01665 711232 ♿) which specialises in seafood. **Seasalt** (104 Queen St, NE65 0DQ ☎ 01665 713569) offers more of a mixture of meat and fish dishes. For take-away fish and chips you can't beat the **Harbour Fish Bar** (corner of Leazes St & Broomhill St, NE65 0AN ☎ 01665 710442). Top off your fish supper with a trip to **Spurreli Ice Cream** (Coquet St, NE65 0DJ ☎ 01665 710890 ♿), a nationally celebrated and award-winning parlour that makes seriously good ices, some of which have a regional twist.

7 COQUET ISLAND

Near Amble 🖉 0300 777 2676 🖑 www.rspb.org.uk/coquetisland

From mid-April, thousands of seabirds descend on this grassy 16-acre lighthouse isle a mile off the coast of Amble and begin squabbling over the best nest site. To see the 30,000 puffins, eider ducks and tens of terns, kittiwakes and fulmars on the RSPB-managed reserve, take a boat tour from Amble (spring and summer only). Landing is not permitted because of the sensitivity of the site, but you'll get excellent views of the birds, and spy-hopping grey seals. **Puffin Cruises** (🖉 01665 711975, 07752 861914 🖑 www. puffincruises.co.uk) operate boat trips out of Amble harbour (not the marina) between Easter and the end of September. The trips last around an hour; call in advance to check sailing times and book tours (just a few pounds). The seabirds depart the island in July and August but it's still possible to see various waterbirds and seals for the rest of the summer.

"Coquet Island is home to the only colony of Britain's rarest breeding seabird, the roseate tern."

Coquet Island is home to the only colony of Britain's rarest breeding seabird, the roseate tern, which nests on this tiny isle and almost nowhere else in Britain. Each pair is provided with a ground nest box that the birds 'decorate' with shells, shingle and objects washed up on the shore. The island's manager, Paul Morrison (aka 'Captain Coquet'), told me that one year he found a nest adorned with daffodils and another with fragments of paint. 'I've also seen a Gothic "hut" decked out with rabbit bones,' he said. Some birds are so particular that they return to the same nest box every year. Warming seas and the fall in availability of sand eels (the main food of puffins and terns) threaten the survival of the seabirds here and elsewhere along the coast.

The **lighthouse** was built in 1841 on top of a Benedictine monastery (the stone base of which is still visible). You will also see recently restored stone cottages (built in 1840 in the ruins of a 15th-century monastic chapel).

8 WEST THIRSTON

🏠 **Northumbrian Arms** (page 272)

Moments from the A1, and south of Felton, is this highly picturesque stone village arranged either side of a wooded stretch of the River Coquet. Spanning the waterway is a 15th-century stone bridge worthy of a few photographs. On the south side, a walkway leads to the river which flows slowly under the boughs of many mature trees. Children may like to while away some time throwing stones from the wide shingle bank here.

St Oswald's Way long-distance path enters the village on the north side of the river, crosses the bridge and then continues to the coast on the south side. The path is well trodden, wooded and makes for a very pleasant riverside wander.

¶¶ FOOD & DRINK

Northumberland Arms The Peth, West Thirston, Felton NE65 9EE ✐ 01670 787370 ⊙ daily ౘ. A busy restaurant full of lively chatter is always a good sign. You'll want to book ahead at peak times for a table in this upmarket old coaching inn by the River Coquet. Traditional British dishes include cod and chips, lamb, steaks and casseroles made with ingredients sourced from Northumberland's coast and countryside.

The Running Fox Café 2–4 Riverside, West Thirston NE65 9EA (north side of the river opposite the old bridge) ✐ 01670 787090 ⊙ daily. Welcoming little coffee shop, café and artisan bakery serving breakfasts and light lunches (soups, sandwiches, quiches). Also doubles as a shop selling newspapers, leaflets about the local area and a small selection of Northumbrian goodies including honey, chutneys and jams.

ALNWICK

🏠 **Courtyard Gardens** (page 272), **Greycroft** (page 272)

'Alnwick is ever under the spell of the dreamy past', a late 19th-century visitor to the town observed. Today, you might also say it is under the spell of *Harry Potter*, whose fans flock to the town's famous medieval castle, better known to some as Hogwarts. For others, even without its fortress and celebrated gardens, Alnwick (pronounced 'Annick') is one of the most vibrant and historically interesting market towns in the North East, and easily reached from the coast in 15 minutes by car.

9 ALNWICK TOWN, CASTLE & GARDENS

At its centre, three venerable streets wrap around a piazza which boasts a market, summer folk music festival and outdoor café culture. To the north are the castle, gardens, museum and church. The most memorable approach to the town centre is from the south under the **Bondgate Tower** – a mighty stone gateway which has served as a main entry point into the once walled town since its construction in 1450.

ALNWICK MARKETS

A very good **farmers' market** fills the Market Place from 09.00 until 14.00 on the last Friday of the month (in December it's held on the last Friday before Christmas) where you'll find plenty of Northumberland's finest local produce on sale. The regular markets on **Saturday** (all day year-round) and **Thursday** (all day from April to Christmas) are a mixture of craft, cake, artwork and clothing stalls with the odd local produce table.

Before you reach the arch, you'll pass the acclaimed secondhand bookshop, **Barter Books** (opposite), on **Bondgate Without**. Opposite is a moving **war memorial** designed by Ralph Hedley in 1921. The three bronze figures of a soldier, sailor and airman warrant close inspection. Close by is the **Percy Tenantry Column**, a fluted pillar surmounted with a lion and guarded at its base by four other feline beasts. It was erected in 1816 by the tenants of the 2nd Duke of Northumberland after he reduced rents during tough economic times. The lion is the emblem of the Percy family of Alnwick Castle and crops up in many places about town, notably on **Lion Bridge** (seen as you're heading north over the River Aln).

Art buffs should head up Prudhoe Street to the **Bakehouse Gallery** (NE66 1UW ✆ 01665 602277 ☉ Tue–Sat ♿). Some of the region's well-regarded painters display their work here, alongside ceramics, handmade jewellery and various other quality craftwork.

Bondgate Without becomes **Bondgate Within** (that is, within the town walls) after you pass under the medieval arch. Here, a wide thoroughfare of Georgian and Victorian buildings leads to the **Market Place** where you'll find the **tourist information centre** (page 40), the imposing Georgian Town Hall and a couple of good eateries. One building on Bondgate Within to look out for is the **White Swan** (NE66 1TD ✆ 01665 602109). In the 1930s, the then owner of the hotel bought all the fittings and artworks from the decommissioned *Olympic* cruise liner (the *Titanic*'s sister ship) and reconstructed them to make an opulent dining room. You don't need to stay at the hotel to dine in the sumptuous oak-panelled restaurant which transports you back to the era of transatlantic cruises, Edwardian style.

Behind the Market Place is **Fenkle Street** – a long run of old merchants' houses with a chocolaterie on the corner. The street curves to meet **Narrowgate** where there's a scattering of tea rooms, interiors shops, an antiques emporium, art gallery and deli. The dusty bottles in the window of **Ye Olde Cross** pub at the junction with Pottergate are said to be cursed and have not been touched in 200 years.

St Michael's Church and Alnwick Castle stand either end of **Bailiffgate**, Alnwick's most elegant street of sandstone houses. The former Catholic church is now the **Bailiffgate Museum** (NE66 1LX ✆ 01665 605847 ⊘ www.bailiffgatemuseum.co.uk ☉ Tue–Sun ♿), which gives a comprehensive introduction to the history of Alnwick district – its buildings, industries and people – and puts on special art and craft exhibitions.

St Michael's Church
Opposite end of Bailiffgate from the castle ☉ May–Sep, most afternoons ♿
'Don't tell me the Victorians were good engineers,' said the church warden pointing to a bowed wall which began to tilt in the years following a 19th-century reconfiguration of the medieval edifice. Despite this, St Michael's certainly gives the appearance of strength and steadfastness with its short, castellated tower supported by wide buttresses. The unusual turret on the southeastern corner of the church served as a lookout point during the centuries of Border fighting.

Inside, the faces on some stained-glass windows have faded because an inferior black pigment was used in their creation. Those corner-cutting Victorians have caused no end of strife for the current warden. Take a closer look at the stone effigy of a knight: his buttons look unremarkable but back in the 14th century they were quite novel, having only come to Europe in the previous century.

Barter Books
Alnwick Station, Bondgate Without, NE66 2NP ✆ 01665 604888 ⊘ www.barterbooks.co.uk ☉ daily (until 19.00 in summer); café; ♿
You have to wonder how many customers to this characterful secondhand bookshop in a former Victorian railway station are here to buy books. Children sit on the floor picking through the shelves like they're in a library, locals wander in for lunch in the old waiting rooms, tourists stand still, necks craned to the ceiling admiring the station architecture, and lone visitors sip coffee by the open fire in the entrance reading the papers. 'I wanted it to be a place people could just go and be

ALNWICK INTERNATIONAL MUSIC FESTIVAL

A market town in Northumberland is an unlikely venue for an international gathering of musicians, but Alnwick is a vibrant place. It's a folk dance and music festival really, with performers from Eastern Europe, North America, Scotland, Northumberland and elsewhere. Expect swirling dresses, traditional costumes, sword dancers, fiddle players and concertinas and ukuleles to be out in force. The popular eight-day event is usually held early in August at a few venues around the town (weekend performances mainly in the Market Place). See www. alnwickmusicfestival.com.

left alone and stay all day if they want', says the founder of Barter Books, Mary Manley, who began converting the station rooms into a bookshop with her husband in 1991. She's certainly achieved that.

Barter Books oozes old-world charm with its decorative ironwork, working station clocks, waiting room **café** (over 100 cakes are baked on site every day), open fires and model train that trundles along all day on a track above the rickety bookcases. Between two bookshelves is a stone water basin (still with its brass cups attached to chains) once used by railway passengers.

On the books front, 'it's a bit of luck' what you'll find says Mary. There's something for everyone with most shelves stocked with non-fiction according to theme. You'll find antique books for upwards of £10,000 and those costing just a few pounds.

Barter Books is also home of one of the original 'Keep Calm and Carry On' World War II posters, which was found among a stash of books bought at auction. The crinkled poster is displayed in a frame. It's not for sale of course, but the owners are doing a roaring trade in facsimile copies of the posters as well as mugs and the other Keep Calm paraphernalia that has become so ubiquitous.

House of Hardy

Willowburn (south Alnwick, off the A1) NE66 2PF 01665 602771 www.hardy fishing.com

Even those not particularly interested in fishing may find this small museum and large showroom appealing. Anglers will be in heaven. For those not in the know, Hardy is a well-regarded Alnwick company making fishing rods and reels. Old black and white photographs of the company's craftsmen at work over 100 years ago and exhibits displaying the evolution of the famous Hardy rods and reels (the 'Rolls Royce of fishing reels' the chap behind the counter proudly described them) are displayed next to the shop. The Hardy traditional bamboo rods cost thousands but are still sold to those with a fondness for the craftsmanship of yesteryear; American visitors and Prince Charles, for example.

Hulne Park
Ratten Row, Alnwick ⊙ generally all year from 11.00 until sunset; no dogs or bicycles; free admission ♿

Not far from St Michael's Church is the imposing gateway to Hulne Park – a huge area of woods and open parkland enclosed by walls and owned by the Duke of Northumberland. Several miles of footpaths and paved tracks wind through the trees, over stone bridges, past dells and across open grasslands.

If Alnwick wasn't already stuffed with so many old buildings, perhaps more would be said of the romantic ruins of **Hulne Priory** founded by Carmelite friars in 1265. Also in the park is one of the most outlandish Gothic follies in England, **Brizlee Tower**, and the imposing 14th-century **gatehouse** of Alnwick Abbey, a striking turreted tower that stands alone in open parkland by the River Aln. Once you're past the working sawmill, you'll find the parkland a wonderfully tranquil place to visit for an extended walk or morning jog.

Alnwick Castle
Where Bailiffgate meets Narrowgate, NE66 1NQ ✆ 01665 510777 ⊘ www.alnwickcastle.com
⊙ end Mar–end Oct; café & restaurant (page 59); free guided tours; ♿ grounds only

Alnwick Castle is often referred to as the 'Windsor Castle of the North' in tourism literature on account of its size and imposing buildings. Like Windsor, it's home to royalty; well, Geordie royalty at least. The Duke and Duchess of Northumberland are historically one of the most powerful aristocratic families in England; they own huge amounts of land and property, including this almighty fortress.

Alnwick has been the Percy family's principal seat for 700 years ever since Henry de Percy bought the castle from the Bishop of Durham in 1309. Stonework from the earlier Norman building is seen in the archway into the keep, but the castle was extensively rebuilt in the 14th century and again in the latter half of the 18th century.

HARRY 'HOTSPUR'

I'll empty all these veins, And shed my dear blood drop by drop in the dust.

William Shakespeare *Henry IV, Part One*

Of all the Percy men through the centuries, the most legendary is Harry 'Hotspur', a fearless and impulsive knight who fought in several conflicts at sea and on land during the 1300s, including the midnight Battle of Otterburn in 1388. Hotspur went on to lead the rebellion against Henry IV in the Battle of Shrewsbury in 1403 and like all infamous knights he died in combat when an arrow pierced his skull (I'm not sure how historically accurate this detail is, but it has certainly helped to perpetuate the Hotspur legend). Shakespeare immortalised Hotspur in *Henry IV, Part One*.

Today, Hotspur is remembered in many place and building names in the North East and in the London football club, Tottenham Hotspur, so called because the Percy family owned the land where the club originated.

The present buildings are largely medieval and the castle roughly retains its original layout with a circular keep about a courtyard and an inner and outer bailey. Miniature stone warriors guard the parapets. From a distance, they look life-size and were intended to give the impression of a well-armed castle. Indeed, Alnwick was very much built with military use in mind, and its strength has been tested several times by the Scots. The formidable **barbican** is said to be one of the best examples of its kind in the country.

Inside the **keep** hangs a Canaletto depicting the ruinous castle as it was in 1750 before the Georgian restoration under the 1st Duke of Northumberland. He directed the transformation of the castle into a stately home, and the countryside beyond the castle's north walls into landscaped parkland.

The current 12th Duke and Duchess of Northumberland have certainly left their mark. The Duchess is responsible for the much-publicised £42-million redevelopment of the gardens and establishing Alnwick Castle and The Alnwick Garden as the North East's leading paid-for attractions and two of the top ten attractions in Britain. The former head of Disneyland Paris was employed as chief executive and is said to be behind some of the attractions. There's no denying the castle has a theme-park edge.

Ever since the filming of *Harry Potter* in 2000, the fortress has become known to many young visitors as Hogwarts School of Witchcraft and Wizardry. The managers are only too happy to indulge them and you'll find broomstick-riding lessons (as entertaining for spectators) among the array of wizard- and medieval-themed activities.

Alnwick Castle is clearly a huge hit with families, but there's also much to interest those with a love of porcelain, fine art (the castle houses a distinguished collection of Renaissance art, including eight paintings by Canaletto and three Titians) and, of course, gardens (see below).

A taste of the Duke of Northumberland's riches are revealed in the **State Rooms**. The dining room, library and drawing room are sumptuously furnished with highly decorative ceilings, fireplaces and wall hangings, etc. When the dining room underwent restoration in 2005–06, it took five men five weeks just to polish the ceiling. Paintings by Canaletto, Velasquez and Turner hang on the walls and an extensive collection of Meissen porcelain is displayed in the **China Gallery**.

Two of the most treasured items in the castle are the ornately carved and painted Italian Cucci cabinets, made out of ebony for Louis XIV's palace at Versailles in the late 17th century. They are thought to be two of the most valuable pieces of furniture in the world.

The **Inner Bailey** is spectacular – for its size, tremendous walls and the 18th-century view from the ramparts. Below, expansive tree-studded **parkland** falls away from the walls and rolls to the River Aln and beyond. It is one of the most beautifully designed landscapes in Northumberland and, not altogether surprisingly, the work of local landscape architect, Lancelot 'Capability' Brown. The parkland can be enjoyed along a public footpath north of the river which requires the visitor first to cross the showy **Lion Bridge** on the B6346. Castellated parapets, faux arrow slits and the arresting statue of a lion guarding the crossing and entrance to the town add to the appeal of this much-photographed bridge dating to 1773. The view looking south with Alnwick Castle rearing above the River Aln is highly memorable.

The Alnwick Garden

Denwick Lane, NE66 1YU ♪ 01665 511350 ⊘ www.alnwickgarden.com ⊙ Feb–Dec, daily; café & restaurant (page 59); &

The newly restored gardens at Alnwick are unashamedly bold and contemporary and designed to thrill. In 1997, Jane Percy, the 12th

ALN VALLEY RAILWAY

Lionheart Enterprise Park (southeast of Alnwick) NE66 2HT ☏ 0300 030 3311 🖥 www.
alnvalleyrailway.co.uk ☉ Easter–Sep, Sun and all weekend on bank holidays; Tue–Thu in
school holidays ♿

From the 1850s a four-mile branch line operated from Alnwick town to the coast at Alnmouth for 110 years. Restoration of the heritage line by a dedicated team of volunteers is currently underway with new sections opening in stages (at the time of writing, trains travelled for half a mile – a ride costing just a few pounds). Steam and diesel locomotives run from the new Lionheart Station (Alnwick's original Victorian station now houses Barter Books) where there's also a small museum, shop, 'bring and buy' stall and café. What will really interest railway enthusiasts though is the loco shed where you can observe the restoration of carriages and engines. Special events include classic car shows, summer markets, Easter egg hunts and so on.

Duchess of Northumberland began steering the development of the overgrown gardens into the pleasure grounds experienced today, but not without criticism.

The centrepiece is the **Grand Cascade**, a huge modern waterfall lined with fountains that plunges over many tiers into a pool. The cascades must have been designed with families in mind because the layout makes it possible for parents to sit in the outdoor café and keep an eye on their children driving toy dumper trunks under the spray of water. The same children will probably enjoy **Splash! Alnwick**, an organised water fight that takes place every hour in spring and summer (water pistols supplied) on the lawns between the Pavilion and the Poison Garden.

"Only at Alnwick can you walk through a dark maze created in a thicket of bamboo, experience a display of the world's most toxic plants and wander in the largest orchard of its kind in the world."

Around the Grand Cascade are a number of distinctive gardens which, with the exception of the more traditional enclosures like the **Rose Garden** and **Ornamental Garden**, are all novel and exciting (a sensory garden is next to be laid out). Only at Alnwick can you walk through a dark maze created in a thicket of bamboo, experience a display of the world's most toxic plants in the **Poison**

Garden and wander under the boughs of cherry trees in the largest orchard of its kind in the world. The **Serpent Garden** uses water to creative effect in a sequence of mesmerising contemporary installations and is not to be missed. Ditto the Treehouse restaurant which is quite magical (see below).

A steward told me the quietest time to visit the gardens is on Fridays. I visited late one Friday afternoon in August and can accurately report that I was one of very few people there.

FOOD & DRINK

Bari Tea 28 Narrowgate, NE66 1JG ✆ 01665 510508 ♿. 'Each tea is timed for three minutes for a perfect brew,' says the owner of this contemporary café specialising in posh tea (loose-leaf and not cheap). Also on offer are cakes and homemade soups. 'Bari' ('baa-ree'), incidentally, is a Northumbrian word meaning 'delicious'.

Carlo's Fish and Chips 7–9 Market St, NE66 1SS ✆ 01665 602787 ⊙ daily. Really good fish and chips (take-away or eat in) at reasonable prices. I reckon Carlo's gives some of the Seahouses restaurants a run for their money.

Grannie's Tearoom 18 Narrowgate, NE66 1JG ✆ 01665 602394. The smell of fresh bread and tea wafts up the stairs of this tiny café hunkered down on the ground floor of a 400-year-old building. It looks straight out of the pages of a nursery book with copper kettles hanging from the ceiling, a drying rack with knickerbockers and a range among its furnishings. Homemade cakes, scones, pies and soups.

Lilburns Bar Restaurant 7 Paikes St, NE66 1HX ✆ 01665 603444 ♿. This is a great find, tucked away on a pedestrian lane connecting the Market Place and Bondgate Within. Lilburns feels more like a café inside but it's earned a good reputation for its evening menu (steaks, lamb, seafood). Expect to pay around £16 for mains. Fish and pasta dishes as well as burgers, baked potatoes and paninis served at lunchtime.

The Cheese Room 5 Paikes St, NE66 1HX ✆ 01665 604000. Picnickers should stock up at this great deli that also makes sandwiches to order and sells crackers, chutneys, olives and so on. You'll find all the Northumberland Cheese Company and Doddington's offerings as well as plenty of regional cheeses from around the UK.

Strawberry Lounge 20 Narrowgate, NE66 1JG ✆ 07845 216810. This little lunchtime gem is hidden from view down a side alley. Cheap sandwiches, jacket potatoes, quiches and fish cakes are served in the small café but what the Strawberry Lounge is best known for are its smoothies and unusual scones (about ten different types such as sultana and pear, and chilli and cheese).

Treehouse The Alnwick Gardens, NE66 1YU ✆ 01665 511852 ⊙ Thu–Sun evening, & from noon–15.00 daily for lunch. You'll need to book far in advance to secure an evening table in this enchanting tree-top restaurant within the grounds of Alnwick Gardens (no ticket required for evening meals). Dishes prepared using local seafood and Northumberland meats are not cheap, but the surroundings are very special, with trees protruding through the floor and an open fire. For breakfasts and light lunches you may like **The Potting Shed** which is great for families (kids will love the rope bridges and walkways), and in the evening those dining in the Treehouse can enjoy a cocktail here.

Turnbull's of Alnwick 33–5 Market St, NE66 1SS ✆ 01665 602186. For a bite to eat while you wander through Alnwick, try this well-known butchers opposite the Market Place. Turnbull's has been here for over 100 years and sell inexpensive take-away sandwiches (cold or with hot meats) and pies. Their steak and ale pie made with Farne Isle ale costs little more than £1.

Yan's Restaurant 10 Bondgate Within, NE66 1TD ✆ 01665 603888 ◷ Wed–Mon. Popular Cantonese restaurant recommended by lots of locals, and probably one of the best places for dinner in Alnwick town centre.

THE HERITAGE COAST

🏠 **Grace Darling Holidays** (page 272), **Coastal Retreats Northumberland** (page 272)

Northumberland's beaches don't get creamier or softer than those between Warkworth and Berwick-upon-Tweed within the Area of Outstanding Natural Beauty – also known as the 'Heritage Coast'. The likes of Sugar Sands, Embleton Bay and Beadnell Bay are popular with families and walkers and often top polls of Britain's best beaches. Despite this reputation, they are surprisingly crowd-free, even in high summer. Family-friendly seaside villages include Alnmouth, Seahouses and Bamburgh. Heritage hunters and nature watchers are spoiled with the renowned Farne archipelago, Lindisfarne National Nature Reserve, and a string of fantastically arresting castles punctuating the coastline (four within 20 miles).

10 WARKWORTH

🏠 **Roxbro House** (page 272)

Warkworth Castle rears over the rooftops of a long row of sandstone houses that step down to the River Coquet, linking the parish church at the bottom with the castle at the top. The Coquet forms a hairpin loop around the village, protecting it on three sides (the castle guards the fourth base to the south) before opening to the sea a mile or so beyond the 14th-century bridge. Warkworth's medieval layout is one of the most intact and celebrated in the whole of England.

WARKWORTH OLD BRIDGE

Clearly a venerable structure, Warkworth's 14th-century bridge over the River Coquet features cutwaters between its two arches and a fortified tower (once used as a toll house). It's a cobbled pedestrian bridge these days but you get good views as you enter the village from the newer road bridge (the B1068/continuation of Bridge Street).

At the foot of the village, the Coquet flows around **St Lawrence Church**, making coastal Warkworth feel much more like a riverside settlement. Despite its protective loop, the river was not enough of a barrier to keep the Scots out in 1174 when they raided Warkworth and massacred the men, women and children sheltering inside St Lawrence's. A church has stood here since Saxon times, but the present building dates to 1130 with medieval and Victorian modifications. Its Norman origins are immediately apparent in the chancel with its, now slightly crooked, arch and impressive stone vaulted ceiling. The only medieval stained glass to survive is in the top of the east window.

"At the foot of the village, the Coquet flows around St Lawrence Church, making coastal Warkworth feel much more like a riverside settlement."

Opposite the church is the **market cross** where, on 9 October 1715, Warkworth became the first public place in England to proclaim James III as king during the fated Jacobite Rebellion. The night before, the legendary Earl of Derwentwater (pages 117–18) and 40 rebels dined at the nearby Masons Arms. The event is recorded on a beam inside the pub and described on a plaque outside.

On the **main street** leading away from the church and market cross, you'll find a few pubs and shops, a contemporary art gallery selling pottery, jewellery and paintings, a chocolaterie and a few cafés.

The **river** is crowded with trees and is a pleasant place to go for a walk, feed the ducks, picnic or row a boat (the hire station is close to the hermitage landing). Half a mile or so upriver from the church is the crossing point for the medieval **hermitage** (✆ 01665 711423 ☉ Apr–end Sep, Sun–Mon & bank holidays; English Heritage) – a 15th-century rock-cut chapel concealed by trees on the north side of the river. To get there, you must take the rowing boat operated by English Heritage (small charge).

Warkworth Castle

Castle Terrace, NE65 0UJ ✆ 01665 711423 ☉ Easter–end Oct & school holidays, daily; weekends only in autumn & winter; English Heritage

worm-eaten hold of ragged stone
William Shakespeare *Henry IV, Part One*

Warkworth is a fortress to be reckoned with. Though much ruined internally, its 14th-century keep still maintains a heavy presence at the head of the village. The perimeter walls and restored gatehouse date from around 1200 and have resisted the ravages of time better than many of the medieval buildings inside.

Percy is a name you will have heard on your travels along the coast, especially if you've already visited Alnwick Castle, currently the Duke of Northumberland's main seat. Several centuries ago, Warkworth was the Percy family's principal residence, hence the lion motif stamped about the place. Nowhere else is the beast more strikingly carved than above the doorway to the Lion Tower at Warkworth.

The impressive **keep** is formed of four polygonal wings arranged around a central square. Its roof, battlements and turrets are long gone, exposing the building's ribcage to the sea air, but you still get a good sense of the layout of rooms and can imagine the Duke of Northumberland's medieval banquets in the Great Hall. From his private chamber, he could look over the village and, as today, see all the way to Coquet Island and beyond.

Warkworth's beach (Alnmouth Bay)

From Warkworth, a glorious long stretch of pale sand backed by thick dunes shoots north to Alnmouth. To reach the beach, take the paved track heading east from the north side of the medieval bridge. After half a mile you come to a parking area with toilets. From here it's a short downhill stroll to the beach.

When you meet the dunes, a fingerpost directs you to Alnmouth (4½ miles) along the coast path. If there were a footbridge crossing the estuary at Alnmouth, this would be one of the most popular beach walks in Northumberland. Unfortunately you get within a hop, skip and a jump (almost) of Alnmouth and have to turn back unless, that is, you're prepared to remove your socks and shoes, roll up your trousers and wade through the fast-flowing water that crosses the bay (see opposite).

¶¶ FOOD & DRINK

For a smart village popular with tourists, it's surprising that there aren't better places to eat in Warkworth. This is particularly true when it comes to evening dining. Your best bet is the **Old Post Office B&B** (32 Castle St, NE65 0UL ☏ 01665 711341) which has a small menu (and only six or seven tables) offering a couple of meat, vegetarian and seafood dishes on Friday and Saturday evenings (book in advance). A couple of fair pubs and cafés are dotted about the main street. Also consider restaurants in Amble (page 49).

11 ALNMOUTH

⌂ The Red Lion (page 272)

Some London to Edinburgh trains stop at Alnmouth, but note that the station is a few miles inland from the village

Alnmouth's pastel-coloured cottages crowded above creamy sands and the Aln Estuary make this old village one of the most distinctive (and photographed) places on the Northumberland coast. An unbeatable vantage point (apart from if you're passing on an East Coast Main Line train) is **Church Hill** (a grassy knoll with a cross and ruined Victorian chapel). A much older church once stood on this hillock but it was destroyed during a storm in 1806 that was so violent, it changed the course of the river, cutting off Church Hill from the village.

The usual approach for those travelling by road is across a multi-arched Victorian bridge that skims the River Aln. If travelling on foot over dunes and **beach** from Warkworth (pages 60–1), you get tantalisingly close to Alnmouth only to find that you can't cross the estuary which is fast-flowing and dangerous because of quicksand, and have to backtrack on the long and unappealing coast path that follows the main road. If you are going to attempt the beach crossing, your best bet is probably to go barefoot at the shoreline when the tide is really far out (don't attempt to cross further up the estuary because the current is very strong and locals warn of quicksand).

"Its pastel-coloured cottages crowded above creamy sands and the Aln Estuary make this old village one of the most distinctive places on the coast."

Alnmouth's main road, **Northumberland Street**, opens generously to sand dunes at its southern end. Along its length are shops, a church and a number of pubs and cafés. The sharp-eyed visitor will notice that a few buildings have irregular-shaped windows (the row leading away from the post office on the main street, for example).

They were built as granaries during the 18th century when Alnmouth was a busy port and exported large amounts of corn.

At the sand dune end of the main street in the side of a stone house is a small window displaying an old barometer that was given to the Alnmouth coastguards in 1860 by the Duke of Northumberland. It is a pleasing object, as is the description of its history.

FOOD & DRINK

For a small town, Alnmouth has a fairly large selection of tea rooms, pubs and restaurants, most of which are strung out along Northumberland Street.

Beaches Restaurant 56 Northumberland St, NE66 2RJ ✆ 01665 830006 ○ Thu, Fri & Sat evenings. There's nothing fancy about this small bring-your-own restaurant in the front room of a B&B but the food is really quite good. Seafood is their speciality (North Sea crab, hake and ling were being served up when I visited) and there's always smoked fish from Craster, and lobster in early summer.

Bistro 23 23 Northumberland St, NE66 2RJ ✆ 01665 830393 ○ Wed–Mon for lunch; Wed & Sat for dinner, plus Thu in summer. This is the place to eat in Alnmouth. It's a fairly simple eatery (tea room in the daytime serving sandwiches; restaurant come nightfall) with a limited menu and opening hours but the owners prepare dishes from scratch using local ingredients such as Cheviot lamb, crab from the North Sea and cheeses from Blagdon. Northumberland beef is always on the menu.

Red Lion 22 Northumberland St, NE66 2RJ ✆ 01665 830584 ♿. Alnmouth is not short of pubs, but the Red Lion is probably the best. It's a traditional old inn with a low-beamed ceiling, open fire and laid-back atmosphere. There's an outside drinking area overlooking the estuary. Good local ales and traditional pub fare (some dishes prepared with Northumbrian beef and fish). Above average B&B accommodation (page 272).

✳ ✳ ✳

A CIRCULAR COASTAL WALK FROM ALNMOUTH

✻ OS Explorer map 332; start: The Wynd, Alnmouth, ♥ NU246106; 2 miles; difficulty: easy; refreshments at the Red Lion (see above)

This is a fairly easy family route with expansive sea views, beach walking, rockpools and a good real ale pub at the end.

At the north end of Northumberland Street, Alnmouth's main thoroughfare, wander down The Wynd towards the sea. When you come to a junction, turn left and continue to the golf club entrance where there's a footpath fingerpost by a road hump. Veering left here will lead to an uphill dirt path offering good views of the coastline. After half a mile or so you'll reach a fork in the path by a golf green. Go straight downhill here, crossing the green until you reach the beach which opens by Marden Rocks (good for rockpooling). Turn right and walk back to Alnmouth along the beach, re-entering the village at the southern end. A pint and hearty lunch await at the Red Lion.

* * *

12 SUGAR SANDS & AROUND

Whin Sill outcrops and limestone between the villages of Boulmer and Craster come together to create a very striking and unusual shoreline particularly near Craster where horizontal sheets of rock heave in great shelves on to the beach. Hidden along this coastline are three sandy bays perfect for families. The middle beach is Sugar Sands – one of Northumberland's finest secluded coves.

The bays are reached in quick succession from the coast path (a rough track for most of the way from Boulmer to Howick and suitable for cyclists). If driving or cycling to Sugar Sands, take the paved lane east from Longhoughton where there's a rough parking area at the end of Howdiemont Sands.

Boulmer

This straggling old fishing village with a rocky shore and RAF base was once legendary for its smugglers. 'As many as twenty or thirty of them, mounted on horseback, would come to Boulmer for gin, and carry it to the centre of the county and the wilds of Coquetdale, not without many hair-breath escapes and lively encounters with the excisemen',

THE GREAT WHIN SILL

Three hundred million years ago, hot, molten rock from the Earth's core surged through to the surface and solidified, forming hard basaltic outcrops rising sporadically – and dramatically – throughout Northumbria. These ridges have caught the eye of emperors, Saxon settlers, dukes – and seabirds. It is what Hadrian's Wall teeters along, Bamburgh Castle rises from and what makes the Farne Islands such a special sanctuary for wildlife. On the coast near Craster the combination of hard Whin Sill outcrops and softer limestone has created many contorted, serpent-like formations on the shoreline. For more information and guided walks by an expert geologist, see Northumbrian Earth ⬧ www.northumbrianearth.co.uk.

HOWICK SHIPWRECK

Just south of Rumbling Kern there's an old ship's boiler that belonged to a French steam trawler that hit rocks nearby in March 1913 on its way to Icelandic fishing grounds. According to a newspaper report at the time, the lifeboat from Boulmer and many local people came to the aid of the fishermen. They rescued 25 men but five sailors (one just 16 years old) drowned. A few of the deceased had tied themselves to the rigging and mast to avoid being washed away in the storm and had to be cut down. The newspaper described the scene as so harrowing that the coastguard ordered all local children away from the shore. The Frenchmen are buried in the church on the Howick Hall estate and the event summarised on the memorial stone.

says Tomlinson in his *Comprehensive Guide to Northumberland*. The centre of the illicit activities was the Fishing Boat Inn, which is still in business today (mediocre pub with a great view of the North Sea from a conservatory). Tomlinson says casks of liquor are sometimes still dug up on the coast – but he was writing in 1888, so there's little chance of contraband finds today.

Rumbling Kern

Such an evocative name for a beach (just north of Sugar Sands) piled with rocks and with plenty of holes and channels for the sea to roar through. At low tide, this is a great bay for rockpooling and beachcombing. At the north end of the cove, there's a tempting swimming hole cut into the rock.

The Victorian house on the headland (now a very popular holiday cottage, see ⊘ www.northumbria-byways.com) is the **Bathing House**, built by the 2nd Earl Grey of nearby Howick Hall for his 15 children to stay in while enjoying a dip in the sea below.

13 HOWICK HALL GARDENS

Howick NE66 3LB ⊘ 01665 577285 ⊘ www.howickhallgardens.org ⊙ early Feb & Mar Wed–Sun, daily during British Summer Time until mid-Nov; tea room (open to visitors to gardens only); ⊙

In the grounds of an 18th-century manor a few miles from the sea is one of Northumberland's finest gardens open to the public. Howick's flowering season starts with a dazzling display of snowdrops followed by daffodils then flowering rhododendrons, camellias and magnolia trees. In high summer, the **Bog Garden** is a visual treat: a water garden with a lake surrounded by bushy lupins, roses, delphiniums and poppies spilling over into grassy paths. Some 11,000 trees and shrubs were planted in the **arboretum** by the current Lord Howick who is an ardent collector of exotics. Many specimens were grown from seeds gathered on expeditions to China and elsewhere which you can read about in the visitor centre next to the tea room.

The **Woodland Garden** is one of the highlights, especially for its eye-catching stone bridge, spring-flowering shrubs and the way it merges naturally into the woods beyond the road. Here, a path called the **Long Walk** takes a meandering route to the

"A path called the Long Walk takes a meandering route to the sea, roughly following the bubbling Howick Burn."

sea, roughly following the bubbling Howick Burn that comes in and out of view for the 1½-mile stroll to Sugar Sands. You are permitted to walk its length under certain conditions, enforced by a couple of gates. When the gardens are closed in winter, the gates are always open and you can walk in either direction. When the gardens are open (early February to mid-November), the gates permit one-way travel (from the estate to the coast) for those who have paid to see the gardens. I've described the circular walk on page 71.

The house (not currently open to the public) was built in 1782 and rebuilt following a fire in 1926. It has been a home, first to the Grey family and later inherited by the Howicks, since 1319. The most illustrious figure was **Charles, 2nd Earl Grey**, who served as prime minister from 1830 to 1834, and is best known for the Great Reform Bill of 1832 which influenced the development of our modern democracy. He loved the family home at Howick and stayed in Northumberland as much as

EARL GREY TEA

This delicate tea was especially blended with bergamot to offset the taste of the lime-rich water from the spring on the Howick estate. Earl Grey tea became popular among London's political elite when Lady Grey served the brew at social events. Twinings were brought in to market the blend but, sadly for the ancestors of the Grey family, the trademark was not registered and no royalties have therefore ever been received.

Leaf Earl Grey tea is served in the old ballroom on the Howick Hall estate (page 68).

he could, to the frustration of colleagues in London. Described in an estate leaflet as 'one of Britain's greatest Prime Ministers, and one of the century's greatest truants', he is buried in the estate's church. Incidentally, he had an unusual way of preventing his children from developing a fear of the dark. On the first full moon in the July following their tenth birthday, they had to walk to the sea on this trail at midnight and return with a stem of grass of Parnassus, a white flower that grew (and indeed grows to this day, albeit in an inaccessible location) on rocks at the coast.

14 CRASTER

ⱔ Proctor's Stead (page 273)

The smell of burning firewood wafts through the streets of stone cottages gathered around a snug harbour in the fishing village of Craster. There's no mistaking where the famous **smokehouse** is situated: it's the stone building with white plumes pouring out of wooden vents in the roof. Herring has been smoked here by L Robson & Sons (see opposite) for over 100 years.

Today, the fish are split using machines and hung on hooks above smouldering oak sawdust and whitewood shavings for up to 16 hours, but once local 'herring girls' did the unenviable task by hand. You can buy kippers over the counter or have them for lunch in the adjoining restaurant or in the Jolly Fisherman (see below).

Craster has become somewhat gentrified in recent years, hence the contemporary café, gastro pub and art gallery. West of Craster harbour is the main visitor car park with a **tourist information centre** (page 40).

⫟ FOOD & DRINK

In and around Craster there are a few places to eat and drink including the contemporary **Shoreline Café** (corner of Church St & Haven Hill, NE66 3TH ⌀ 01665 571251 ⱔ) that sells coffees, sandwiches and cakes.

Earl Grey Tea House Howick Hall, Howick NE66 3LB ⌀ 01665 572232 ☺ see times for Howick Hall on page 66 ⱔ. A cup of leaf Earl Grey tea served in the home of the famous brew is a real treat – as are the sumptuous surroundings of the old ballroom with its floor-to-ceiling windows looking out over the estate gardens. Howick Hall's cream tea is one of the best in Northumberland (the fruit scones are particularly delicious) but to eat here you must purchase a ticket for the gardens, which isn't cheap.

Jolly Fisherman Haven Hill, NE66 3TR ⌀ 01665 576461 ⱔ bar area only where you can also eat. Once a routine pub in a prime seafront location and now a much-improved place

🌾 RENNINGTON SCARECROW FESTIVAL

If you're in the area during August bank holiday weekend, drop in to the village of Rennington to see the scarecrows. Visit ⊘ www.bradtguides.com/renningtonscarecrows for more details.

to eat with an expansive view of Dunstanburgh Castle. The owners have built an outside terrace and brought in the decorators ('rustic chic') and a reputable chef. You'll still find old favourites though like crab soup, crab sandwiches and kipper pâté (now served on a wooden board with toasted sourdough bread). Seafood is their thing but red meat and a couple of vegetarian options also feature on the evening menu.

L Robson & Sons smokehouse Haven Hill, opposite the pub, NE66 3TR ⊘ 01665 576223 ⊘ www.kipper.co.uk ⊙ daily, but in autumn and winter closes on Sun & early afternoon on Sat 👍). Craster kippers are the obvious choice if cooking up your own seafood lunch, but the famous smokehouse also sells fishcakes, kipper pâté, baked herring, mussels, scallops and smoked salmon among other seafood delights from their on-site shop. The restaurant is sadly rather tired-looking.

Dunstanburgh Castle

Craster; no road access, 1¼-mile walk north from Craster across grassland ⊘ 01665 576231 ⊙ Apr–end Oct & Feb school holidays, daily; weekends only in winter; toilets; free admission for National Trust members; English Heritage

Viewed from the north, Dunstanburgh is a shattered ruin clinging to the edge of a cliff formed of Whin Sill rock. Through sun haze or sea fret, the medieval edifice rarely looks anything but rough and moody: its crumbling turrets and curtain walls are almost always seen in silhouette form. But from the south, Dunstanburgh bares its formidable chest, appearing more brutish – and terrifically romantic. The sight of the huge drum gate towers greeting the sun, and the sea pounding nearby rocks, cannot be beaten. It doesn't matter that most of the fortress has succumbed to the wind and sea and is now under the ownership of fulmars and kittiwakes.

"Viewed from the north, Dunstanburgh is a shattered ruin clinging to the edge of a cliff formed of Whin Sill rock."

But for all its might, the 14th-century stronghold of Thomas, Earl of Lancaster, the richest man in England after the king, was more a show of power than an important military base. Dunstanburgh never came under attack by the Scots (though plenty of local inhabitants and their livestock were driven by Scottish raiders to within its protective walls); but it was besieged during the Wars of the Roses in 1462. On one of two attacks, the garrison, which had taken to eating their horses, only really surrendered to the Yorkists out of starvation. After the execution of Lancaster for treason, the castle was inherited by John of Gaunt, son of Edward III, who built a gateway bearing his name in the west curtain wall (still visible today). By the mid 1500s, Dunstanburgh was a ruin, and, in any case, after the Union of England and Scotland in 1603 it had become militarily redundant.

"After the execution of Lancaster for treason, the castle was inherited by John of Gaunt, son of Edward III, who built a gateway bearing his name in the west curtain wall."

For a castle of which little remains, Dunstanburgh still holds its own in the line of Northumberland's great coastal fortresses. But, unlike Alnwick, Bamburgh or Lindisfarne, it has not been patched up or altered much over the centuries by its owners. You'll find, firstly, that most of what you see today dates from its original construction in 1313, and secondly that there's not much to see behind its walls, besides a view of the coast from Liburn Tower and a number of medieval garderobes.

The legend of Sir Guy the Seeker – and his ghost which is said to haunt Dunstanburgh – is immortalised in a ballard that begins:

Sir Knight! Sir Knight! If your heart be right,
And your nerves be firm and true,
Sir Knight! Sir Knight! A beauty bright
In durance waits for you.

Searching for shelter one stormy night, the knight met with a wizard who ushered him through Dunstanburgh Castle to the bedside of a maiden lying asleep under a spell. She was guarded by two skeletons: one holding a sword and the other a horn. The fate of the maiden rested on the knight choosing the sword or the horn. He wrongly opted for the latter and spent the rest of his life being taunted by the wizard's words:

Now shame on the coward who sounded a horn
When he might have unsheathed a sword.

* * *

CRASTER, HOWICK HALL & BEACH CIRCULAR WALK

※ OS Explorer map 332; start: Whin Hill, Craster, ♀ NU258198; 6 miles; difficulty: easy walk on flat paths that are mostly well marked; refreshments at Howick Hall tea room, & the pub & café at Craster ♨ for a longer version of this walk, see ⊘ www.bradtguides.com/crasterwalk

This is one of my favourite coastal walks because of the variety of scenery (woodlands, coastal flower meadows, historic gardens, sandy beaches, bird cliffs, castle views) and the lovely tea room and pub in the middle and at the end of the walk respectively.

Owing to the one-way gates on the Howick Hall estate (pages 66–8), in spring, summer and early autumn you must walk in an anti-clockwise direction (ie: north on the coast path on the return leg), the route described here.

Set foot from Whin Hill (opposite the pub) and take the (signed) path for Howick Scar that goes round the back of the houses, crosses a field and then part of a meadow before descending a track and through **Howick Scar Farm**. Cross the road and take the signed footpath to Howick Hall along the edge of a field. Skirt the rocky gorse-covered Hips Heugh and after crossing a dry stone wall, walk through a field and then up a tree-lined track which emerges by **Howick Hall**.

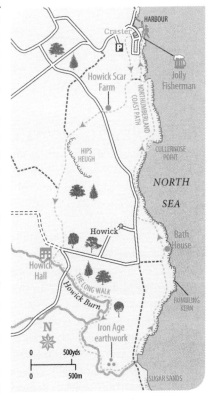

Pay your entrance money and wander through the gardens picking up the wooded **Long Walk**, which is reached by crossing a bridge over the road. There's a one-way turnstile here and another as you near the sea (see page 67 for access).

For glorious **Sugar Sands**, turn right, or if you are returning to Craster, head north on the coast path (signed).

An **Iron Age earthwork** hereabouts is accessed via a gate on the left just north of the footbridge. There are good views of the coast all the way to Seahouses from the top of the earthwork, which is not particularly impressive in itself.

Halfway to Craster the coast path skirts the Bathing House at Rumbling Kern (page 66)

and the **Cullernose Point** bird cliffs where fulmars and kittiwakes nest in summer. Distant views of Dunstanburgh Castle enrich the return route for much of the way. In summer, the flower meadows on the outskirts of the village are stuffed with buttercups, clovers and orchids.

Follow the coast path directly into the beer garden of the Jolly Fisherman.

15 EMBLETON

Set back half a mile from the sea between Craster and Newton-by-the-Sea, Embleton draws in visitors because of its proximity to Embleton Bay, one of the most popular sandy beaches in Northumberland (see opposite), its coastal golf course and its pleasing cluster of pubs and houses set around a triangular village green with a church. There are parts of the **Holy Trinity**, including the nave arcades, that date from the 13th century and the lower sections of the tower date from even earlier.

FOOD & DRINK

If you're looking for a pub, the **Greys Inn** (NE66 3UZ ✆ 01665 576983) at the top end of the green is your best bet. For good coffee, try **Eleanor's Byre** (Spitalford NE66 3DW ✆ 01665 571371), an unexpected café (and gift room) with a sunny courtyard by the roadside south out of Embleton.

16 LOW NEWTON-BY-THE-SEA

Newton hasn't always been so gentrified. Despite second-home owners from Newcastle swallowing up the place and the reinvention of the much-loved shabby pub into more of an upmarket restaurant, the hamlet's square of whitewashed stone cottages a few yards from the beach is still very appealing.

In 1859, the travel writer Walter White in *Northumberland, and the Border* observed boys coming and going from herring boats and the cottages in the square where 'women fling their household slops and fish offal' and 'are content to live within sight thereof'. White was not impressed. 'Newton is not pretty or pleasing', he wrote. He never would have guessed that 150 years later, well-off families would be hob nobbing on the green, eating lobster in the pub, attending folk music concerts in the tiny corrugated iron church by the side of the road as you enter Newton (and, incidentally, bought in kit form over 100 years ago), and paying extortionate prices to buy the holiday shacks in the dunes.

BIRDLIFE AROUND EMBLETON BAY & NEWTON

In summer, watch gannets plunging into the sea in open water and cruising terns along the shoreline (all five British breeding species could show up). Fulmars and kittiwakes nest on the cliffs under **Dunstanburgh Castle** and at **Cullernose Point** (south of Craster). In winter, the wave-washed rocks at **Newton Point** are reliable for eider ducks, turnstones and red-breasted mergansers.

Behind the dunes and north of the boat park at Newton is a freshwater **lake** overlooked by a couple of bird hides (one is wheelchair accessible). All the usual suspects are found here, including coots, swans, geese and gulls.

The surrounding damp fields are often more exciting though, especially in winter when flocks of wading birds and migrating geese gather to feed. Don't overlook the scrubland as you walk to the bird hides; migrant passerines rest here in autumn on their journey south.

Embleton Bay & Newton Haven

Car park at Newton-by-the-Sea; bus stops at High Newton & Embleton

Between Newton-by-the-Sea and Dunstanburgh Castle is a glorious stretch of buttery-coloured sand (technically two bays) and one of the most popular family beaches in Northumberland. That said, even on hot days in summer, kite-boarders can still find an empty run of sand, and children can be lord of their own dune. The most accessible rockpools are at the northern end by Newton but the Emblestones (halfway along) are also full of anemones, starfish, hermit crabs and so on. Look out for grey seals hauled up on the furthermost rocks.

Surfing lessons can be arranged along some of Northumberland's beaches, including at Embleton, through Northside Surf ($\mathscr{O}$ 01665 713146, 07944 398115 $\mathring{\mathscr{O}}$ www.northside-surf-school.co.uk) – a company based in Amble.

If it gets too crowded at Newton, wander north over the headland to **Football Hole** – a small, secluded bay – and hunker down in the dunes.

🍴 FOOD & DRINK

Joiners Arms High Newton-by-the-Sea NE66 3EA $\mathscr{O}$ 01665 576112 ⬤. There's a gastropub feel to this revamped inn at the bottom of the hill as you approach Low Newton. It's always busy with families (book ahead at weekends) and has gained a good reputation for its food (fish dishes as well as Northumbrian beef burgers, steaks and so on). On the beer front, there are usually a few North East bitters on tap. Boutique-style B&B rooms upstairs.

Ship Inn Low Newton-by-the-Sea NE66 3EL ✆ 01665 576262. You may see a local fisherman walking up Newton's beach with a few lobsters for the restaurant. It almost goes without saying that if you want lobster for dinner (Wednesday to Saturday), you'll need to put your order through in advance. Apart from the fresh seafood, most meats and dairy products are also sourced in Northumberland and the beer comes from the on-site brewery. Unsurprisingly, the Ship is always overflowing with cheerful families and walkers. What's not to like? Fighting for a table at lunchtime (you can't book).

✻ ✻ ✻

☗ BEACH, CASTLE & SMOKEHOUSE WALK: NEWTON TO CRASTER

☀ OS Explorer maps 332 & 340; start: Newton-by-the-Sea, ♀ NU241245; 4½ miles one-way; difficulty: easy; refreshments at Newton & Craster

The return linear walk to Dunstanburgh Castle and Craster from Newton-by-the-Sea is one of the most popular on the Northumberland coast and has all the ingredients of a perfect coastal trail: a super sandy beach, shallow waters, a castle and a great pub at either end. It's also straightforward to navigate and you can do away with your maps – just head for the ruined fortress in the distance.

From Newton, walk for 1½ miles south along the beach until Embleton Bay comes to an abrupt end by a mass of boulders. Note that a rivulet runs across the sands and can be crossed when the tide is very low (you'll probably have to go barefoot); otherwise head inland along the edge of the golf course and over a couple of little bridges.

Once at the end of Embleton Bay, climb on to the headland, skirting the golf course on your right and a World War II pillbox before making your way under Dunstanburgh Castle's walls to its mighty south entrance. Craster is just over a mile to the south and reached on a well-worn grassy track across farmland.

✻ ✻ ✻

17 PRESTON TOWER

☗ **Joiners Shop Bunkhouse** (page 273)
Preston, near Cathill NE67 5DH ✆ 01665 589227 ⧉ www.prestontower.co.uk ⦿ daily until dusk or 18.00, whichever is earlier

A well-preserved medieval tower dating back to 1392 stands in landscaped parkland a couple of miles southwest of Beadnell. Very few fortified towers quite as special as this are open to the public and provide such a vivid sense of the border clashes that were so frequent in Northumbria until the 17th century. Rooms are furnished with items typical of the period, including animal skins, wood stools and a spinning wheel. I like the way you are free to visit on any day and enjoy the tower at leisure; just remember to pop your entrance fee into the honesty box (just a few pounds) and switch off the light when you leave.

Though Preston Tower looks like a complete building, it is in fact one half of a four-turreted 'castle', part of which was pulled down when the threat of violence from marauding clans waned. At one time the entrance would have been on the first floor (accessed by way of ladders which were then lifted off the ground). Livestock was housed on the ground floor. The slit windows and seven-foot-thick walls would have been very difficult to penetrate.

From the turrets, you can see all the way to the sea (the coastguard cottage at Newton-by-the-Sea is just visible).

A clear highlight is the 1864 **clock** which, the information panel tells you, has a similar mechanism to Big Ben. On the hour, cogs start spinning and a metal arm is depressed, triggering another lever that pulls a cord that moves the hammer which strikes the deafening half-ton bell at the top of the tower – to the great excitement of both children and adults. The dilemma you'll have is whether to watch the whirring mechanism or experience the powerful, bone-vibrating gong of the bell. Fortunately, you can see both if you are quick enough up the stairs (be careful – there's no hand rail at the top). Note that there's a pause between when the mechanism kicks into gear and when it really gets going. I stood for what felt like a few minutes with my hands clasped over my ears waiting for the bell to strike.

Three short **trails** lead around the estate, providing a view of the mansion house, built in 1802, and the mature ornamental trees including redwoods and a beautiful copper beech. Look out for red squirrels.

18 BEADNELL

Å **Annstead Farm** (page 273), **Beadnell Bay Camping and Caravanning Club Site** (page 273), **Tewart Arms Cottage, Camping & Caravan Site** (page 273)

Beadnell has two pleasant enough historic areas (the harbour and village) connected by a number of roads with modern houses. This one-time fishing village is now mainly a holiday area which boasts one of the most unspoilt sandy beaches in the North East. The **village centre** is to the north and set back from the seafront.

COASTAL FLOWERS

In late summer, bloody crane's-bill puts on a deep pink-purple display among the marram grass, sea campion and the odd burnet rose in dunes along the Northumberland coast. **Orchids** are also not difficult to spot. A couple of noteworthy sites include the grasslands behind Beadnell Bay, which are covered in pyramidal orchids in localised areas (visible from the coast path from June to August). You'll also see masses of orchids in buttercup meadows on the southern fringes of Craster.

Perhaps the most special is the **Lindisfarne helleborine** (lime green flowers with a white 'lip' coloured brown inside), an endemic species that flowers on the island (and nowhere else) along with ten other orchids (a huge number of marsh helleborines in July, for instance). If visiting Lindisfarne in spring, an abundance of pink thrift covers the saltmarshes.

Whin grassland is an important habitat in Northumberland. It appears where outcrops of the dark grey volcanic Whin Sill break through the sea and land (around Dunstanburgh Castle, Craster and Lindisfarne's castle, for example). Associated plants include common rock rose, maiden pink, chives, purple milk-vetch and field garlic.

Those who make the approach on foot from the south across Beadnell Bay will find the knot of curious buildings above the tiny **harbour** rather appealing. They include 18th-century lime kilns, a turreted stone guesthouse and a 13th-century chapel, now completely ruined. If you continue north along Harbour Road with the sea to your right, you'll come across a couple of ramshackle 19th-century fishermen's huts (there used to be more but some were demolished in 2011). Unfortunately they are not protected and are in a poor state of repair. Below them is **Beadnell Haven**, once used by fishermen (see box, opposite).

Beadnell Bay

A pristine sandy beach padded with dunes and lapped by blue water is not easily found anywhere in England, but to come across one as crowd-free as Beadnell is rare indeed. Families, walkers and birdwatchers will love it here.

Halfway along is Long Nanny – an inlet by a hut that is well known for its colony of over 2,000 pairs of **arctic terns** that nest in the dune grasses. This is probably the largest colony on mainland Britain. The hut is manned by National Trust wardens around the clock and it is the best place to watch the birds at close range without disturbing them.

19 SEAHOUSES

🏠 **St Cuthbert's House** (page 272) ⛺ **Springhill Farm** (page 273), **Stewart Arms Cottage, Camping & Caravan Site** (page 273)

Seahouses is a bustling fishing town, now busier with tourists popping into gift shops for buckets and spades than with fishermen, but its harbour is still very much a working port. Ten fishing vessels were docked when I last visited and, as always, the lobster pots were stacked

FISHING HERITAGE

Katrina Porteous

Local historian, poet and editor of The Bonny Fisher Lad

Most of north Northumberland's coastal villages have been strongly shaped by fishing. Traditionally this was carried out from 'cobles', small open wooden boats launched from the beach. The fishing year was divided into the winter season, when long lines were used to catch cod and haddock, and summer, when herring were caught using drift nets. All the family was involved: women sold fish inland and, with their children, gathered mussels and limpets to bait the 1,400 hooks of each line.

Herring became a major industry from the early 19th century, and villages such as Seahouses prospered. In summer the men fished at night, and women worked in teams, gutting and packing herring into barrels for export, or smoking them as 'kippers'. Although herring are no longer caught locally, Craster and Seahouses still have active smokehouses. In Seahouses the remains of several 19th-century herring yards can be seen, now converted into cottages. Walk along South Street looking for blocked-off 'bowly-holes' in the walls, where cartloads of herring were shovelled into troughs for

gutting. Nearby, the gateway of Chapel Row is marked by grooves made by generations of fisherwomen sharpening their limpet-picking tools on their way to the rocks.

On Lindisfarne, old upturned herring drifters are used as sheds, and on Harbour Road at Beadnell two tarry fishermen's huts, now disused, mark the Haven where cobles were launched. Near them, beside the footpath to the sea, stand the remains of a row of 18th-century 'bark-pots'. These square structures consisted of a hearth, chimney and large metal tank, and were used to boil nets, ropes and sails in a tannin-rich liquid to preserve them. This seashore is full of hidden clues to its past, such as mussel-beds, lobster ponds and rectangular troughs called 'bratt holes', only visible at low tide, where fish were stored for live export in sailing sloops to London.

Today, fishing on this coast has greatly diminished. Where it still exists, it is mostly confined to catching crabs and lobsters. But look out for cobles still working traditional summer salmon nets in Boulmer Haven.

WHALES, PORPOISES & DOLPHINS

Martin Kitching is a wildlife expert and director of Northern Experience Wildlife Tours (✆ 01670 827465 ◊ www.northernexperiencewildlifetours.co.uk), which runs pelagic boat trips from Seahouses and North Shields near Newcastle to look for cetaceans and seabirds, as well as wildlife-watching trips elsewhere in the county.

The diminutive harbour porpoise can be seen along the Northumberland coast all year round, and minke whales appear from mid to late summer with late August being the peak time for sightings. Stunning white-beaked dolphins swim close to the shore in June and July, then they move offshore into deeper, cooler water and have been the highlight of trips to the Farne Deeps since 2010. Bottlenose dolphins, from the population around Fife and Tayside in eastern Scotland, seem to be taking a shine to Northumberland's coastline. Above the waves, pelagic wildlife trips are often accompanied by fulmars, kittiwakes and squabbling gulls, while rarer sightings have included storm petrels, long-tailed skuas, sooty shearwaters, grey and red-necked phalaropes and, in August 2013, a lone orca. You just never know what you'll see ...

on the harbour wall. A couple of fishermen with caps and waterproofs stood around chatting: a timeless scene.

The **tourist information centre** is in Seafield car park (page 40).

One of the greatest pleasures at Seahouses is to sit on the terrace of benches facing the harbour eating some of the best fish and chips you will find anywhere in the UK.

Seahouses grew as a holiday resort in the 1920s. Then, as now, the Farne Islands were the reason many people came here and today you'll find a number of boat tour companies around the harbour. Opposite the kiosks are Seahouses's well-preserved **lime kilns**, dating to 1841. As at Beadnell and Lindisfarne they were ideally situated for the easy transportation of lime by boat.

A short walk south from the harbour along a row of cottages lined with starlings and jackdaws provides a good view of Bamburgh Castle and the Farne Islands. Depending on whether the tide is high or low, there are between 15 and 28 islands in the chain. On **South Street** you'll see evidence of the 19th- and 20th-century fishing industry, including a very old **smokehouse** (page 77). Continuing south on the headland, the wind picks up as you press on to Beadnell Bay (see page 76).

🍴 FOOD & DRINK

Neptune's or Pinnacles for fish and chips? That's the dilemma that faces every visitor to Seahouses. I usually opt for a take-away from **Pinnacles** on Main Street (NE68 7RE ✆ 01665 720708) and plonk myself on one of the benches overlooking the harbour, but **Neptune's** (NE68 7SJ ✆ 01665 721310) on the other side of the road has a dining area where you might want to shelter if a fret is rolling in off the sea. Really, you can't go wrong anywhere in Seahouses: the fish comes straight off the boats a few hundred yards away and most restaurants have had decades of perfecting the batter.

The Fisherman's Kitchen 2 South St, NE68 7RB ✆ 01665 721052 🖱 www.swallowfish. co.uk ♿. Herring have been smoked here since 1843. It's worth visiting the smokehouse even just to see the photos on the wall above an old iron range, and herring baskets and anchors hanging from the ceiling. You can buy everything you need for a seafood barbecue: locally caught mackerel, scallops, king prawns, whole crab and lobster.

Olde Ship Inn Main St, NE68 7RD ✆ 01665 720200 ♿. This is a great seafarers' pub with bags of character (and nautical artefacts), overlooking the harbour. Expect real ales, an open fire, a beer garden and convivial chatter.

20 FARNE ISLANDS NATIONAL NATURE RESERVE

✆ 01665 720651 ○ Apr–end Oct; toilets on Inner Farne; boat prices do not include admission on to the island, which must be paid on landing; no refreshments; National Trust

'A boat may be secured for fifteen shillings. In addition to this charge, the boatmen expect to be provided with refreshments, solid and liquid.' Visitors to the Farne Islands no longer need to supply the skippers of the Seahouses tour boats with food and drink, as they did in the late 19th century, but little else has changed here since Victorian tourists came to experience the famous bird islands.

Boat trips, such as **Billy Shiel's Boats** (✆ 01665 720308 🖱 www. farne-islands.com) depart hourly between 10.00 and 15.00 depending on the weather and can be booked from the kiosks at Seahouses harbour. Note that most seabirds will have left the islands before the end of the summer but eider ducks, cormorants, shags and seals can be seen throughout the year, and there are winter migrants from early autumn. Allow for a round trip (including the Inner Farne stop-off) of three hours. Birdwatchers and photographers may want to combine a trip to Inner Farne with Staple Island.

Everyone who has visited these rocky isles scattered a couple of miles northeast of Seahouses will remember ducking and flinching from the dive-bombing arctic terns. A wave of the hands usually keeps the birds,

CUDDY'S DUCK

Several hundred eider ducks nest on the Farne Islands. Most of them inhabit Inner Farne, where they have received sanctuary for over 1,300 years ever since St Cuthbert lived here in the 7th century. The saint afforded the ducks special protection and is sometimes referred to as the first bird conservationist. His love of eiders is the reason why Cuthbert is sometimes depicted with the bird at his feet and the origins of the local name: Cuddy's Duck.

which are ever so protective of their chicks running at your feet, from striking, but you might want to wear a hat just in case.

From the moment you step ashore, you'll see puffins crash-landing with beaks stuffed full of sand eels, terns wheeling in the sky or spearing fish from the sea, cormorants sitting proud on their castles of dried seaweed, and guillemots standing on rock stacks painted white with guano. There is no other wildlife experience quite like this anywhere else in Northumberland. But only for a few months of the year. Come mid-August, the birds depart for open waters, abandoning their empty nests to the wind and sea.

The islands are divided into two main groups by Staple Sound. **Inner Farne**, the closest island to the mainland, is of most interest to visitors and is also the disembarking point for boat tours. Boardwalks guide visitors on a half-mile long circular walk around the island. Tens of thousands of puffins nest here in burrows they dig themselves (not old rabbit burrows as is sometimes thought), while razorbills, kittiwakes and guillemots lay their eggs on the columnar sea-facing rocks (part of the Great Whin Sill that peaks in several places along the Northumberland coast). Sea campion covers much of the ground that isn't bare rock.

Inner Farne was inhabited by hermits and monks for 900 years; the most well known was **Cuthbert**, who lived twice on the island before and after he became Bishop of Lindisfarne. The second time, in AD687, he returned to his much-loved sanctuary to die. The only other person to have lived on the island for as long as Cuthbert is the lively National Trust Head Ranger, David Steel.

Nothing remains of Cuthbert's simple shelter and prayer room, but you will see a few old stone buildings, including a chapel built around 1300. The 17th-century wood stalls inside came from Durham Cathedral.

Two **lighthouses** still operate on the Farne Islands, both dating to the early 1800s. The red and white beacon on Longstone is the famous 'Grace Darling lighthouse' from where the lighthouse keeper and his daughter rowed through a storm in 1838 to aid survivors of a shipwreck (page 82). In the years following the rescue, Victorian tourists would visit the famous family at the lighthouse and delight in hearing of the extraordinary event first hand. Today, you'll need to visit the Grace Darling Museum in Bamburgh.

21 BAMBURGH

The wind can really kick up on the wide, long bay connecting Seahouses and Bamburgh and you can find yourself walking through streamers of sand being blown lengthways down the beach like wisps of smoke. The bracing walk is rewarded with the sight of Bamburgh Castle rising majestically from the dunes – all rock, turrets and battlements. It is undoubtedly one of Britain's most romantic castles and this is one of the most unspoilt and dramatic coastal panoramas, with the Farne Islands visible to the south and Lindisfarne Castle silhouetted on its rocky perch to the north. The view is most expansive from the castle's Battery Terrace.

In the **village**, the fortress maintains its heavy presence despite keeping close watch over the North Sea. My 19th-century travel guide describes Bamburgh as 'clean and cheerful' and a 'model village'. Nothing has changed in that respect. The centre is almost entirely made of stone and centred about a wooded green. **Front Street** has a pleasing run of 18th-century stone cottages, a number of which are now gift shops, eateries and B&Bs.

"The bracing walk is rewarded with the sight of Bamburgh Castle rising majestically from the dunes – all rock, turrets and battlements."

Keep heading uphill and you'll reach **Bamburgh Gallery** on Lucker Road (NE69 7BS ✆ 01668 214420), the sister studio to the Chatton Gallery near Wooler. Most prints and original artworks (many depicting the Northumberland coast) are by well-regarded painters, Robert Turnbull and Zana Juppeniatz.

Bamburgh does get a little crowded in summer, but if you're feeling hemmed in, just wander down to the generous **beach** or cycle along **The Wynding** (a quiet paved lane north out of the village that hugs the seafront and provides a superb view of the coastline all the way to a light beacon and golf course). Walkers can continue ahead to Budle Point and drop down on to the sandy shore. A beach towel comes in handy here.

Facing the sea to the northwest of the village on Radcliffe Road, is the modern RNLI station and enchanting **Grace Darling Museum** (NE69 7AE ✆ 01668 214910 ⌖ www.rnli.org.uk/gracedarling ☉ Easter–end Oct, daily; closed Mon at other times ♿) that perpetuates the memory of the Victorian heroine who helped saved shipwrecked passengers off the Farne Islands. The collection of memorabilia in the small museum is elegantly presented. You'll find out about events on that fateful night, the life of the lighthouse keeper and his family and Grace's rise to fame in the years following the rescue – an intriguing tale in itself. For more details, see the box below.

GRACE DARLING

I had little thought of anything but to exert myself to the utmost, my spirit was worked up by the sight of such a dreadful affair that I can imagine I still see the sea flying over the vessel.

From a letter by Grace Darling in her namesake museum at Bamburgh

In the early hours of 7 September 1838, the paddle steamer SS *Forfarshire* hit the corner of Big Harcar off the Farne Islands. Knowing that the lifeboat from Seahouses would not be able to reach the stricken vessel in such poor conditions, William Darling, the lighthouse keeper on Longstone Island, launched his wooden rowing boat and, with the help of his daughter, Grace, they rowed for a mile through choppy waters to reach the nine shipwrecked survivors. The Darlings' boat could only carry five passengers so they had to make a second trip in order to bring all the survivors to the lighthouse.

The story was widely printed in the papers and it seems the Victorian readership couldn't get enough of the romantic tale of the lighthouse keeper's daughter, who became famous in her lifetime. She sat for endless portraits and received many gifts including £50 from Queen Victoria. Four years later, she died of tuberculosis aged 26 (in the building that is now the Pantry deli on Front Street). Her story endures, though the events and Grace's character have been much romanticised. Wordsworth penned the following verse, an extract of which appears on a memorial on the Farne Islands:

Pious and pure, modest and yet so brave,
Though young so wise, though meek so resolute –
Might carry to the clouds and to the stars,
Yea, to celestial Choirs, Grace Darling's name!

The main exhibit is the famous Darling rowing boat, a shapely old coble. Around the boat are paintings depicting the rescue, including Carmichael's romantic scene of Grace and her father rowing through violent waters away from the lighthouse. Also on display are letters and clothes including Grace's black cloak.

Next door but one is **3 Radcliffe Road**, where Grace was born (a plaque above the doorway gives the date: 24 November 1815) and, in the churchyard opposite, is where she is buried, facing the sea, as is fitting. Her **grave** is reached by following the trampled grassy trail to a large Gothic memorial (rebuilt in 1993 to the same design as the older sandstone structure that had become worn by the weather).

Inside **St Aidan's Church**, Grace Darling is represented in a series of stained-glass windows in a small chapel to the left of the altar.

The church dates for the most part from the end of the 12th century and is notable for many reasons, including its long chancel and many arcades. It stands on the site of a much earlier church founded by St Aidan in AD635. The only relic from that time is thought to be the wooden girder in the baptistery. According to legend, it was the same beam the saint died leaning against and is said to have survived two fires.

Bamburgh Castle

Bamburgh NE69 7DF ✆ 01668 214515 ⟨ www.bamburghcastle.com ◔ mid-Feb–early Nov, daily; weekends at other times; café; ♿ grounds & some rooms including the Kings Hall

Many writers and architectural historians have declared Bamburgh the most wondrous of all England's coastal castles. You may well agree when you see the mighty edifice strikingly situated on a fist of dolerite rock thrust 150 feet from sea level through sand dunes. Bamburgh is certainly the stuff of fairytales.

Its enviable situation proved a valuable vantage point for settlers from ancient times and almost certainly the Romans. From the Anglo-Saxon period to the present day, Vikings, kings, earls and dukes have seized, pounded and abandoned the castle in various states of ruin. Some of the Anglo-Saxon objects retrieved from the fortress are on display inside the castle's Archaeology Room, including part of a stone throne.

After the Viking raids, the Normans rebuilt the castle in stone. The keep you see today dates to the reign of Henry II. Bamburgh stood strong for several hundred years and survived invasions from north of the border until 1464 when its walls were razed by the Earl of Warwick during the Wars of the Roses. Connoisseurs of trivia will take pleasure in knowing that Bamburgh was the first castle in England to fall to cannon fire.

The fortress was extensively rebuilt in the 18th century and contains later additions, such as the stables, added by the Victorian industrialist Lord Armstrong, whose family has owned the castle ever since. As a rule of thumb, the pinkish outer walls are medieval, and those with a grey hue are Victorian. Much of the interior dates to this latter period, including the **King's Hall** (the former banqueting hall), a magnificent wood-panelled room of ballroom proportions with a false hammer-beam roof and stained glass. A newspaper report from 1932 describes the annual Bamburgh Castle Ball as 'a beautiful fashion parade at which quite the most swagger gowns imaginable were worn'.

In addition to the King's Hall, don't miss the views from the **Court Room** and the intriguing **bottle-shaped doorway** at the bottom of the stairs. This allowed knights on horseback to swiftly enter the building without having to dismount (how's that for style?). The **Billiard Room** and adjoining **Faire Chamber** evoke the era of high-society social events where aristocratic men played pool in one room and ladies gossiped in the sumptuous surroundings of the chamber next door.

The **Armstrong and Aviation Artefacts Museum**, housed in the old castle laundry gives visitors a glimpse into the life of First Lord Armstrong and houses a collection of aviation artefacts donated and salvaged from World War I, including the wreckage of a Spitfire.

¶¶ FOOD & DRINK

You'll find a couple of tea rooms and restaurants on Front Street, including the **Lord Crewe Hotel** (NE69 7BL ✆ 01668 214243) which has a contemporary hotel restaurant and bright tea room on the same road. For picnic food, try the tumbledown **greengrocer** (also a newsagent) opposite the church. Out the back there are crates and carts stuffed with fruit and veg and an old man of an apple tree standing among fallen fruit. Also try **Carters** ('Butcher Baker Sausage Roll Maker') on Front Street. **The Pantry**, on the same street, sells local cheeses, pies and sandwiches. A hot kipper bun or crab sandwich is a bargain at under £3. **Mizen Head** Lucker Rd, NE69 7BS ✆ 01668 214254. 'You can't get fresher,' the manager says of the hotel's seafood dishes, many of which are prepared using produce straight from the North Sea, including lobster from Seahouses and salmon and kippers from Craster. On the downside, the contemporary restaurant is somewhat soulless and a little out of the way at the western end of the village.

SCENIC ROAD: BUDLE BAY TO BAMBURGH

There is an outstanding view of Bamburgh Castle from the B1340. As you reach the brow of a hill, the sight of the mighty fortress raised above the sea will make you want to pull over and grab your camera. If you can time your journey for late in the afternoon on a clear day, you'll see the castle wondrously lit by the sun, making this one of the most arresting panoramas on the coast.

22 BUDLE BAY

By road from Bamburgh to Belford or on the coastal footpath, you enjoy far-reaching views of the swirling sand and mudflats sheltered in this deep, wide bay. Non-birdwatchers travelling with birders in autumn and winter beware: from here to Lindisfarne and beyond is serious binocular and field guide country. One of the best places to see some of the thousands of ducks, geese and waders that descend on the flats is from the roadside path and pull-in areas along the coast road east of Waren Mill. As the tide comes in, the birds are pushed closer to land.

23 ROSS BACK SANDS

⌂ **Outchester and Ross Farm Cottages** (page 272)

The beach at Ross is a gloriously deserted sandy spit that extends for three breezy miles from Budle Bay almost to Lindisfarne. Access is via a mile-long footpath through Ross Farm and across the dunes, which puts off the few travellers who venture to this remote place. Your reward, however, is an unbeatable panorama: all sky, sea and white sands with Lindisfarne Castle at one end and Bamburgh Castle and the Farne Islands at the other. One Saturday afternoon in winter, I walked for over two hours without seeing another person.

A pair of binoculars will come in handy, both to check out the seals lazing on sand humps in Lindisfarne's bay (best viewed from Guile Point) and to scan the sea for divers, grebes and scoters in winter, and terns in summer. At the northern end of the spit on **Guile Point** (out of bounds from May to July because of nesting birds) you'll see two triangular navigation towers. They help keep mariners on the right course through the dangerous waters which have claimed many boats, including the remains of two shipwrecks you see by walking the length of the beach. Keep in mind that from the main access point on to the

LINDISFARNE OYSTERS

Oysters have been harvested for hundreds of years on the mudflats of Lindisfarne bay. Past owners of the oyster beds include the monks in the 14th century and a Victorian landowner. The industry died out but was resurrected in 1989 by a local farmer who spotted oyster shells on the sand. Current owners, Christopher and Helen Sutherland, inherited the business in 2003. You can buy their oysters at the Lindisfarne Oysters smokehouse in Seahouses, online, or direct from Ross Farm (between Budle Bay & Lindisfarne, NE70 7EN ✆ 01668 213870 ⌨ www.lindisfarneoysters.co.uk) if ordered in advance.

sands (roughly the midway point of the spit) the towers look deceptively close but they take over an hour to reach.

A word of caution: make a mental picture of where the footpath enters the beach as it is difficult to find on your return. At the time of writing it was marked by a bough in the sand.

24 BELFORD

Since the A1 was diverted away from this old market town between the coast and the Cheviot Hills, it's become very quiet in Belford … The High Street is a long row of grey stone houses curving away from the Market Place where there's a stone cross (at least 200 years old).

When Belford was a coaching stop on the old Edinburgh to London road, horses were fed and watered in stables (now somewhat changed) by the side of the Blue Bell Hotel.

Those interested in the history of the town should step round the corner to **Belford Hidden Histories** (adjacent to the inn on Church St ☉ daily). Among displays is an intriguing photograph of suffragists standing outside the Blue Bell, which is thought to date to October 1912 when a group marched from Edinburgh to London with a Votes for Women petition.

Also close to the Blue Bell is the parish church which was rebuilt in 1828 by John Dobson, the architect responsible for many churches and country houses in Northumberland. Note the Norman chancel arch.

¶ FOOD & DRINK

A couple of places serve coffees on the main road running through the town. Families might want to travel a bit further to **Sunnyhills Farm Shop** (South Rd, NE70 7DP ✆ 01668

219662 ⊙ daily ♿) on the southern outskirts of the town where there's an adventure playground and café set in farmland.

St Cuthbert's Cave

St Cuthbert's Way long-distance path (page 41) from the Cheviot Hills to Lindisfarne passes a small wood near Holburn Grange (four miles west of Budle Bay and also accessible along a grassy track from the car park at Holburn Grange) where there's a cave set within a huge sandstone outcrop. Monks carrying Cuthbert's body are said to have rested here (locally known as 'Cuddy's Cave') when they fled from Viking invaders on Lindisfarne at the end of the 9th century. If you continue on St Cuthbert's Way over the hills, you gain a spectacular panorama of Lindisfarne and Bamburgh castles.

Nearby (a mile north of St Cuthbert's Cave) is **Holburn Moss** – a wetland nature reserve with an artificial lake supporting many overwintering ducks and geese.

25 LINDISFARNE (HOLY ISLAND)

⌂ **Hunting Hall** (page 272), **Lindisfarne Bay Cottages** (page 272) ⋀ **The Barn at Beal** (page 273)

Lindisfarne Castle seemingly rises out of the sea off the coast of north Northumberland, but from the causeway that connects the island to the mainland at low tide, it sinks out of view and Lindisfarne as a whole appears as a long grey-green streak across a glistening expanse of sea, saltmarshes and sandflats. It's one of the most striking and beautiful panoramas on the Northumberland coast, so slow down and drink in

LINDISFARNE GOSPELS

It is remarkable that this exquisite illuminated manuscript survived 600 years of battles, invasions and unrest in this once lawless region. The gospels are considered one of the most treasured religious and artistic works in the UK and for that reason are stored for safe-keeping at the British Museum in London. Durham Cathedral, Chester-le-Street and Lindisfarne all have facsimiles of the book; the last is displayed in the Lindisfarne Centre on Marygate. The highly decorative pages were painted using animal and vegetable dyes in one unified style by Eadfrith who was Bishop of Lindisfarne in the late 7th and early 8th centuries.

the view. Beyond the grasslands and dunes on the north side of the island are some of Northumberland's finest and whitest sandy **beaches** that are often empty even in high summer.

When the tide retreats over **Lindisfarne National Nature Reserve** (the waters, mudflats and saltmarshes between the island and the mainland), it exposes a seabed that stretches for what appears to be several miles, though it is impossible to tell where the flats meet the sea when the tide is out. Even when it's overcast, the reflected light is sharp and the sky perfectly mirrored in the silvery expanse. For ducks and waders, this is a giant bird table with enough marine creatures on offer to support tens of thousands of birds. Their numbers swell from early autumn until spring when migrant birds from the continent join in the banquet. Seals rest on exposed sandbanks here.

Lindisfarne, however, is best known as a place of **Christian pilgrimage**. For over 1,000 years, worshippers have travelled to the island on foot across the mud and sands – a tradition that continues today by following a line of posts that steer walkers around dangerous quicksand.

THE WILDLIFE OF LINDISFARNE

Ducks, wading birds and geese begin arriving from late summer and early autumn on the saltmarshes, grasslands and tidal mudflats surrounding Lindisfarne island (a National Nature Reserve) where they spend the winter. Most of the time they are busy prodding the mud for food or avoiding death by peregrine. On the occasions that a raptor does swoop by (sparrowhawk and hen harrier are also possible), a pandemonium of birds takes to the sky.

There are so many vantage points, but some trusted favourites are the mainland shores of the Fenham Flats where shelduck, redshank, wigeon, bar-tailed godwit and curlew congregate in good numbers. This is a popular feeding area for light-bellied Brent geese. You can walk along the shore here though the ground is very muddy.

Lindisfarne causeway (from the bridge) is good for close-up views of waders and ducks on your way to the island, as are the damp fields on the approach to the castle (masses of teal, wigeon, lapwing and golden plover here). If walking across the island's dunes in November and December you have a very good chance of seeing the day-flying short-eared owl. The last time I visited, I saw at least three individuals here.

The reserve is also known for its grey seals and flowering plants. Dunes on the northwest side of Lindisfarne Island blossom with 11 varieties of orchids in summer. Look out for the Lindisfarne helleborine (see box, page 76).

A monastic community led by St Aidan was established on Lindisfarne under the instruction of Oswald, King of Northumbria, in AD635. St Cuthbert came to the island 50 years later when he left the Farne Islands to become Bishop of Lindisfarne.

On Cuthbert's death in AD687, his body remained perfectly preserved – an apparent miracle that inspired thousands of pilgrims to travel to the island, and the creation of the celebrated Lindisfarne Gospels.

"Danish raids forced the monks of Lindisfarne to flee the island, carrying Cuthbert's coffin and the gospels."

Danish raids forced the monks of Lindisfarne to flee the island, carrying Cuthbert's coffin and the gospels. Over 100 years later they finally came to rest in Durham where a shrine was constructed that was later rebuilt (the same magnificent Norman cathedral you see today). The Viking invaders are depicted on a 9th-century stone carving, now housed in the **Lindisfarne Priory Museum** (Church Lane TD15 2RX), which shows a line of rudimentary figures waving swords and axes.

Lindisfarne village

Most visitors arrive by car and some take the infrequent 477 bus from Berwick to the village centre where there's a lively local community, post office, a few eateries, pubs, holiday cottages and a couple of places offering B&B accommodation. Opposite the village green is **St Aidan's Winery** (TD15 2RX ℘ 01289 389230 ♂ www.lindisfarne-mead.co.uk ☉ daily ♿), distillers of the famous Lindisfarne Mead, a fortified wine made with honey. The **Lindisfarne Centre** (Marygate, TD15 2SD ℘ 01289 389004 ☉ daily ♿) serves as a **tourist information centre** and has a very good bookshop selling local guides as well as three exhibition spaces, one of which is devoted to the story of the **Lindisfarne Gospels** and includes a facsimile of the AD698 illuminated manuscript.

Lindisfarne Priory & church

Church Lane TD15 2RX ℘ 01289 389200 ☉ Mar–end Oct, Feb school holidays & Easter, daily; weekends only in winter; English Heritage

The ruins of the early 12th-century priory and 13th-century parish church face each other on the southwestern tip of the island, just a few steps away from the village green. Nearly 900 years of wind and rain as well as damage during the Reformation have badly worn the stones of the arcades and arches of the **priory**, which was founded by Benedictine monks from Durham Cathedral. Enough structures and geometric patterns remain to appreciate the layout of the building and recognise its architecture as Norman – and even to notice similarities with the nave at Durham. At dusk, the naturally blushed sandstones deepen in colour to that of a red night sky. The view from the churchyard looking over the gravestones with the priory to the left and the castle and boats in the bay to the right, is exceptionally picturesque.

"At dusk, the naturally blushed sandstones deepen in colour to that of a red night sky."

The oldest parts of **St Mary's Church** date from the time of St Aidan in the 7th century, but most of it is 13th century. Notice the different style of the facing arcades: the arches on the south side are pointed and date from the 13th century while those on the north aisle are Romanesque. There's an eye-catching stained-glass window above the north altar of fishermen, and 20th-century glass in the west wall depicting St Aidan and St Cuthbert. The wood sculpture of monks carrying Cuthbert's coffin is identical to the bronze version in Durham city. They mark the start and end points of the monks' journey.

Lindisfarne Castle

TD15 2SH ☏ 01289 389244 ○ early Feb–early Nov, Tue–Sun & Bank Holiday Mons; selected weekends in winter; check website or call ahead for times which are dependent on the tides; National Trust

Lindisfarne Castle crowns a conical-shaped mound of Whin Sill rock at the south of the island. The Tudor fortress appears to naturally emerge from the dolerite, rather than being built upon it, which is all rather pleasing from a visitor's point of view. The castle dates from 1542 and was fortified in Elizabeth I's reign but the strength of the impenetrable-looking walls has never been fully tested.

For many visitors, the most intriguing period in the building's history was the evolution of the castle into an Edwardian house by architect Edwin Lutyens under the instruction of Edward Hudson, editor of *Country Life* magazine. He created domestic rooms in every chamber, connected by way of passages.

The interior has much rustic appeal and is simply furnished, including with items designed by Lutyens. Uncluttered rooms allow appreciation

LINDISFARNE CAUSEWAY

A good service of horse-drawn traps, and a car, runs during low-tide, the charge being 6s. per conveyance, each holding three passengers.

Robert Hugill *Road Guide to Northumberland and the Border*, 1931

It's frustrating to reach the causeway to find you've missed the safe crossing time by minutes, but I can say from experience that the crossing times listed on the information board at either side of the causeway are usually very accurate, having myself made a foolish dash for it many years ago in a car and almost conked out. I was not ten minutes over the safe crossing limit, but the sea was already rushing across the paved road frighteningly quickly. If you get caught out, there's a refuge on stilts and the RNLI will take care of you, but your car will be washed away. A couple of dozen cars are usually abandoned every year. Plan ahead by checking the timetable online at www.northumberlandlife.org/holy-island.

Walkers following the **Pilgrims' Way** across the tidal mudflats should be very cautious. It takes around an hour to walk the three miles from the mainland to the island. This should only be attempted if you can reach the other side by the mid point of the safe crossing period. There is a refuge for walkers accessed by ladders halfway across.

of details like the arcades, spiral staircases, vaulted ceilings and patterned flooring made with bricks arranged in herringbone formation (a Lutyens trademark). 'I want to amuse myself with the place,' said Edward Hudson. He certainly did that – not just in transforming the castle, but by holding summer parties.

In farmland on the north side of the castle is a pretty little **garden** designed by Gertrude Jekyll in 1911 and protected on four sides by dry stone walling. Roses, sweet peas, fuchsias and delphiniums bring colour and scent to the isolated enclosure in summer. The story of the garden's creation and restoration to the original layout is told in an informative leaflet you can pick up near the shed.

 FOOD & DRINK

A couple of cafés, a restaurant and two average pubs on Lindisfarne serve food. **Pilgrims Coffee House** on Marygate (TD15 2SJ ✆ 01289 389109) is home to the best latte on the island (the café also sells their own coffee beans, scones, cakes and sandwiches).
Barn at Beal Beal Farm, TD15 2PB ✆ 01289 540044 ⊙ daily & Fri & Sat evenings ♿.
On the approach to Lindisfarne Causeway, road travellers pass this large eatery housed in

a modernised 19th-century cart shed which stands on a hill gazing at the island. Monks at Lindisfarne Priory are said to have kept their beehives here. The busy café/restaurant serves very good lunches prepared with local meats, cheeses and fish and there's a roast on Sundays. You'll also find a small vintage shop, bird of prey centre and tiny camping area here.

Bean Goose Restaurant Market Sq, Lindisfarne TD15 2RX ✆ 01289 389083 ⏲ Tue–Sat. This laid-back restaurant with a real fire is your best bet on Lindisfarne for an evening meal but lots of people know this so make sure you book. Locally caught lobster, crab and fish, oysters from across the bay, vegetables grown on the island and Northumbrian meats and cheeses earned the Bean Goose a gold award from the Green Tourism Business scheme for their commitment to sourcing local produce.

✳ ✳ ✳

🚶 ROUND-ISLAND WALK OF LINDISFARNE

✳ OS Explorer map 340; start: first public car park you come to on reaching the island from the causeway, 📍 NU125424; 5 miles; difficulty: fairly easy but paths through the dunes are undulating; for refreshments, see pages 91–2

It takes a couple of hours to complete this circular trail which is a beautiful walk with constant views of the sea, and culminates in the priory and castle. The last time I walked around the island on a gloriously sunny morning in September, I didn't meet anyone for the first hour and had the beaches on the north side of the island all to myself. As for the route, you hardly need a map; just a sense of the shape of the island and the location of the village and castle in relation to the dunes and causeway.

Several yards south of the first ticketed car park you come to on reaching the island, there's a footpath by a kissing gate that crosses into farmland and over dunes. Keep on this undulating path through the extensive dunes, passing a stone ruin on your way to the sea. By now your shoes and ankles may well be covered in the seeds of piri-piri burr – an invasive plant that you should steer clear of to avoid spreading its seeds.

Eventually you'll come to the first of a string of pristine **sandy bays** that fringe the north of the island. Turn right and cross the beach before climbing back up on to the dunes and continuing on your way eastwards over the sandy grassland, keeping the sea on your left. Head towards the white triangle day marker at Emmanuel Head.

Continue southwards, with the Farne Islands, Bamburgh Castle and the Cheviots all within view. Where the path peters out, cross over a fence into a field using the stile and continue in the same direction. There's a gate at the end and beyond that a fingerpost by another gate. For the most direct route to the village and car park, go through this gate and follow a farm track; for the castle, continue straight on for a quarter-mile.

As you near the castle, the path curves towards **lime kilns** on a raised embankment (an old waggonway that was used during the late 19th century for the transport of lime). According to the National Trust, they are some of the best examples of Victorian lime kilns anywhere in England. Also note the remains of two timber jetties – or staiths – near to the gate at the bottom of the castle path. Lime was loaded on to moored ships from wagons which ran along the structures.

The three **upturned boat hulls** (now storage sheds) are much photographed. The path to the left leads to the castle. With the castle behind you, continue downhill to the little harbour. A pleasant approach to the priory and village green is made by walking around the harbour and up and over the grassy heugh. Skirt the priory and turn right on to Church Lane from where you'll find the entrance to the ecclesiastical buildings.

To return to the car park, work your way through the village streets and follow the main road (Chare Ends) towards the causeway, passing The Lindisfarne Hotel on your right.

✱ ✱ ✱

26 CHESWICK SANDS & AROUND

⚐ **Pot-a-Doodle Do Wigwam Village** (page 273)

Located far from any settlement of note means that those who do make it to this three-mile-long stretch of desolate coastline between Goswick and Scremerston find it blissfully free of people. Apart from the golf club at Goswick and the distant view of Berwick, your contact with the built world is minimal. A paved track running along the inland edge of the dunes makes getting here by bicycle straightforward; drivers can park at several rough pull-in areas reached from Cheswick and Scremerston.

At its northern end, Cheswick Sands merges with **Cocklawburn Beach** beyond some impressive limestone rocks (crumbling lime kilns are evidence of past industry on this stretch of the coast). And to the south, at low tide, the vast expanse of **Goswick Sands** north of Lindisfarne reveals itself. Take care here: the incoming tide progresses quickly across the beach.

27 BERWICK-UPON-TWEED

🏠 **The Anchorage** (page 272)

The salmon-fishers rowing in their boats from Spittal Snook, looked strange and spectral through the mist; and if Tweed had anything to say concerning his birthplace in the western hills, and his travel along the Border land, it was stifled by the gloom, and I heard it not.

Walter White *Northumberland and the Border*, 1859

Salmon are still caught on the Tweed in the time-honoured way using nets and traditional wooden boats, but on a sunny day, the river is nothing like as brooding as the description above. The same is true of the town itself, which is really a very cheerful-looking place with its red-tiled Georgian houses gathered along the river's edge and colony of swans. The approach from the south is made all the more memorable by an old stone bridge that skims across the water in 15 low leaps leading you into the centre of Berwick in the most pleasing of ways.

Berwick has an uneasy identity because of its position on the wrong side of the river. Scottish or English? A lot of folk to the north and south are never quite sure because the northern banks of the Tweed are in Scotland, except at Berwick. At least that's the case today. But, this is a town that has yo-yoed from one side of the border to the other some 13 times. It doesn't help that Berwick's football team plays in the Scottish league and that the town has various other allegiances to north of the border. It's understandable therefore that many locals don't affiliate themselves to either country, preferring the description: 'Berwicker'. Their accent is equally non-committal: neither Northumbrian nor Scottish Borders.

Border disputes in the Middle Ages eventually led to the complete fortification of the town under Elizabeth I. These distinctive 16th-century **ramparts** remain largely intact and are said to make Berwick an outstanding example of a fortified town.

A wander on Berwick's ramparts

From a visitor's point of view, the ramparts encircling the town make a great walk offering views through Berwick's streets. This is the best way to get to know England's northernmost town. Without deviation, the circuit takes an hour or so, but most likely you'll want to hop off and on and see places of interest as you go. Information panels explain the form of the curtain wall, moat and impressive artillery bastions.

Starting at the eastern ramparts, your first calling point should be
Berwick Barracks (Parade, TD15 1DF ✆ 01289 304493 ○ mid-Mar–
end Oct, Mon–Fri; English Heritage) the oldest post-Roman army
barracks in Britain, dating to 1719. The quadrangle houses a museum
which traces the military history of the King's Own Scottish Borderers
regiment, formed in 1689 to defend Edinburgh against the Jacobites.
This isn't just a military heritage centre, however: in the clock building,
you'll find the **Berwick Museum & Art Gallery** with its small recreated
garrison town and fine art gallery. **The
Burrell Collection** (an offshoot of the   *"The Burrell Collection*
magnificent Burrell Collection in Glasgow)   *includes paintings from*
includes paintings from the 16th century   *the 16th century to the*
to the early 20th century from Britain,   *early 20th century from*
France and the Netherlands. Works include   *Britain, France and*
those by local artist James Wallace who   *the Netherlands."*
painted scenes of everyday life in the 1900s,
including salmon fishermen on the Tweed. One of the most eye-catching
(and slightly random) objects housed in the museum is Lindisfarne's old
telephone exchange on the ground floor which stands around eight feet
high and is complete with all its many switches and plugs.

Annexed to the barracks and outside of the quadrangle by the ramparts'
path is the **Gymnasium Gallery** (○ when exhibitions are showing; contact
the tourist information office) which puts on contemporary shows. Some
of the fittings from when the building was used as a gym remain *in situ.*

Don't miss the **Holy Trinity Church** on Wallace Green (opposite the
barracks). The mid 17th-century building is one of very few churches
constructed in Cromwellian England and is strikingly different from
any other church you will see in the North East, particularly because it
has no tower or spire. The interior is a mix of Gothic and classical styles.

THE LOWRY TRAIL

Berwick's many cobbled lanes and irregular-shaped buildings caught the eye of L S Lowry who painted some of his most memorable street scenes here from the mid 1930s until his death in 1976.

The **Lowry Trail** (pick up a leaflet in the tourist information office on Marygate) allows you to compare his paintings (shown on panels at each stopping point) with reality.

When you reach **Scot's Gate**, one of the main entrance archways into the town, you are pretty much in the centre of Berwick. If you continue south on the ramparts towards the river, you'll reach **Meg's Mount** (the westernmost bastion on the ramparts and one of Berwick's finest vantage points).

Berwick's centre

If approaching Berwick's centre from the train station, you'll probably end up walking down **Marygate**, which is basically the town's high street and is where you'll find the **tourist information office** (page 40). There's a **market** on Wednesdays and Saturdays mainly with clothes and fruit and veg stalls.

Besides the mid 18th-century **town hall** – easily the most prominent historic building on the street (tours daily in summer at 10.30 and 14.00) – Marygate does not hold huge appeal for tourists. The street is mainly lined with budget chain stores and charity clothes shops.

Sloping downhill from Marygate to the Tweed is **West Street** – a narrow, cobbled lane worthy of a few photographs. Congratulations if you manage to get to the bottom without stopping for fish and chips or a divine hot chocolate at the chocolaterie (page 99).

Bridge Street is set behind the river and Quay Walls and has a run of great independent shops, galleries and eateries. A few businesses really stand out such as **Bridge Street Bazaar** (℘ 07581 778568), a fantastic vintage antiques emporium with plenty to catch the eye: church pews, crockery, milk churns, 1950s wooden chairs, baskets full of ribbon, and old lanterns – all fairly reasonably priced. **The Treasure Chest** (℘ 07720 986127) is worth a peek if you like vintage clothes, jewellery and china. Health food shops don't get better than **The Green Shop** which is probably the most well stocked of its type I've ever come across (page 99). **Marehalm** (℘ 01289 332723) is a very tasteful craft and interiors shop selling pottery, paintings, furnishings and decorative glass pieces. Next door is **Twenty Five**, a gallery run by painter Scot Robinson who lives in Spittal and paints local scenes: mainly the North Sea looking wild and wintry, and Berwick's streets which have a Lowry-esque touch. 'I don't need to go far to find inspiration. Your eye is always

"Bridge Street is set behind the river and Quay Walls and has a run of great independent shops, galleries and eateries."

GEMMA HALL

SAVOURING THE TASTE

Fishing villages along the coast ensure a ready supply of fresh crab, lobster, oysters and fish to Northumberland and Tyneside's restaurants and B&Bs. Game from the moors and regional cheeses also regularly appear on menus.

1 Eat or sleep at a working farm and enjoy the fresh local produce on offer. 2 Pick up Lindisfarne oysters near Ross Back Sands. 3 The smokehouse in Craster is home to the famous kippers. 4 Regional favourites are sold in this fantastic Morpeth cheese shop. 5 Berwick-upon-Tweed has a growing Slow Food movement with a farmers' market on the last Sunday of the month.

MOVING MOVEMENT/S

GEMMA HALL

SUSAN MCNAUGHTON/BFF

VN

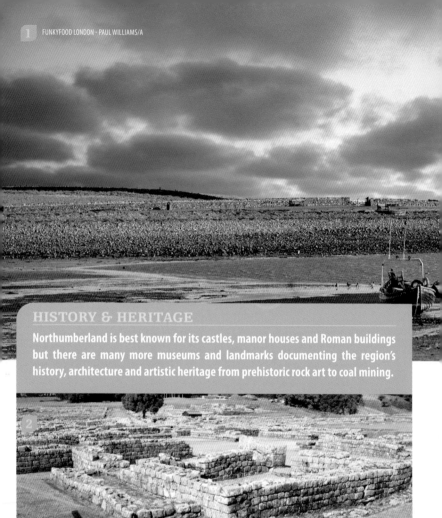

FUNKYFOOD LONDON - PAUL WILLIAMS/A

HISTORY & HERITAGE

Northumberland is best known for its castles, manor houses and Roman buildings but there are many more museums and landmarks documenting the region's history, architecture and artistic heritage from prehistoric rock art to coal mining.

JAIME PHARR/S

1 Cross the causeway on St Cuthbert's Way to the Holy Island. 2 Vindolanda Roman Fort is one of a number of fascinating historical sites to visit along Hadrian's Wall. 3 The church of the Holy Paraclete in Kirkhaugh. 4 The annual Festival of the Heavy Horse at Hay Farm Heavy Horse Centre. 5 Thomas Bewick's *History of British Birds* on display at Cherryburn.

CAROL STEVEN/HFHHC

GEMMA HALL

GEMMA HALL

DAVE HEAD/S

ISLANDS

Birdwatchers are in for a treat in Northumberland with the renowned Farne Island archipelago, Coquet Island bird reserve and Lindisfarne's castle isle all within easy reach of the mainland.

1 St Mary's Lighthouse and rocky reef is popular with families. Go rockpooling at low tide. 2 Grey seals bask on the rocks of the Farne Islands. 3 Puffins can be seen in abundance on Coquet Island. 4 A highlight of a trip to the coast is taking a boat from Seahouses to the Farne Island seabird colonies.

CRAIGBIRDPHOTOS/S

MARTIN KITCHING/NEI

GEMMA HALL

NEWCASTLE TO BERWICK BY TRAIN

From Newcastle to Berwick, the East Coast Main Line service from London to Edinburgh offers a tantalising view of some of Northumberland's finest dune-backed beaches and seaside villages during the 45-minute journey. Stone viaducts, wooded riverbanks, 19th-century station houses and sheep grazing in fields pepper the landscape between glimpses of the sea. Look out for Alnmouth's picturesque cluster of red-tiled houses stacked above the river and white sands, and Lindisfarne with its castle rising from the water on a fist of rock and long streak of bumpy dunes.

As you near Berwick, the line is all of a sudden right up against the shore and you can look down and see waves hammering the rocks below. But none of these sights is quite as spectacular as when the train drops its speed on crossing Stephenson's lofty viaduct into Berwick from where passengers gain a plunging view of the town and River Tweed. Looking south, the silhouettes of some of Northumberland's castles are just visible.

caught around here,' he says. Lowry must have thought the same judging by the number of times he painted the town. Sallyport and Dewar's Lane, both reached from Bridge Street, were famously depicted by the artist. The latter is a tight little cobbled alley with a bulging 200-year-old granary, now an excellent, modern YHA which also houses the **Granary Gallery** (TD15 1HJ ✆ 01289 330999 ☺ phone for opening times ♿) which puts on a few well-regarded art shows every year. Access to the granary is from the Tweed-facing **Quay Walls**, itself worth a stroll for its handsome row of Georgian houses.

Along the riverside: Berwick's bridges

East Coast Main Line trains from Edinburgh to London chug across Robert Stephenson's 1850 **Royal Border Bridge**, offering a spectacular view of the Tweed. The clear problem here is that you only very briefly see its 28 towering arches, but the bridge's magnificence is sensed in the way it makes you feel at 126 dizzying feet above the river. It's such a Victorian pleasure.

The other way to get up close to those long, colourful stone legs is to stroll downhill on a leafy path that connects the station with the river. Cowering underneath the Border Bridge arches is the ruin of **Berwick Castle**, founded in the 12th century. Those ruthless Victorians bulldozed the fortress to make way for the bridge and station.

Continuing downriver on the promenade, you'll pass a boathouse and then **New Bridge** (opened 1928). Its sculptural undersides won't go unappreciated by photographers.

The 17th-century **Old Bridge**, last in the trio of Berwick's bridges, skims across the Tweed in 15 graceful arches.

Tweedmouth & Spittal Beach

Facing Berwick on the south side of the river is Tweedmouth – a largely residential area but with many 19th-century buildings near the river which serve as reminders of the area's once thriving grain, herring and salmon fishing industries. Here, **Brewery Lane** has an intact run of 19th-century brewery buildings; it's rare to find all the elements of a Victorian brewery (drying sheds, malt kilns and the 'brewery tap' – the nearest pub to the brewery) as well preserved as this.

On Tower Hill, and with an expansive view of the Tweed, is **Tower House Pottery** (TD15 2BD ✆ 01289 307314 📖 www.towerhousepottery.com ⊙ Mon–Fri). When I visited, the owners were immersed in their craft, painting vases, plates and cups with their trademark floral designs and local scenes.

Keep going along Dock Road to reach **Sandstell Road** with its old herring sheds and salmon fishermen's shiel. **Spittal's beach** and its Victorian promenade (painted many times by L S Lowry) was once a very popular seaside resort. It's still well visited by Berwickers and is recommended for a blustery walk. ♿ The promenade is paved and easily accessible in a wheelchair.

▮▮ FOOD & DRINK

Fish and chip shops in Berwick are plentiful. In recent times I've tried **Cannon's** (11 Castlegate, TD15 1JS ✆ 01289 331480) which was recommended by several locals, and the **Fish Restaurant** (33–41 West St, TD15 1AS ✆ 01289 306149). Both were very good.

FOOD & BEER FESTIVAL

Berwick has an active Slow Food movement and an annual **Food and Beer Festival** in September (📖 www.berwickfoodfestival. co.uk) which brings together the best local food and drink producers and musicians for a weekend of tasting. In previous years the event was held in Berwick Barracks but do check the website.

UPDATES WEBSITE

For additional online content, photos, accommodation reviews and more on Northumberland, visit ⊘ www.bradtguides.com/northumberland.

Incidentally, the latter still serves take-aways in newspaper, something I haven't seen for a long time. **Prior Chippy** (9A Grove Gardens, Tweedmouth TD15 2EN ⊘ 01289 308936) also has an excellent reputation.

Audela 41–47 Bridge St, TD15 1ES ⊘ 01289 308827 ♿. Two ladies digging into a plate of langoustines caught my eye on passing this bright, contemporary café-cum-restaurant on Berwick's best independent shopping street. Audela's breakfast, lunch and evening menus are peppered with seafood dishes prepared with local produce, including lobster and crab from Berwick's waters and fish from Eyemouth. Hearty meat-filled sandwiches and a variety of salads also feature on the lunch menu, with lamb, steak and fish dishes in the evenings.

Barrels Ale House 59 Bridge St, TD15 1ES ⊘ 01289 308013. Characterful pub full of local chatter just off the Old Bridge. Inside, vintage skis and a big fish hang from the wall and ceiling along with a load of other random objects. Punters sit on barrels and in an old barber's (dentist's?) chair enjoying a (cheap) pint of real ale.

Cocoature 18 West St, TD15 1AS ⊘ 01289 308821. Milk or dark hot chocolate or a mixture of both? That's the dilemma when ordering a take-away at this little chocolaterie. I recommend the dark only for a rich-tasting hot drink.

The Corner House Café 31 Church St, TD15 1EE ⊘ 01289 304748. On cold days, the flickering of flames from an open fire in front of leather Chesterfield sofas and the smell of home cooking lure pedestrians in off the street to this snug café. It's the sort of place you could end up for several hours reading the papers or one of the secondhand books for sale. Though not extensive the menu includes soups, sandwiches and cakes – all made in-house.

The Green Shop 30 Bridge St, TD15 1AQ ⊘ 01289 305566 ♿. A very well-stocked eco shop selling fruit and veg, local cheeses, ice creams and crafts as well as an array of green and fair trade household goods and beauty products.

Queen's Head Hotel 6 Sandgate, TD15 1EP ⊘ 01289 307852. It's not cheap (most mains upwards of £15), but the food is made with care by good chefs and many of the ingredients are sourced locally. French and traditional British dishes (steak, venison, salmon, etc).

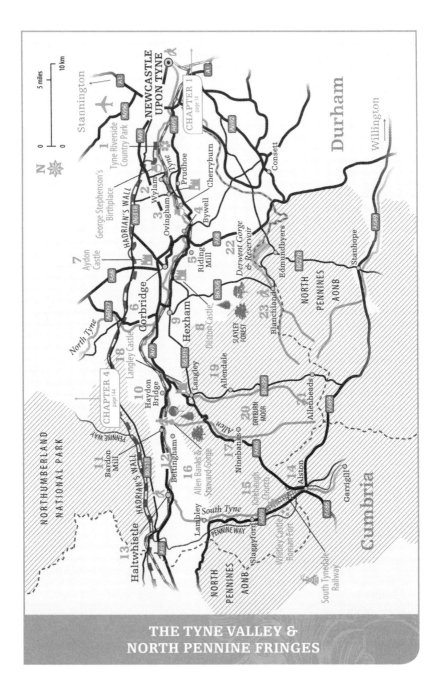

THE TYNE VALLEY &
NORTH PENNINE FRINGES

3
THE TYNE VALLEY & NORTH PENNINE FRINGES

From Carlisle to Newcastle, road, river and railway ribbon across the neck of England through a wide, fertile valley with fields, pockets of woodland and a scattering of farms and settlements hunkered down by the water's edge. **Hexham** and **Corbridge** are the most prominent and visited market towns on the River Tyne.

From Haltwhistle, the South Tyne hurries eastwards past ruined castles, manor houses and historic market towns on its way to meet the North Tyne near Hexham. Here, the two rivers become one, forming the **River Tyne** for the final run through Newcastle and on to the coast. The countryside is not remote and neither is it dramatic, but there is much beauty in this broad-sided valley that is filled with light owing to the relative flatness of the land.

"Heather becomes increasingly dominant as you gain altitude, and, from some moors, you can see all the way into Scotland."

Mining and industrial production over the last few hundred years greatly changed the character and fortunes of settlements in the Tyne Valley and North Pennines. These industries expanded with the aid of the railways in the 19th century and towns and villages grew as a result. Many places, particularly along the Tyne corridor, have retained their characterful uniform terraces of sandstone and brick, village greens and stone bridges.

Visitors who wander into the **North Pennines** hills which stretch across the southernmost flank of Northumberland and into Durham, will discover some of the region's most remote and beautiful upland scenery. Heather becomes increasingly dominant as you gain altitude, and, from some moors, you can see all the way into Scotland. For the most part, however, the North Pennine fringes are characterised by wooded gorges, flower-filled meadows and a pastoral landscape reminiscent of the Yorkshire Dales with dry stone walls criss-crossing farmland.

GETTING AROUND

Undoubtedly, the most reliable and frequent public transport option in the Tyne Valley is the train (see below) though Hexham is also well serviced by bus from Newcastle. As for travel in the North Pennines, you really need your own transport.

One **bus** that may be of help is the 688 from Hexham to Allenheads via Langley, Allendale and a few other places. It runs several times a day Monday to Saturday. Alston is reached from Carlisle by taking bus 680, which also stops at Lambley.

TRAIN

The best way to get a sense of the lie of the land and enjoy the big, bright views in the Tyne Valley is to take the frequent **Newcastle–Carlisle** train on what is sometimes referred to as the Tyne Valley Line (and occasionally the slightly misleading Hadrian's Wall Country Line). Railway and river intertwine the whole way and the train stops at most riverside towns and villages. The surrounding green and yellow fields dotted with sheep, cows, woods and farmsteads are just lovely. On the downside, it's no Bullet Train and it rattles along like a tin can.

A Hadrian's Wall Country Line **Day Ranger ticket** (www. northernrail.org) allows unlimited travel between Newcastle and Carlisle stopping at Prudhoe, Corbridge, Hexham, Haltwhistle and a few other stops. Buy tickets at the station or on board trains where stations are unmanned. Incidentally, you are never far from a 'proper' pub in the Tyne Valley. A good number are conveniently located close to train stations, as detailed in a leaflet produced by CAMRA (Campaign for Real Ale). Download *Whistle Stops* at www.cannybevvy.co.uk.

The Tyne Valley Line

The Newcastle–Carlisle railway, dating from the 1830s, was one of the earliest railways ever built. The stations have retained much of their original Victorian character and North Eastern Railway Company architecture. Waiting rooms with tall chimneys, big station clocks, signal towers, water tanks and decorative iron footbridges painted cream and red add to the historic appeal of the villages and towns the stations serve. At Haltwhistle station all the above elements come together, making it one of the most interesting on the line.

CYCLING

The River Tyne corridor offers the day cyclist some pleasant easy routes along the river to market towns and villages where there are plenty of watering holes. If you can't manage the return ride, take your bike back on the train. I've described the popular **Newcastle to Wylam** cycle ride on page 112.

Thigh-busting moors and long exhilarating downhill stretches abound in the North Pennines. Hundreds of cyclists take on the 140-mile **Coast-to-Coast** (Whitehaven to Tynemouth via Alston and Allenheads) and the 150-mile **Pennine Cycleway** (**NCN Route 68**; Appleby or Penrith to Berwick-upon-Tweed via the North Pennine moors, Redesdale and Wooler) every summer and you'll find good facilities along the way. There are many day rides of course: around the reservoirs, along disused railway lines (see a description of the **South Tyne Valley Trail** on pages 127–9 which follows the Pennine Cycleway), and country lanes above wooded gorges. Five **guides** produced by the North Pennines AONB are available to download from the cycling pages at ∅ www.northpennines.org.uk.

CYCLE HIRE & REPAIRS

In addition to the places listed below, there are a couple of options in Newcastle (page 17).
ActivCycles 17 Watling St, Corbridge NE45 5AH ∅ 01434 632950. Repairs.
North Pennine Cycles Nenthead CA9 3PF ∅ 01434 341004. Repairs and bike hire.

ℹ TOURIST INFORMATION

Alston Town Hall, bottom of Front St, CA9 3RF ∅ 01434 382244 ☉ daily in spring & summer, closes on Sun at 15.00; Oct–Easter, Tue, Wed & Thu 10.00–15.00, Mon & Fri 10.00–17.00 ♿

Corbridge Hill St, NE45 5AA ∅ 01434 632815 ☉ end Mar–end Oct, Mon–Sat; at other times of the year, Wed, Fri & Sat ♿

Haltwhistle Westgate, NE49 0AX ∅ 01434 322002 ☉ Easter–end Oct, Mon–Sat ♿ access through side entrance of library

Hexham Wentworth car park, NE46 1QE ∅ 01670 620450 ☉ daily ♿

Online, the **North Pennines AONB** website (∅ www.northpennines.org.uk) has a huge amount of information about the landscapes, geology and wildlife of the region. The AONB also produces many high-quality guides, booklets and leaflets on sale online or by phone (∅ 01388 528801) and found at tourist information centres.

WALKING

Around the towns and villages in the **Tyne Valley**, there are plenty of options for short walks along the riverside, some of which I've mentioned in these pages (Cherryburn to Ovingham and Riding Mill to Corbridge, for example). Beautiful mixed woodlands crowd smaller rivers like the **West Dipton Burn** and **Devil's Water** just south of Hexham – both of which offer walkers several miles of riverside rambles. The advantage of following the West Dipton Burn is that you pass Dipton Mill pub which serves food and has its own brewery (page 123). Further west is **Allen Banks**, another stunning wooded valley easily reached from Haydon Bridge (page 134).

The North Pennines presents some of the best opportunities for moorland and valley walks in England. From the River Tyne, the **Pennine Way** heads due south roughly following the course of the River South Tyne from Lambley to Alston before climbing across some of England's highest and most desolate fells; **Isaac's Tea Trail** makes a circuit of the beautiful Allen valleys. This 37-mile circular trail (marked on OS Explorer maps) follows in the footsteps of Isaac Holden, a devout Methodist who travelled the Pennine moors in the mid 19th century selling tea and raising money for good causes.

TAXIS

Advanced Taxis Hexham ✆ 01434 606565. Journeys to Housesteads, Hadrian's Wall or Allendale cost around £25, for example.
Alston Taxis Alston ✆ 07990 593855. Alston to Haltwhistle costs £30.
Corbridge Village Taxi Corbridge ✆ 01434 634006. Similar prices to the above.
Diamond Private Hire Haltwhistle ✆ 07597 641222. Can take up to two bikes.

THE TYNE VALLEY

As you travel upriver from Newcastle, the landscape becomes increasingly rural from Newburn onwards. Some of the greenest and most tranquil stretches of the River Tyne are found here and are easily reached by following the riverside path out of Newcastle city centre (page 112), or by taking the train to Wylam or Prudhoe.

Hexham and Corbridge hold instant appeal for visitors because of their historic market squares, venerable buildings and easy access to Newcastle, the North Pennines and Hadrian's Wall.

NEWCASTLE TO OVINGHAM

Little effort is needed to lure passing tourists to Wylam and Ovingham with their affluent Victorian terraces, riverside settings and old pubs. However, there are a few other places nearby that should not be overlooked, including Bywell.

1 Tyne Riverside Country Park

From Newcastle the Country Park is signed from the A6085; car park off Grange Rd, NE15 8ND (close to the Big Lamp Brewery & Keelman pub)

You'd never guess a coal mine once stood on this 200-acre meadow and wetland parkland near Newburn, unless, that is, you look carefully for clues in the landscape (the remains of four beehive coke ovens can still be seen at Blayney Row, for example).

Today, the site, which extends to the south side of the Tyne at Prudhoe, is popular with dog walkers, families and those cycling and walking Hadrian's Wall.

"If visiting at dusk in winter, you'll walk under the noisy flight-path of hundreds of jackdaws and rooks."

From Newburn, two trails keep tight to the riverbank (one exclusively for walkers). The Tyne flows lazily here, tugging the branches of overhanging shrubs and trees. If visiting at dusk in winter, you'll walk under the noisy flight-path of hundreds of jackdaws and rooks roosting in nearby trees.

¶¶ FOOD & DRINK

The Keelman's Lodge Grange Rd, Newburn NE15 8NL ℰ 0191 267 1689 𝄐 www. keelmanslodge.co.uk ♿. The large playground next to an outdoor seating area shouts 'family-friendly pub'. The Keelman is not really in the countryside as such but the leafy riverbank setting gives that impression. The building dates back to the mid 19th century and was formerly a water pumping station. Decent, inexpensive pub dinners (and breakfasts) are served all day and into the evening (scampi, fish and chips, steaks, burgers) along with beer produced on site in the Big Lamp Brewery.

2 Wylam

For a small place, Wylam has produced a surprising number of the great railway pioneers of the 18th and 19th centuries. **George Stephenson** and **Timothy Hackworth** were both born here and **William Hedley**, who was raised in nearby Newburn, worked at the Wylam Colliery and tested his famous steam engine prototypes on the Wylam Waggonway.

Those with an interest in railway history should visit the **museum** in the library on Wylam's Falcon Terrace.

The town itself makes a very pleasant stopping point on your travels along the Tyne. Grand stone houses and brick terraces either side of the river reflect the affluence that came with being a railway town in the 19th century.

Two **bridges** span the Tyne at Wylam. The more striking is the 1876 railway bridge (now only open to cyclists and pedestrians) at Hagg Bank (west of Wylam Station and the road bridge, and reached from the riverside path). The single-span structure is reminiscent of Newcastle's Tyne Bridge which was built half a century later. The crossing further east by the train station directly links the two sides of Wylam town and retains its 1899 Toll House.

Wylam's **centre** is on the north side of the river and accessed by following the Main Road north from the station and memorial green. It's attractive enough with a few restaurants, shops, a post office and a couple of pubs but unless you need some food, there's not a great deal to warrant the uphill walk.

On the south side of the Tyne is Wylam Station, which conveniently stands next to a great real ale pub, The Boathouse (page 108).

Wylam Waggonway

Today it is a recreational path surrounded by trees that runs for a few miles between Wylam and Blayney Row but at the turn of the 19th century, this waggonway (that then extended to Lemington) played an important role in the development of modern railway travel.

Wagons were used to transport coal from Wylam Colliery to ships docked at Lemington staiths on the River Tyne, some five miles away. Originally they were pulled on wooden rails by horses, until the owner of the colliery, Christopher Blackett, set his mind to making the transfer of coal more efficient.

"Wagons were used to transport coal from Wylam Colliery to ships docked at Lemington staiths on the River Tyne."

In 1808, he replaced the wooden rails with cast-iron ones and enlisted the engineering skills of his colliery manager, William Hedley, to develop an engine to replace his horses. Hedley experimented with different designs until the *Puffing Billy* was unveiled in 1814. The stout locomotive (now housed in the Science Museum in London) was created

THE SALMON RUN

For a month from mid-October, salmon turn upriver and embark on an arduous journey to their breeding grounds, leaping over rapids and boulders as they swim. The Tyne, being the number-one salmon river in England and Wales, is a good place to witness the spectacle (try Hexham weir or Wylam Bridge).

In the early 1800s, the Tyne was, as it is today, very good for salmon. On one day in June 1833, between 400 and 500 salmon were fished from the river · and taken to market in Newcastle. But, back in the 1950s there were virtually no salmon left, owing to pollution. Cleaner water and the hatchery in Kielder (page 171) have reversed the salmon's fortunes quite dramatically and record numbers were recorded in the Tyne in recent years.

with the assistance of two local engineers, Timothy Hackworth and Jonathan Forster, and is the oldest surviving steam engine in the world. The train carried coal along the Wylam Waggonway for 50 years, but its greatest contribution to the Industrial Revolution was in demonstrating that smooth iron wheels could run on flat iron tracks without derailing. This was an important step in the evolution of the modern train, enabling the locomotives of the future to travel at high speeds.

George Stephenson's Birthplace

Wylam Waggonway NE41 8BP (a pleasant half-mile walk east of Wylam village)
🕾 01661 853457 ☉ Feb school holidays & early Mar–end Oct, Thu–Sun; weekends only at other times of the year; tiny café selling a small selection of drinks, cakes & snacks also open every weekend in winter; ♿ National Trust

Halfway along the old waggonway to Wylam is a small limewashed stone cottage built for mining families around 1760. It was here, in 1781, that the great railway engineer George Stephenson was born. In his early days, he would have watched horses outside pulling wagons laden with coal from Wylam Colliery.

Stephenson lived with six other family members in one room of the four-bedroom building. It has been furnished in the style of an 18th-century dwelling and houses George Stephenson's Jacobean rocking chair, but the floor was bare earth back then. With just one room open to the public, there is little to see inside, but the National Trust stewards really go to town bringing the legacy of George Stephenson and the golden era of railway development to life.

Bradley Gardens

Sled Lane, Wylam NE41 8JH ℘ 01661 852176 ✐ www.bradley-gardens.co.uk ⊖ Tue–Sun
& bank holidays (closed Tue after a bank holiday); ♿

Since undergoing restoration, this enchanting walled garden dating to
1749 and its **tea room** and nursery have expanded to include upmarket
home stores including a cook shop, garden shop and Bridgewater
Interiors showroom. The gardens and wonderful Victorian glasshouse
(the same as the one at Wallington Hall) have been given much-needed
TLC where you can enjoy lunch or afternoon tea and admire the
flowerbeds and walkways draped in climbers. On sunny days outdoor
seats provide a view of the green hills rising beyond the old brick walls.
The entrance is tucked away down a quiet lane south of Wylam train
station and next to a lake where there are many water birds.

▟ FOOD & DRINK

Even if you don't go inside **George Stephenson's Birthplace** (page 107), there is a tiny
garden café next to the cottage, serving a small selection of cakes, teas and cold drinks.

In Wylam you have the choice of a couple of pubs, as well as cafés and restaurants including
Bistro en Glaze (Main Rd, NE41 8AJ ℘ 01661 852185 ⊖ Tue–Sat), which serves mainly
French dishes but also burgers and some Northumbrian/Border specials including haggis
with pan haggerty. **The Wood Oven's** (Main Rd, NE41 8DN ℘ 01661 852552 ⊖ Wed–Sun
(evenings only) ♿) inexpensive pizzas are made the traditional way and are popular with
locals. **The Boathouse** (Station Rd, NE41 8HR ℘ 01661 853431) is a rather tatty but well-
loved traditional pub next to Wylam's eye-catching train station. It holds much appeal on
account of its wide selection of drinks, laid-back atmosphere and open fires. The 12 ales on tap
change regularly except for the popular Tyneside Blonde, which is always available.

Three miles south of Wylam is the lovely Victorian glasshouse tea room at **Bradley
Gardens** (page 108).

3 Ovingham

By any Northumbrian standard, the lively riverside village of Ovingham
('Oving-jum') is one of the most appealing to visitors in the region. The
area around St Mary's Church is particularly quaint with its red phone
box, cottage gardens and streamside pub (the Bridge End Inn).

Those who arrive by train, or by bike along the traffic-free route from
Newcastle via Wylam, will enter the village over the **Ovingham Bridge**
from Prudhoe. The single-lane rickety road crossing, dating to 1883,
doesn't strike one as particularly sturdy, especially when cars cross and

the whole structure shudders. The adjoining pedestrian bridge (added in 1974) is worth walking over for the river views (and bone-rattling sensation when cars pass on the road bridge). The Tyne is extremely lush and overgrown here. Mature trees and bushes crowd the riverbank where fly-fishermen whip the water with their lines and kayaks take it in turn to whoosh down the rapids.

"Fly-fishermen whip the water with their lines and kayaks take it in turn to whoosh down the rapids."

St Mary's Church is built on the site of an early Saxon building of which the tower is the only relic. It is thought that part of the west side of the tower was built using Roman stones and the structure may have been designed with habitation in mind during the post-Roman centuries when invasions were feared. As you walk to the main doorway, you'll see the grave of the celebrated 18th-century nature artist, Thomas Bewick, who lived at Cherryburn over the river and went to school in Ovingham.

The last time I visited, I was drawn from the busy streets into St Mary's churchyard by the sound of children singing along to a piano. Despite the commuter traffic outside and the mini-scooters stacked in the church porch (the same entranceway that Thomas Bewick used as a canvas for his chalk drawings when he had run out of notebook pages), there was something quite old-fashioned about the scene.

Whittle Burn is crossed by way of a fetching old packhorse bridge formed of two narrow stone arches. From here you can trace the waterway upriver along a quiet footpath. Nineteenth-century records of Whittle Burn note the occurrence of fairies. If a quiet woodland with a shallow, stony stream and overhanging trees is the kind of place that attracts fairies, then this should indeed be a favourite haunt.

OVINGHAM GOOSE FAIR

The tradition of selling birds and other livestock at the village's annual Goose Fair seems to have died out some time in the early 20th century but was revived in the late 1960s; the fair is now held on the third Saturday in June. Visitors are entertained with Morris and Rapper dancers and traditional Northumbrian folk music, with a procession beginning from the old Goose Fair Cross. Cakes, plants, ice creams and crafts can be purchased from stallholders, while children can have their faces painted and participate in the fancy dress competition. It's all good, traditional country fun.

Cherryburn

Station Bank, Mickley, Stocksfield NE43 7DD ✆ 01661 843276 ☺ Feb school holidays—end Oct, Thu—Tue; Jul & Aug daily; café; ♿ National Trust

> The eventful day arrived at last ... I can only say my heart was like to break; and, as we passed away, I inwardly bade farewell to the whinny wilds, to Mickley bank, to the Stob-cross hill, to the water banks, the woods, and to particular trees, and even to the large hollow old elm, which had lain perhaps for centuries past, on the haugh near the ford we were about to pass, and which had sheltered the salmon fishers, while at work there, from many a bitter blast.
>
> A Memoir of Thomas Bewick Written By Himself, 1862

The year was 1767 and 14-year-old Thomas Bewick was leaving his birthplace on the banks of the River Tyne to begin an apprenticeship at an engraving workshop in Newcastle. His fondness for the family home at Cherryburn and the woods and rivers surrounding the farmhouse stayed with Bewick for the whole of his life. Though he is most famed for his woodcut blocks of birds and his celebrated 1797 book, *A History of British Birds*, on every other page of the book there is a vignette depicting rural scenes typical of the Tyne landscape in the 18th century: boys sail toy boats on the river in one picture while in another a farmer cuts his meadow with a scythe. There is humour too, like the man holding on to a cow's tail while crossing a river with a drunkard on his back.

Bewick's engravings evoke nostalgia for the rural way of life and draw us seemlessly into his childhood in the Tyne Valley where fishermen stand knee-high in water, men play the fiddle and it is almost always summertime.

THE SPETCHELLS CHALK GRASSLANDS

Dubbed 'The White Cliffs of Tynedale', this grassy embankment that runs parallel to the river between Hagg Bank and Prudhoe was created by waste chalk from an ICI chemical factory that became colonised by shrubs, trees and lime-loving plants. Walkers and cyclists will find an assemblage of plants more usually found in the downlands of southern England, including wild marjoram, St John's wort, bird's foot trefoil and kidney vetch. Also look out for unusual butterflies including the dingy skipper, a brown butterfly with beige speckles.

The National Trust looks after Bewick's much-loved Cherryburn with great care and makes much of the stone cottage, cobbled courtyard and farm outbuildings huddled near the Tyne. It's a very appealing museum with a fascinating print room (demonstrations every Sunday), displays of Bewick's works, and live folk sessions in the garden (first Sunday of the month from May to October). Children will enjoy the farm animals and playing in the cherry orchard.

From here, you can **walk** through countryside and along the river to Ovingham on the north side of the Tyne where Bewick went to school.

Prudhoe Castle

NE42 6NA ✆ 01661 833459 ⊙ Easter–end Oct, Wed–Sun ♿ access to ground floor of the house but outside areas difficult on a rough track; English Heritage

From the valley basin, Prudhoe Castle is seen poking through the trees at the top of a steep bank. The 12th-century ruin is easily the most striking historic attraction in Prudhoe (pronounced by locals as 'prudha'), not that it has much competition in this modern settlement and former coal mining town, known today for the manufacture of paper towels and its ferret rescue centre.

The castle, said to be the only fortress in the North never to be taken by the Scots, is really very impressive, even more so close up than from a distance. Its ten-foot-thick curtain wall, elevated position and moat no doubt provided good protection. Originally the stronghold of the Umfravilles, it was eventually inherited by the powerful Percy family of Alnwick Castle.

Allow about an hour or so to walk around the grounds (where there are plenty of nice picnic spots), tour the keep and visit the exhibition room.

⅋ FOOD & DRINK

Bridge End Inn West Rd, Ovingham NE42 6BN ✆ 01661 832219. Friendly local pub serving regional ales (no food). On weekend evenings in summer there's always a convivial atmosphere on the patio outside by the old stone packhorse bridge.
Duke of Wellington Newton, near Corbridge NE43 7UL ✆ 01661 844446 ⊘ www.thedukeofwellingtoninn.co.uk ⊙ daily, from breakfast ♿. Gastro pub (with a view of the Tyne Valley) serving regional ales and decent traditional pub fare like steak and chips. Good B&B accommodation upstairs.

✳ ✳ ✳

🚶 NEWCASTLE TO WYLAM
BY BICYCLE OR ON FOOT

❀ OS Explorer map 316; start: Newcastle quayside; 10 miles; difficulty: easy/moderate; refreshments: the Keelman (Tyne Riverside Country Park), Wylam Waggonway, Wylam village &, best of all for a drink, The Boathouse next to Wylam station

This easy, off-road cycle path takes you west along the Tyne Valley under Newcastle's famous bridges and into tranquil countryside. It follows the well-signed **Hadrian's Cycleway** (NCN Route 72). The footpath for walkers (**Hadrian's Wall Path**) follows the same route, except between Scotswood and Newburn Bridge (the section you may wish to cover by bus 22 from Newcastle Central Station because it follows a busy road).

From Newcastle's quayside, follow the riverside promenade west from the **Tyne Bridge** passing under the High Level, Metro, Rail and Redheugh bridges in that order. The countryside doesn't get going until your back is to Newburn, but the urban fringes should not be overlooked as you hurry towards the leafy banks of the Tyne further west.

At the Newcastle Business Park (not as ugly as it sounds) you'll get a good view of the **Dunston Coal Staiths** (page 30). In winter, shelduck, teal, lapwing and the odd curlew dabble in the exposed mud at low tide.

The mile-long stretch to the ancient woodland of **Denton Dene** is a big, busy concrete affair (albeit one on a footpath and cycle path), but once you enter the Dene's woody confines, the Scotswood Road and its juggernauts seem far away. If you've heard the famous North East song 'The Blaydon Races', you'll recall the often recited line: 'There were lots of lads and lasses there, all with smiling faces, ganning along the Scotswood Road, to see the Blaydon Races.'

Just after Blaydon Bridge, the cycle path turns to the river and follows it closely to Newburn. Continue straight ahead if you want to see the 120-foot-high **Lemington Glass Works cone** – the only one of four late 18th-century brick cones still standing here and one of the last remaining in England.

The historic **Tyne Rowing Club** is just beyond the Newburn Bridge. After a very pleasant half mile through the **Tyne Riverside Country Park** (page 105), the path swings north where you will meet with the old **Wylam Waggonway** (pages 106–7). The café at **George Stephenson's Birthplace** (page 108) is a welcome stopping point.

Return the same way or by train (bikes permitted) from Wylam. If you continue west for another couple of miles to lovely **Ovingham**, you'll cross Wylam's eye-catching old railway bridge at Hagg Bank and a manmade limestone grassland (page 110). NCN Route 72 goes past Prudhoe train station on the south bank of the Tyne from where you can return to Newcastle.

✳ ✳ ✳

CORBRIDGE, HEXHAM, HALTWHISTLE & AROUND

Following the river from Ovingham to the western edge of Northumberland, the traveller dips in and out of a string of market towns and hamlets with plentiful historic buildings and attractions. Almost anywhere along this stretch of the wide, low-sided valley, you will find far-reaching views of farmland and glimpse church towers and manor houses peeping through the trees.

4 Bywell

'Bywell is the most beautifully placed and the most picturesque and architecturally rewarding of all Tyneside villages', wrote the architectural writer, Pevsner. Technically Bywell is a village but it's not easily recognisable as such in the sense that there is no local shop, row of cottages or post office, but it does boast two churches. Why two churches within such close proximity? Experts say they may have existed in two separate villages many years ago.

St Andrew's is fascinating on account of its extensive Saxon stonework. According to Pevsner it has a 'first-rate Saxon tower, the best in the county'. Let's overlook the fact that there are few competitors, even if we're flexible with the county borders (St Andrew's at Corbridge, Ovingham's church and St Paul's of Bede fame at Jarrow come to mind), and instead admire the 9th-century tall tower with its irregularly shaped stones and rounded windows that give it a characteristic Saxon appearance. The base of the cross in the chancel is also Saxon and retains some fine stone detailing but the rest of St Andrew's mostly dates to the 13th and 19th centuries. Note the collection of medieval grave slabs set into the exterior walls and displayed inside.

"Its castellated turrets are pretty impressive and the roofless building is of considerable age."

As for **St Peter's** – identified by its comparatively squat, wide tower – well, it's largely 13th century (with some Norman masonry) and was built on the site of a Saxon church.

The other prominent building in Bywell is the **castle**. I say 'castle' but it's really just the gatehouse to a castle that was never built. Still, its castellated turrets are pretty impressive and the roofless building is of considerable age (early 15th century). It's said that Henry VI took shelter here on fleeing the 1464 Battle of Hexham and left behind his sword, helmet and crown.

5 Riding Mill

When you arrive by train from Newcastle, Riding Mill feels like the first stop in the Northumberland countryside. There are no attractions to speak of in the village except for a couple of defensive **bastle houses** in Broomhaugh, the 17th-century **Wellington Inn**, a decent pub for Sunday lunch (Main Rd NE44 6DQ 🖉 01434 682531 🖢) and the old **mill house** opposite, but the leafy setting, stone cottages and closeness to the River Tyne make this an appealing stopping point. The construction of the Newcastle–Carlisle line made it possible for Tyneside businessmen and their families to live in the countryside, hence the tall townhouses you see today that were built with Victorian commuters in mind.

The **riverside** is easily reached from the station. From the platform on the north side of the line, take the paved footpath that continues for a few hundred yards to Broomhaugh. Turn left at the Methodist church and continue to the end of the street where a dirt path near an old bastle house leads to the river.

A very pleasant, albeit muddy, **walk** follows the southern bank of the Tyne to Corbridge. A longer route could encompass Devil's Water (a wooded gorge) and Hexham; return by train from either town.

🍴 FOOD & DRINK

Wheelbirks Ice Cream Parlour Stocksfield NE43 7HY 🖉 01661 842613 🖄 www.wheelbirks. co.uk 🕘 Tue–Sun 🖢. Cheerful café serving sandwiches, burgers, cakes and farm-produced ice cream in a converted Victorian stable. The beef used in the burgers and for Sunday roast are from the farm's Jersey cattle. Exceptionally family-friendly with plenty of play areas (inside and out).

6 Corbridge

🏠 **Angel Inn** (page 273)

On entering this historic market town from the east, the wide main thoroughfare with its large double-fronted houses makes quite a first impression. In the **centre**, art galleries sit next to an upmarket delicatessen on Hill Street, where you'll also find the **tourist information centre** (page 103); ladies chat outside smart dress shops on Middle Street; and several vintage-inspired cafés, a florist, bookshop and 1950s-style sweet shop circle the busy Market Cross. A number of shop fronts have original 18th- and 19th-century wood detailing and a few are among more than 60 listed buildings in Corbridge.

Prosperity has not always been associated with Corbridge, however. In the 14th century, the town was attacked and ransacked by the Scots on several occasions. The Black Death later wiped out much of the remaining population. For several hundred years, Corbridge remained a small, insignificant settlement, until 1835 when the Newcastle–Carlisle railway opened. Wealthy businessmen moved here from Newcastle, gentrifying Corbridge into the smart town it is today. Most of the streets date to this period though the layout is medieval.

There were several earlier booms in the town's history that ought to be mentioned, notably during Roman times and again in the 13th century, when Corbridge was said to be (regionally) second only to Newcastle in wealth.

The **Tyne** flows fast over rapids as it passes Corbridge and it is not difficult to imagine the destructive power of the waterway after prolonged rain. In 1771, the flooded river was strong enough to wash away every crossing along the Tyne, except for the magnificent seven-arched **bridge** you see today at Corbridge which has spanned the Tyne since 1674. You can access the northern banks by walking down the path at the side of the bridge.

The **riverside trail** is tranquil and especially beautiful late in the afternoon when the sun turns the sandstone bridge a deep gold. Late one October afternoon, I walked this path and met some young boys fishing. The bridge in the background and the ducks that had gathered under a willow added to the timelessness of the setting. If it weren't for the BMX bikes on the ground, it could have been a rural scene from any autumn day in the last few hundred years.

St Andrew's Church

Before you enter St Andrew's, note the **vicar's pele tower** in the churchyard (now housing a tiny vintage antiques shop). The defensive structure, where clergymen of centuries past would have taken refuge during attacks on the town, is thought to date to around 1400. English Heritage ranks it as the best example of its kind in Northumberland.

The walls of **St Andrew's Church** date mainly to the 13th century, though there is evidence of Norman construction as you enter the south porch, and the tower is Anglo-Saxon. Perhaps most striking of all is the 16-foot-high Roman arch which forms the entrance to the baptistery. Like many buildings in Corbridge, we can hazard a good guess as to where this stone treasure was sourced. Equally as impressive and standing over double the height is an Early English archway dating to the 13th century.

As you depart the church grounds, turn right to see the exterior of the Saxon tower and the intriguing 700-year-old **King's Oven** built into the church wall. A plaque explains that it was 'the communal oven for the baking of the village's bread and meat'.

Coria Roman Fort

Corchester Lane, Corbridge NE45 5NT ✆ 01434 632349 ⊙ early Apr–end Oct & school holidays, daily; weekends at other times ♿ museum & 3 sides of the fort but accessing the interior is difficult; English Heritage

Before Hadrian's Wall was constructed, the Roman garrison town of Coria (sometimes known as Corstopitum, but we now know from the Vindolanda tablets that the Romans called it Coria) at the western edge of Corbridge, built circa AD85, was an important settlement at the junction of two major Roman roads: Dere Street and the Stanegate (Old English meaning 'stone road'). It also held a strategic position at a crossing of the river and later acted as a supply town for the Wall.

Visitors can wander around the stone foundations of market buildings and peer underneath the large flagstones covering the granary floor. Also of note is the base of what was once an impressive fountain which was fed by an aqueduct. One of the most treasured finds at Coria is a free-standing stone carving of a lion with a bushy mane poised on top of a captured deer (or is it a goat?). The Corbridge Lion is on display in the on-site **museum**.

¶¶ FOOD & DRINK

A scattering of average cafés dot the streets around Corbridge's St Andrew's Church, including the busy 1940s–60s-styled **Tea & Tipple** (18 Market Pl, NE45 5AW ✆ 01434 632886) where you can grab a scone and fairly decent coffee. The **Artisam** (18–22 Front St, NE45 5AP ✆ 01434 634214) Chinese restaurant is popular with locals and there are also a few pubs worth mentioning. Picnickers or those staying in holiday cottages can pick up supplies in the local Co-op and at the nearby **Corbridge Larder** (18 Hill St, NE45 5AA ✆ 01434 632948), a deli and well-stocked food store selling a range of local produce.

Angel Inn Main St, NE45 5LA ✆ 01434 632119 🖥 www.theangelofcorbridge.com ♿ but disabled toilet a pig to reach. Old coaching inn with two dining rooms: the restaurant/bar area at the front is more casual; at the back is their smart restaurant. Food wise, the menu is the same. Choose from a selection of gastro-pub dishes (fish and chips, Northumberland steak, gourmet

sandwiches and so on) or something from the specials menu which is that bit more upmarket. Lamb is sourced from the Angel's own farm near Ponteland. **Take-away fish and chips** (✆ 01434 634602 ☉ Tue–Sat lunchtime & evenings) are available from the side of the inn.
Black Bull Middle St, NE45 5AT ✆ 01434 632261. Low beamed ceilings, stone walls, a coal fire, real ales and good-value traditional pub food (fish and chips, bangers and mash, burgers and steaks) make this 18th-century pub a favourite with locals.
Brockbushes A69 roundabout east of Corbridge NE43 7UB ✆ 01434 633100 ☉ daily ♿.
A pick-your-own strawberry and raspberry farm with a tea room (coffees, soups, scones, cakes) and farm shop.

7 Aydon Castle

Aydon, a few miles north of Corbridge NE45 5PJ ✆ 01434 632450 ☉ Apr–end Oct, Wed–Sun ♿ ground floor only; English Heritage

Not a true castle as such; really a fortified manor house, albeit one of the most intact and formidable of its period. The stone buildings stand on an elevated fist of farmland overlooking a wooded ravine and are well preserved owing to the fact that they were continuously occupied for the best part of 700 years until the late 1960s.

Aydon Castle was originally unfortified when it was built by a Suffolk merchant in the late 13th century, but that was before warring between Scotland and England threatened settlements across Northumberland. In 1312, the Scots burned nearby Hexham and Corbridge, prompting the construction of a high stone wall around three sides of the manor. The south side was already protected by the steep bank of a ravine.

You can wander through the courtyards and bare chambers, stables, hall and kitchen. The orchard is a nice place to take a rug and some sandwiches. Alternatively, take your packed lunch down to the wooded ravine below and enjoy a **walk** along Cor Burn – a shallow river that rushes over stones and fallen branches on its way to meet the Tyne.

8 Dilston Castle

Dilston Castle: 1½ miles south of Corbridge NE45 5RJ ✆ 01661 844157 ♂ www.friendsofhistoricdilston.org ☉ the castle has opened & then closed a few times in recent years (currently closed at the time of writing) so check the website for details

The ruins of a mid 15th-century castle stand high above the wooded slopes of Devil's Water, surrounded by parkland and a 17th-century chapel and gatehouse. The setting is very fitting for the romantic and tragic tale of the legendary 3rd Earl of Derwentwater, James Radcliffe.

Dilston was the ancestral home of the powerful Radcliffes for 200 years, but its links to the family and the last Earl of Derwentwater were extinguished in the years following the Jacobite Rebellion of 1715.

The Earl's life was cut short for his leading role in the rising against George I. He was just 26 and newly married. The Jacobite army had been initially successful in many towns in Northumberland, but when they proceeded south through Lancashire, they were defeated at Preston. The earl was imprisoned in the Tower of London and later executed.

The wooded slopes rising from **Devil's Water** (name derived from the 12th-century settlement, Dyvelston) are as scenic today as when Tomlinson wrote in his 1888 *Comprehensive Guide to Northumberland* the account below, and many of the same plants, trees and foliage observed then colour Dilston's woods and meadows to this day.

Under the shade of pine, beech, rowan and birch trees the visitor saunters along the winding pathway, by banks covered with the trailing flowers … Crossing a narrow plank, he proceeds to the right, along a rustic pathway, through a tangled copse, perfumed by the honey-suckle and wild rose, until he reaches the haughs already seen from the heights above. Here he seems to stand in the arena of a vast amphitheatre, with tiers on tiers of foliage sloping upwards from the river's edge

Dilston Physic Garden

Dilston Mill House, NE45 5QZ ✆ 07879 533875 🖉 www.dilstonphysicgarden.com ⊙ mid-Apr–mid-Oct, Wed & Sat

Gardeners and those interested in the medicinal use of plants should visit this intriguing two-acre site near Dilston Castle created by a neuroscientist at Newcastle University researching the healing properties of plants. Visitors can wander the winding paths, taking in the profusion of scents and colour produced by some 600 plants with healing properties.

Day courses include tuition on meditation, yoga, foraging for edible plants and medicinal herbs (see website for details).

9 Hexham

🏠 **Langley Castle** (page 273), **Fairshaw Rigg** (page 273) ⛺ **Rye Hill Farm** (page 274)

The Tyne Valley's most significant market town is engulfed by so many trees that it appears much smaller than its true size when approached by train or from the riverside. The historic centre stands on a plateau above the river and is reached by heading uphill in the direction of the abbey tower (one of the few buildings to break the green canopy). You'll pass the **tourist information centre** (page 103) in the car park on your way. On reaching the marketplace – a bustling square with a higgledy-piggledy mix of Victorian, Georgian and medieval buildings – it is clear why Hexham was once voted England's favourite market town by *Country Life* magazine. The criteria were charm, accessibility and sense of community, all of which are apparent to the visitor.

Hexham's buildings have been burned and pillaged many times over the 1,300 years since it began life as a monastery on a terrace above the Tyne. In the Middle Ages, farming and lead mining were the principal industries, but Hexham later became a centre of leather production and was famed for its gloves known as Hexham Tans. According to A B Wright in his 1823 *History of Hexham*, some 280,000 pairs of gloves were produced annually. If you walk down Gilesgate, a narrow alley on the left leads into a large courtyard with a few old buildings and a shallow stream running over a channel of cobbles. Where now you see a car park, until the 1920s animal skins were soaked in large tanning pits here. Wright also notes the town had two woollen manufacturers, two rope makers (one can still be seen on Argyle Street), 16 master hatters and a 'very considerable brewery'. I suppose it would have to be of some size in order to have supplied some of Hexham's 32 inns and pubs. A number of those historic taverns are still extant and serving ale today.

A wander round the streets radiating from the **marketplace** reveals the shops and industries of bygone times. The stone-pillared shelter prominently standing in the market square is known as **The Shambles** – a medieval meat market. Goods are still sold here but you are more likely to find potted plants and clothes. A **farmers' market** runs on the second and fourth Saturday of the month.

One of the most fascinating streets in Hexham, **St Mary's Chare**, is tucked away down a passageway next to Paxton's fish and chip shop, which stands on the site of an old chapel from which the street gets its name. You can see the outline of one of the chapel's windows to the side of the entrance arch. The cobbled lane has many Victorian shop fronts housing the odd antiques emporium and bookshop (**Cogito Books** has a particularly good selection of local guides). Hidden somewhat in a narrow courtyard alley is an enchanting **clock repair shop**. Grandfather clocks stand in the alley ticking away the days.

Running parallel to St Mary's Chare is **Fore Street**, a busier pedestrian street with an equal number of old shop fronts. The **Old Pharmacy** is a curious building: its black and red frontage with decorative grapevines was designed by a Belgian refugee in 1916 and looks totally incongruous – and far too special to be a Poundstretcher.

Snaking downhill from the marketplace is **Market Street** – a road with plenty to tempt shoppers with its art gallery, interiors shops and huge antiques emporium, **Ashbourne House Antiques** (✆ 01434 607294), which is stuffed with china, bric-a-brac, copper pots, furniture and architectural salvage. You could find anything here from a cast-iron Victorian radiator to a hookah pipe.

Film-goers should head to the independent picture house, **The Forum Cinema** (8–9 Market Pl, NE46 1XF ✆ 01434 601144 ⌂ www. forumhexham.co.uk ♿), not least to admire the Art Deco café interior. At the other end of Hexham's market square is the **Queen's Hall Arts Centre** (Beaumont St, NE46 3LS ✆ 01434 652477 ⌂ www.queenshall. co.uk), which puts on regular dance, music and theatre performances.

Hexham Old Gaol

Hallgate, NE46 1XD ✆ 01434 652349 ⊙ Apr–Sep, Tue–Sat; Oct–Mar, Tue & Sat only

'No, people weren't sent here to be punished,' the steward at the oldest purpose-built prison in England (completed 1333) says, correcting my false assumption. 'This was a holding cell until suspected criminals were tried. If found guilty, *then* they were punished.'

It's hard to see how being kept in a windowless stone cellar living on scraps of charity food for sometimes over a year (trials of prisoners were only held every quarter so you can imagine the backlog of cases) cannot be seen as a punishment. Perhaps that is why records show that 75% of prisoners in the Middle Ages were found not guilty when they were shackled and walked the few hundred yards to the Moot Hall where they were brought before a judge. For the remaining 25% who were found guilty, stocks, the ducking stool, branding and the whipping post were some of the punishments they could expect – if they weren't hung. Executions were performed behind the Moot Hall in the marketplace but were rare because the Archbishop of York ruled Hexhamshire, and the Church was not in favour of the death penalty. The Archbishop was, however, in favour of collecting fines and 'board and lodging' from inmates. The gaol was in use until the 1820s.

The stone tower, made with hugely thick walls, has four levels open to visitors. Each floor has an exhibition room dedicated to a different aspect of local history: the Border Reivers, rural life and the history of the gaol itself. The dungeon is reached by way of a glass lift that doesn't open but pauses long enough for visitors to gawp at the impenetrable walls and imagine being imprisoned in the cold, dark surroundings.

Hexham Abbey

Market Pl, NE46 3NB ✎ 01434 602031 ⊛ www.hexhamabbey.org.uk ♿

Founded in AD674 by Wilfrid, Bishop of York, the abbey was originally built as a monastery but very quickly became a church. It was said by a follower of Wilfrid's (Eddius Stephanus) to be of greater beauty than anything 'this side of the Alps'. Today, the only surviving part of Wilfrid's wondrous building is the **crypt**, reached by descending a stone staircase in the nave. The warren of tight passages and chambers was constructed using masonry from nearby Coria, in which you can see Roman carvings and lettering.

Danish raids in the 9th century damaged the original Saxon building, which was restored as a priory some 200 years later (the remains of the priory cloisters lie in the abbey's southwest grounds). Most of what you see today dates to the 12th and 13th centuries.

You may find the view of the abbey from the street underwhelming, but wait until you step inside. What appears from the outside to be a rather stout, manly building with a short tower, is elegant and lofty inside. The best vantage point is from the broad stone staircase in the south transept. The **Night Stair** used to lead to the canons' dormitory and today provides visitors with a superlative view of the crossing and choir. Lancet windows in the north transept and the three tiers of arched windows opposite drive the walls skywards, creating a sense of space and height. At the bottom of the Night Stair is a **Roman tombstone** with a startling engraving of a standard-bearer on horseback trampling over a cowering, primitive-looking Briton.

"The Night Stair provides visitors with a superlative view of the crossing."

Many more treasures are found in the aisles and around the altar, including an **Anglo-Saxon chalice** and a **frith stool** (a bishop's throne) that may have been built for Wilfrid in the 7th century. A number of rare medieval **wood-panel paintings** are nearby.

In the chancel, you'll find the **Dance of Death** painted across four panels; Death is depicted in each hovering next to a cardinal, king, emperor and pope. Above the altar in the **Leschman Chantry Chapel** is an unusual wood painting of Christ emerging from a coffin. Kneeling at the head of the coffin is Prior Leschman whose stone effigy (carved with a hooded robe pulled over his eyes) is also in the chapel. Lastly, note the curious stone-carved figures on the side of the chapel, depicting a jester, harpist and bagpipe player.

Abbey Grounds & the Sele

Every corner of this pleasure ground commands a good view of the abbey and the church. It is now the mall of the fashionables, the privileged playground of the lower classes, and the place of exercise and amusement for all.

This observation of Hexham's historic parkland was made in 1823 and largely rings true today. Twenty acres of green space surrounds the abbey on all but one of its sides, divided into three distinct areas: the Abbey Grounds with its 20th-century bandstand; a large open area of grassland called the **Sele**; and the gardens and bowling green in front of the Georgian mansion, **Hexham House**. Visitors won't struggle to find a tranquil corner to put down a picnic rug. To the side of the bowling green is a wooded area with a lively burn that trickles through a 13th-century archway and under the boughs of oak and fir trees.

A pleasant **stroll** follows the burn uphill past the bandstand on your left and the Sele on your right. At the top, a secluded narrow passage on your left, called Seal Terrace, leads past a row of diminutive early 19th-century cottages. At the Fox pub, turn left on to Hencotes and return to the abbey by continuing downhill to Beaumont Street.

¶¶ FOOD & DRINK

Gusto Mucho on Market Street served up a very good coffee and all their cakes were homemade but at the time of going to press they were changing ownership and becoming the **Small World Café** (✆ 01434 606200 ♿), but things are not expected to change much. It may be a chain pub (Wetherspoons) and the bar area can get rowdy, but walk down the steps at the back of **The Forum** (8–9 Market Pl, NE46 1XF ✆ 01434 609190) into the café area and find high ceilings with geometric features, and gold and mint paintwork that will take you back to the days when this was an Art Deco cinema. Coffees and inexpensive pub grub (burgers, etc).

Hexham is fortunate to have a number of very good country pubs close to town. I've listed a couple of the best ones here but also consider the **Carts Bog Inn** at Langley (page 137).

Bouchon Bistrot 4–6 Gilesgate, NE46 3NJ ✆ 01434 609943 ☺ Mon–Sat for lunch & dinner ♿. Posh French restaurant in Hexham's old town centre, awarded the accolade of 'best local French Restaurant in the UK' on Gordon Ramsey's TV programme, *The F Word*.

Danielle's Bistrot 12 Eastgate (off Battle Hill), NE46 1BH ✆ 01434 601122 ☺ Tue–Fri for lunch & dinner, evenings only on Sat. Fairly pricey, no-fuss Italian popular with locals. No pizzas on the menu; just good Mediterranean dishes served on bare candle-lit tables. Roast duck in an orange and Cointreau sauce, ravioli, roasted guinea fowl and Northumbrian steak were on the menu when I last visited.

Dipton Mill Inn Dipton Mill Rd (a couple of miles south of Hexham), NE46 1YA ✆ 01434 606577 ☺ daily but no food on Sun evenings. Old drovers' pub in a tranquil setting on the outskirts of Hexham serving ale direct from the landlord's Hexhamshire Brewery. Hearty ploughman's sandwiches and a selection of pasta, chicken, red meat and fish dishes – all made on site – are served in this 17th-century former mill. On a summer's day you'll probably want to be outside in the beer garden by the mill stream. Walk off your meal with a ramble through the West Dipton Burn – a beautiful wooded gorge.

The Rat Inn Anick NE46 4LN ✆ 01434 602814 ☺ Tue–Sat & bank holidays lunch & dinner, Sun food served between 12.00 & 15.00. Ask a local or Tynesider which is their favourite country pub in the Tyne Valley and chances are they'll rave about this old drovers' inn (low beamed ceiling, flagstone floors, etc) that sits high above the Tyne. Enjoy exceptional, good-value pub food made with the very best Northumbrian farm meats, and fish from the North Sea. Sit in the sunny garden or inside next to the blazing cast-iron range. Ales are from local microbreweries. Make sure you book for Sunday lunch.

10 Haydon Bridge

🏠 **Grindon Farm** (page 273)

Two **bridges** connect this quiet town, which straddles the River Tyne, including the graceful, six-arched pedestrian bridge built in 1776. From here you gain a good view of Haydon Bridge's old stone houses rising directly from the river, and the hills beyond.

The long, uniform streets of stone make the north side the most appealing. The street backing on to the Tyne is **Ratcliffe Road**. Number 1A was bought in 1962 by Monica Jones, the long-term girlfriend of Philip Larkin. According to the poet's biographer, Andrew Motion, some of the couple's happiest times were spent in Haydon and the surrounding countryside: 'They lazed, drank, read, pottered around the village and amused themselves with private games. The place always cheered them both up.'

A sulphurous spring popular in Victorian times is reached on a short walk east from the Anchor pub (south side of the bridge) via a tranquil riverside path. The **Spa Well** has suffered a few landslides over the years but is currently open.

⫴ FOOD & DRINK

General Havelock 9 Ratcliffe Rd, NE47 6ER ✆ 01434 684376 ⊙ daily but no food on Mon or Sun evenings. 'Proper chef, proper ale, proper crack' reads a chalkboard outside this well-regarded riverside pub (painted black). The interior is not posh, but that does not reflect the food, which is very good. Everything you eat here is made on site by the chef and his wife, even down to the breads, pastries and ice cream, hence the limited menu (all good traditional fare: steak and chips, lamb and veg, fresh fish, etc). The setting couldn't be more appealing, with a garden overlooking the South Tyne.

11 Bardon Mill & Pottery

By road or railway between Haydon Bridge and Haltwhistle, you will pass Bardon Mill, a small settlement with a village store (useful café here), post office, pub and green set either side of a burn.

Next door to the **Bowes Hotel** pub (✆ 01434 344237; serves food ♿) is **Errington Reay & Co pottery** (✆ 01434 344245 ✐ www.erringtonreay. co.uk ⊙ daily Nov–Apr, but closed Sun ♿), which stands on the site of a 17th-century woollen mill. The company started producing ceramic chimneypots and piping in 1878. Look at the roofs of houses in the village and you will see that some are an unusual design, looking a little bit like an upside-down plant pot placed on top of a stump. Known locally as the 'Marriage Save Pot', it was developed at the pottery and remained in production until quite recently. It was a successful solution to the problem of smoke billowing back down chimneys into homes, which was a frequent nuisance in this exposed village.

"Errington Reay & Co pottery stands on the site of a 17th-century woollen mill."

Once there were a number of potteries in the Tyne Valley but they closed when the manufacture of cheap, plastic water pipes took off. Errington Reay survived by clever adaptation of their machinery to make garden plant pots. Five hundred pots are produced here every week, all hand-finished by a couple of men sitting at potter's wheels, and traditionally made using a salt-glaze (one of very few potteries in Britain still producing pots in this way). There's a large selection of seconds for sale.

12 Beltingham

Roughly a mile southeast of Bardon Mill on the south side of the river is Beltingham – a hamlet of half-a-dozen houses about a church and green whose existence is not recognised by Google Maps. But, what it lacks in size, it makes up for in superlatives: Beltingham is home to the oldest yew tree and the only Perpendicular-style church in Northumberland. It also has the smallest village green in England (you could just about pitch a four-man tent on its circle of grass) and is the most picturesque hamlet in

"Beltingham is home to the oldest yew tree and the only Perpendicular-style church in Northumberland."

the county. At least I think so. In truth, I can only objectively verify one of the above claims (the oblong church) but the yew tree at the north end of the churchyard (the one whose torso is being pulled in by metal belts) is truly ancient. The church guide refers to estimates of it being 2,000 years old, though it is more likely to be about half that.

As for the 'most scenic hamlet in Northumberland' award, except for possibly Cambo in Wallington, I can't think of any other place with such an agreeable arrangement of houses, church and green, and where the stone buildings have been quite so faithfully preserved according to their original design. The farmland setting and nearby wooded ravine add to the appeal of this little idyll by a burn.

Of course, there is little to do here, few places to see and nowhere to eat or drink (unless two well-to-do ladies invite you in for coffee with the vicar) but you can stay in the plush **Beltingham House** (✆ 01434 609521 🖥 www.beltinghamhouse.co.uk), a Georgian mansion which was visited more than once by the late Queen Mother who popped in to see her relatives, the Bowes-Lyons. It is now a holiday cottage that sleeps 14.

A wooden lych gate marks the entrance to 16th-century **St Cuthbert's Church**. Some believe an earlier timber structure stood here and was visited by monks carrying St Cuthbert's body in the 10th century, hence the church's name.

There are two very pleasant **walks** from Beltingham. Heading west across farmland you come to **Willimoteswyke Castle** – an impressive, albeit derelict, 16th-century fortified manor house with seven-foot-thick walls and an intact pele tower; going east you descend into the most beautiful wooded gorge in the whole of Northumberland, **Allen Banks** (page 134). I did say this was a hamlet of superlatives.

13 Haltwhistle

🏠 **Ashcroft Guesthouse** (page 273)

'Welcome to Haltwhistle – Centre of Britain.' Most visitors would never have guessed the geographical centre of Britain is so far north. As it happens, it's not. Well, at least if you believe the inhabitants of Dunsop Bridge in Lancashire or Allendale in the North Pennines who also claim the title. It depends on how the centre is calculated, of course.

What is true is that this market town was, for 300 years, the centre of many clashes between the Scots and the English and warring Border clans. The constant threat of violence explains the large number of defensive **bastle houses** (see box, page 181) along the High Street. In fact, Haltwhistle claims (quite accurately) to have more of these defensive buildings in and around its town than anywhere else in the North East. A good number are found clustered about the marketplace. Look for two-storey dwellings with irregular windows and prominent stones at pavement level such as at the Centre of Britain building (also noted for its 15th-century pele tower) and the fish and chip shop. If it weren't for the blue plaques, you might struggle to distinguish them from ordinary domestic dwellings as they have been modified over the years. The Bastle Trail leaflet available in the **tourist information office** on Westgate (page 103) provides more clues.

Haltwhistle's centre is, in essence, one long, main thoroughfare with a park at the western end and the marketplace in the centre. The **railway station** is one of the most unchanged on the Newcastle–Carlisle line and retains its original waiting room, ticket office and cast-iron footbridge, as well as the old water tank (a relic from the days of steam, set back from the line and supported by a square stone building with arched windows all around). Note the engineer's plates dated 1861 with their decorative seahorses. The signal box is an elegant building made of weatherboards that curve outwards from a narrow rectangular brick base.

Tucked behind the marketplace is the early 13th-century **Holy Cross Church**. As you enter the building, you'll see what is clearly a very old stone stoup supported on a column. Its age is disputed though some believe it could be Roman. As you walk down the nave, three lancet windows simply decorated with stained glass by William Morris & Co rise elegantly above the altar.

On passing the pulpit, note the memorial stone standing on the floor. The Latin inscription is translated in the church guidebook and reads:

To God the greatest and the best
After a short, difficult, useless life
Here rests in the Lord
Robert Tweddle
Of Monkhazelton Durham
Dies 1735. Aged 23

Continuing eastwards along Main Street, the shops peter out and domestic dwellings made of sandstone sit side by side with agreeable uniformity. Soon the noises of the town are replaced by the cheerful chatter of sparrows in garden bushes and jackdaws clucking on rooftops.

Mill Lane on the left leads to **Haltwhistle Burn**. A footpath hugs the waterway for 1½ miles upriver passing a number of relics from the days when Haltwhistle was a prosperous industrial town in the 18th and 19th centuries, including a brickworks. If you continue northwards, you will soon reach the Military Road and Hadrian's Wall.

¶¶ FOOD & DRINK

There's not a great choice of places to eat in Haltwhistle. Your best bet is probably the busy **Black Bull** (Market Sq, NE49 0BL ✆ 01434 320463), where you'll find a good selection of real ales and fairly decent pub food. A few cafés are dotted along Main Street.

✳ ✳ ✳

🏃 THE SOUTH TYNE TRAIL BY BICYCLE OR ON FOOT: HALTWHISTLE TO ALSTON

✳ OS Explorer maps OL43 & 31; start: Haltwhistle; 23 miles; difficulty: fairly easy, albeit a long route; cycle ride strenuous in a few places; refreshments at Haltwhistle, Featherstone, Alston

The mixed-use waymarked South Tyne Trail is an ideal way to discover the valley and some of the best river, woodland and hill country in the North Pennines. For the most part it follows the railway path (as far as Alston). If you continue from Alston to Garrigill and on to the source of the Tyne (🖐 this extended route description can be found at 🖉 www.bradtguides.com/sourceofthetyne), walkers stay close to the riverside; cyclists take a quiet hilly lane via Leadgate.

On joining the disused railway line south of Haltwhistle and the A69, thickets of birch and oak and gentle countryside soon give way to more dramatic scenery. The wooded gorge of the South Tyne is most spectacularly viewed from the towering arches of **Lambley Viaduct**. At the far end, you have to carry your bike to the river and then haul it back up the other side because there is no access along the 100-yard stretch of the old trackbed in front of the former train station (now in private hands). If you can't face carrying your bicycle, follow the redirected road route signed just under a mile back at Thorneyhole Wood car park that passes above Lambley village (be prepared for a heck of a climb from river to moor level).

Once you're back on the railway line, the temperature drops as you enter the North Pennine moors proper where heather covers the highest plateaux and woods, and fields descend to the river.

Slaggyford and its quaint old railway buildings and platform are a pleasant place to stop for sandwiches. The South Tyne Trail continues straight ahead on the disused railway line but it gets pretty boggy and almost impossible to ride (fine for walkers with gaiters), so cyclists might want to take the road route by turning left and heading for the river via Slaggyford village. Follow the NCN Route 68 signs, which soon lead you on to a quiet country lane for the last five miles to Alston. This is wonderful cycling. It's quiet with some challenging ascents and descents, and glorious river

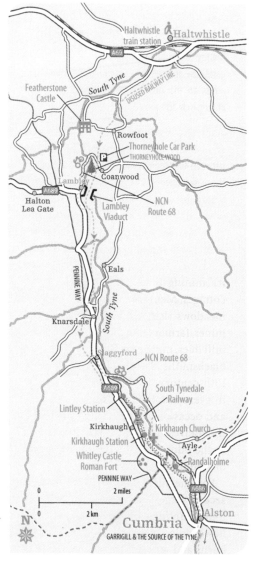

and countryside scenery: pastures divided by dry stone walls, old farm buildings, an unusual church (see *Kirkhaugh*, page 132) and farmers rounding up sheep with Border collies. **Walkers** continue due south at Slaggyford station, eventually meeting the **South Tynedale Railway** (page 131) where the odd narrow-gauge steam engine puffs by. There's a small viaduct

FEATHERSTONE CASTLE & BRIDGE

Featherstone Castle is an imposing 13th-century embattled manor with turrets, a gatehouse and pele tower. There's no general access to the castle but it appears quite impressively across parkland from the banks of the River South Tyne (there's a lovely riverside path for walkers here). Half a mile north is the curious, lopsided 18th-century **Featherstone Bridge** (♀ NY675619), set within a dreamy riverscape lined with mature trees.

between Kirkhaugh and Alston that spans Gilderdale Burn. Below is a secluded swimming pool. The market town of **Alston** and its painstakingly restored Victorian station are ahead.

* * *

INTO THE NORTH PENNINES

It's mining that's responsible for the pitted fells, terraces of stone cottages, Methodist chapels, schools and reading rooms; the way the meadows rising out of the valleys are boxed into 'allotments' where miner-farmers toiled to support their families in lean times; the smelt mill flues, mine entrances and chimneys; the railway lines, workshops, blacksmiths and mine agents' houses. Relics from the 18th- and 19th-century lead-mining and quarrying industries lie scattered in every hamlet and on every hillside in the North Pennine valleys, and occasionally the rich minerals in this European Geopark reveal themselves above ground; but to the casual visitor, with the exception of the odd striking chimney, lime kiln and water wheel, it's far from obvious that this was once the biggest lead-mining region in the world.

For the most part, however, the **North Pennines AONB** – the second largest in the UK, covering 770 square miles and spanning four counties – is characterised by wooded gorges, heather moors, flower-filled meadows, unusual rock formations, whisky-coloured burns and waterfalls.

What really draws outdoor enthusiasts are the wild-looking landscapes that become increasingly rugged as you stray over the border into County Durham. Nowhere in England is truly wild, of course, and even the most desolate-looking Pennine moors are managed, but, nonetheless, the feeling you get when setting foot across

Stanhope Common, coming across alpine plants left over from the last ice age, hearing the drumming of snipe and the courtship display of black grouse is one of supreme detachment and isolation. If there is one corner of Northumberland that gets forgotten about – this is it.

SOUTH TYNE VALLEY & ALSTON

Scenically, the northern reaches of the South Tyne Valley are typical of the wider Tyne Valley and Hexhamshire countryside: green pastures carved by dry stone walls and hedgerows, parkland studded with mature oaks, broadleaved woodland and the odd stone hamlet here and there; but the landscape steps up a gear quite quickly on heading south, and certainly by the time you reach Lambley the Pennine moors are looming tantalisingly close.

Alston, a remote market town (just over the border in Cumbria), is particularly popular with cyclists, railway aficionados and walkers.

14 Alston

The main cobbled street through England's highest market town climbs steeply up a hillside and pauses at a bend in the road, before continuing up and out of the settlement. In the past, horses and carts would rest at this landing by the marketplace; today it's the coast-to-coast cyclists who stop for a breather.

The view of the old stone houses dropping away along the winding road, and the hills rising on the other side of this Cumbrian valley, has Hovis advert charm and there are even a few people pushing their bicycles up the hill just to complete the picture. For all Alston's old-world appeal and run of early 17th-century houses built during the growth of the lead-mining industry, it's still a working town (and not as genteel as some other places in the Pennines) but it caters reasonably well to visitors, with

"The view of the old stone houses dropping away along the winding road, and the hills rising on the other side of this Cumbrian valley, has Hovis advert charm."

cafés, food stores, pubs, craft shops and an outdoor clothing shop. The **tourist information centre** (page 103) is in the Town Hall at the foot of Front Street.

St Augustine Church was rebuilt a few times, notably in 1770 to a design by Smeaton (of Eddystone Lighthouse fame) and again 100 years later – the building standing today. Its most striking feature is its 17th-century single-handed clock which came from Dilston Hall (along with a bell) in 1767 in the decades after the execution of Lord Derwentwater (pages 117–18). Only the bell was installed; the clock forgotten about for 200 years until restoration in 1977. Its single hand operates with the assistance of stone counterweights hanging in leather slings from pulley wheels.

FOOD & DRINK

Alston's Front Street has a couple of cafés, including the friendly **Cumbrian Pantry**, which sells inexpensive scones and sandwiches, and the tea room at **Alston Station**. For something more substantial in the evening, you could try the **Alston House Hotel** (Townfoot, CA9 3RN ✆ 01434 382200) for steak and chips, lasagne, fish dishes, etc. During the day, the café serves sandwiches, baked potatoes, pies and burgers.
Cumberland Hotel Townfoot, CA9 3HX ✆ 01434 381875 ♿. I counted six pubs in Alston (a town with a population of around 1,000 people) and found this freehouse offered something different from the others with bookcases, pew benches, real ales, an open fire and a convivial atmosphere with walkers and cyclists coming and going. Very good-value hearty pub food.

South Tynedale Railway

Alston CA9 3JB ✆ 01434 381696, 01434 382828 (for timetables) ♂ www.south-tynedale-railway.org.uk ☉ Easter–early Nov usually 4 days a week; Jul & Aug daily (check website for operating days at other times of the year such as at Christmas); café

Steam engines trundle through the wooded South Tyne Valley for 3½ miles from **Alston to Lintley** offering glimpses of moorland scenery and passing over the Tyne Viaduct. The return journey takes about an hour but you might want to hop off at **Kirkhaugh Station** and wander up to Whitley Castle Roman Fort (pages 132–3) or down to the river.

Originally a branch of the Newcastle–Carlisle railway, the Alston to Haltwhistle line opened in 1852 and closed in the 1970s, only to reopen a decade later under the care of the local railway preservation society. Trackbeds were replaced and the station buildings restored, allowing the first narrow-gauge steam engines to enter passenger service in 1983. Though just a few miles of the line were originally opened, it keeps getting longer and by 2017 it may have reached Slaggyford where plans are underway to restore the platform and timber station house. Eventually it is hoped the line will open all the way to Haltwhistle.

The Hub museum

Station Yard, Alston CA9 3HN ✆ 01434 381609 ⊗ www.alston-hub.org.uk ☺ generally Jun–end Sep, daily; Easter–Christmas, weekends, but phone to check ♿

Round the back of Alston's restored train station is this fantastic little museum in an old goods shed dedicated to transport heritage. Filling every space inside The Hub are vintage motorbikes and a few cars, as well as a large collection of bicycles showcasing in a roundabout way the evolution of this most enduring form of transport from the penny-farthing to a 1972 Raleigh Chopper. A mass of memorabilia hangs from the walls and ceilings: model aeroplanes, black and white photographs, road signs and vintage advertisements.

15 Kirkhaugh Church

Unusually dedicated to the Holy Paraclete (in other words, the Holy Ghost), this secluded Victorian church with a distinctive needle-like spire (apparently the rector was influenced by churches he'd seen in Germany's Black Forest) stands in farmland by the River South Tyne and adjacent to a grand villa with shuttered windows. A stone cross in the churchyard dates to before the Norman invasion, reminding visitors of the Anglo-Saxon church that once stood here. Inside, a hammerbeam roof and the chairs instead of pews will catch your attention, as will the wood-burning stove which shows just how cold it gets up here.

"A stone cross in the churchyard dates to before the Norman invasion, reminding visitors of the Anglo-Saxon church that once stood here."

The countryside around Kirkhaugh is extremely pretty: fields with mature trees leading to the river, a scattering of old farm buildings, 17th-century bastle houses and a pele tower at **Randalholm**. Quiet lanes connect all these places which are within walking distance of Alston and can be incorporated into a circular jaunt via the Roman fort at Whitley Castle (see below).

Whitley Castle Roman Fort

📍 NY694486

All that remains of Britain's highest built Roman fort that once housed a garrison of 500 men (and was probably connected with lead- and silver mining) are its impressive earthen ramparts and the faint outline of the foundations of barrack blocks (now turfed over). Roman altar stones, masonry from a bath house hypocaust and smaller finds have been recovered over the centuries although no major excavation has ever taken place.

By road, you can reach the fort from the A689. Park at the bridge over the Lort Burn next to Castle Nook farmhouse (♀ NY696490) and follow the footpath up the side of the burn. This brings you out in the field above the farmyard and from there you can walk uphill to the northern ramparts.

"All that remains of Britain's highest built Roman fort are its impressive earthen ramparts and the faint outline of the foundations of barrack blocks."

If **walking** from Alston, pick up the Pennine Way at the south end of the town and head north for 2½ miles. If you time your walk well, you can return by steam train on the South Tynedale Railway from Kirkhaugh station; alternatively cross the River South Tyne (a short walk from the station across a field) and return to Alston on Isaac's Tea Trail by way of quiet country lanes and a waterfront footpath.

THE ALLEN VALLEYS

The rivers East and West Allen run off the central moors and flow through farmland and woodland until they converge south of Haydon Bridge, forming the River Allen. **Cupola Bridge** – a magnificent trio of arches built in 1778 – spans the confluence of the Allens and marks the head of **Allen Banks** and **Staward Gorge** (one of the region's oldest and most enchanting woodlands).

Travelling upriver into the heart of the North Pennines – and the southern reaches of Northumberland – the scenery in both the east and west valleys takes on an increasingly wilder look where meadows become rough grasslands and ramshackle barns replace cottages. Snow markers line the sides of the highest roads and a ski-tow appears above Allenheads.

On high slopes, evidence of lead mining is glimpsed here and there, and many buildings associated with the industry are found in the now quiet settlements, particularly at Allenheads. You might well spot the odd bastle house and defensive tower, evidence that farmers and landowners in the late medieval period once feared the appearance of Border Reivers riding over the hills on horseback to steal their livestock – and worse.

16 Allen Banks & Staward Gorge

South of the River Tyne, between Haydon Bridge & Bardon Mill, ♥ NY798640

Under the boughs of oak trees and around boulders and shingle banks where herons stand by the river's edge and dippers dive from rocks into the water, the River Allen (north of the convergence of the West Allen and East Allen) flows lazily through a steep-sided, wooded gorge on its way to the Tyne. In spring, the familiar tunes of woodland birds are occasionally interrupted by a more exotic song: the rhythmic notes of a pied flycatcher or the coin-spinning song of a wood warbler, both birds newly returned from Africa and infrequently heard elsewhere in Northumberland. In wood clearings look out for wild pansies – this area is well known for them – and, in the conifer trees, red squirrels.

Allen Banks is a precious broadleaved woodland – ancient in places – and utterly enchanting: visit on a balmy summer's evening when swifts are gliding high above the canopy and the first bats have emerged to catch insects by the river, and you'll see what I mean; glimpsing an otter on an evening like this would not be unheard of.

⁂ ⁂ ⁂

🏃 ALLEN BANKS CIRCULAR ON FOOT

❋ OS Explorer map OL43; start: National Trust car park near Ridley Hall, ♥ NY798640; 3 miles; difficulty: fairly easy except for the optional strenuous hike to Staward Peel; refreshments at The Garden Station café & Langley Castle (page 137)

Start from the National Trust car park, keeping to the riverside path for just over a mile to **Briarwood Banks** (do not cross the suspension bridge). Continue through this ancient tract of woodland, cross a burn via a little metal bridge, then turn immediately left and take the larger wooden footbridge over the River Allen to **Plankey Mill**.

To extend this walk to **Staward Peel**, turn right, go through the gate and follow the lazy river to the woods ahead. It's a steep climb through the wooded Staward Gorge Valley but the views over the canopy from the pele tower at the top are magnificent.

To **return** from Plankey Mill, head to the farm buildings and take the lane on your left uphill for a short distance until you see a track on your left that leads down to a kissing gate by the river. Walk through damp meadows (gaiters come in handy here) fringed with alders and keep an eye out for field pansies in summer. Enter tranquil woodlands and continue to the suspension bridge over the River Allen. Once you've crossed the rushing river, turn right and retrace your path to the car park.

Alternatively, you could return the same way from Plankey Mill (on the west side of the river) but vary the route slightly by taking the high path at the top of the gorge which trails beneath many elderly beech trees.

✳ ✳ ✳

17 Ninebanks & around

🏠 **Ninebanks** (page 274)

The quiet sheep-grazed meadows and steep wooded slopes of the West Allen Valley are sparsely populated – and very beautiful in summer (access on foot by following Isaac's Tea Trail). One conspicuous building in the hamlet of Ninebanks stands out from the 18th-century miners' houses and farm buildings: a defensive pele tower dating to the times of the Border Reiver conflicts in the 16th century. The church, half a mile south, is notable for its hearse house (a stone building that once housed the village's horse-drawn funeral cart), built in the 19th century with money raised by local philanthropist and tea peddler, Issac Holden.

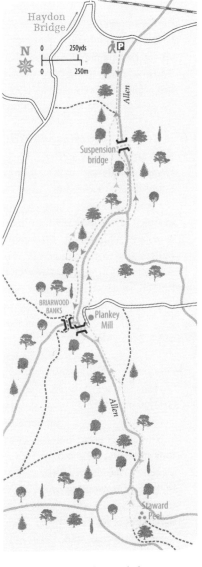

Whitfield is scattered about a bit with a pub, an unusually grand church out on a limb by the river (a nice place for a wander or a picnic), a fist of houses and a village shop-cum-café and crafts workshop on the main road (A686). If you turn uphill here, you'll eventually reach a stone school and a tiny 18th-century church high above the lapwing-populated valley.

🍴 FOOD & DRINK

Whitfield Village Pantry Whitfield NE47 8HA ✆ 01434 345709 🖥 www. whitfieldvillagepantry.co.uk ◷ daily, but on Mon & Sun mornings only ♿. Pleasant little café in a village store that serves breakfasts and lunches. Upstairs is MAKE, where recycled haberdashery items are 'waiting to be recycled into new things' by visitors sitting by the log stove knitting and sewing with a cup of tea and slice of cake. Open workshop sessions on Thursdays; on other days you must book courses (felting, patchwork, making clothes) in advance.

18 Langley Castle & some mining heritage

🏠 **Langley Castle** (page 273)

Places of interest around **Langley**, not far from Hexham, must be hunted out – some more than others. Langley Castle is signposted off the A686, as is the charming railway station café (see opposite), but finding the old lead smelt mill, flue, and one of the most complete (and now sadly abandoned) 19th-century collieries in England, requires a bit of detective work with an OS Explorer map.

Medieval **Langley Castle** (NE47 5LU ✆ 01434 688888) is somewhat hidden in woods a couple of miles south of Haydon Bridge. It's one of the most impressive defensive towerhouses in Northumberland, with embattled turrets on each corner of a central block, and immediate wow factor. Though restored in the 19th century, much of what you see is the original 1350 building with seven-foot-thick walls, huge fireplaces, a chapel and some of the best-preserved medieval garderobes you will find anywhere.

"Medieval Langley Castle is one of the most impressive defensive towerhouses in Northumberland."

Now an upmarket hotel (page 273), the owners have gone to town with faux medieval furnishings (rich red fabrics and dark wooden furniture) to reflect the castle's 14th-century origins. Non-guests can dine here or take afternoon tea in the drawing room which is heated with open fires and lit with wrought-iron chandeliers. Ask to visit the roof terrace which offers views for miles around.

Like many manmade pools in the North Pennines, **Langley Reservoir** was built to power the now demolished **smelt mills**, but you can walk up to a surviving **chimney** by taking the B6305 away from the reservoir in the direction of Hexham. You can't miss it at the top of the hill, but you might overlook its **flue** – a 'horizontal chimney' that runs across the fields for nearly a mile (now cut by the B6305), connecting the mill to the vertical chimney. Like those elsewhere in the Pennines, it was designed to release harmful lead and silver vapours and particles away from human habitation and farmland. You can see the grassy mound from the road (♀ NY838611) and its opening at The Garden Station café.

Most remarkable of all the industrial buildings and structures remaining in this area is the **Stublick Colliery** (500 yards north of the B6295/B6304 crossroads) that once extracted coal to power the smelt mills. It retains its engine houses and chimneys and, though there's no public access to the derelict site, you can view the group of buildings from the road.

The Garden Station

Langley NE47 5LA ✆ 01434 684391 ○ Mar–Oct, closed Tue

The clock at old Langley Station near Hexham always tells the correct time at 11.30. It hangs outside a quaint former waiting room and ticket office dating back to 1860, which is now a sweet **café** specialising in afternoon tea and cake (served on vintage china inside the waiting room or outside on the platform). It's wonderfully secluded along this old railway line, with high banks thickly planted with shrubs and shade-loving species, and you can walk on the woodchip path and under stone bridges arching over the line. Look for sculptures in the bushes and an old smelt flue that connects with Stublick Chimney.

FOOD & DRINK

Carts Bog Inn Langley NE47 5NW ✆ 01434 684338 ♿ through the back door. Two things worth bearing in mind if you're planning on eating at this 18th-century country pub: book in advance and come with an empty stomach. It's one of the best pubs for miles around and is really popular, both for the quality (and quantity) of the food and the real ales from the likes of Wylam and Allendale breweries. Much of the food comes from the local area, with beef from the landlord's farm, game from the Northumbrian hills and fish from North Shields. Expect good, uncomplicated dishes (cottage pie, lamb and mash, steak, Cumberland sausage, etc). Bog Pie (beef and mushrooms) is their speciality.

The Garden Station (see above).

Langley Castle Near Hexham NE47 5LU ✆ 01434 688888. Intimate evening tables in a medieval towerhouse. Expect to pay close to £50 per person for a three-course dinner (the lunch menu is less expensive). Example dishes are saltmarsh lamb with vegetables, and halibut with samphire and razor clams. Scones and afternoon teas are served in the medieval-styled drawing room for those just wanting to pop in and savour the surroundings.

ALLENDALE BA'AL FESTIVAL

New Year's Eve in Allendale is a spectacle of fire, light, ceremony and drunkenness which begins long before local men dressed in costume called 'Guisers' (a hereditary position) parade in a circuit around the town centre with flaming tar barrels on their heads, and ends in a raucous celebration in the streets and pubs. The procession, thought to have Pagan origins, is timed so that the men return to the centre and tip their barrels into the huge bonfire in the marketplace, setting it alight on the stroke of midnight.

19 Allendale

High Keenley Fell (page 273), **High Broadwood Hall Cottages** (page 273)

A tangle of streets at the heart of Allendale reveals the town's medieval origins but most of the buildings date to the 19th century. Squeezed among them are a scattering of 18th-century houses, a couple of Methodist chapels, a reading room, an old pharmacy with heritage features including vintage bottles in the window, a village hall, an original Co-operative food store, a post office (where you can hire electric bikes), and a handful of venerable inns. Many buildings still have their original lettering and frontages. One fetching detail worth mentioning is the sundial on the south aisle wall of **St Cuthbert's Church**. Inscribed on the face are the co-ordinates '54 50' to reflect the (much-debated) claim that Allendale stands at the centre of Britain.

The **Allendale Forge Studios** (✆ 01434 683975 ◷ daily ♿) is an artists' co-operative on the site of an old blacksmiths in the marketplace. Besides working studios, there's a gallery, café and craft shop selling knitted Alpaca clothes (from nearby Fairshaw Rigg farm), handmade soaps and jewellery.

♥ FOOD & DRINK

Allendale does not excel on the food front, but if you're just after an inexpensive sandwich, scone or bowl of soup, there are three perfectly fine places to choose from in the marketplace, including the **Allendale Tearooms** (✆ 01434 683575 ◷ Tue–Sun), which is recommended for tea and homemade cake, and the **Allendale Forge Studios** (see above). **The Crown** Catton NE47 9QS ✆ 01434 618351 ♿. The view here is a huge draw for those visitors looking for a pub lunch in the Allendale area, particularly on sunny days when you can sit in the garden looking out over fields and the heather-topped Pennine moors. If there's a nip in the air, diners inside can enjoy the same panorama through wall-to-wall glass doors. Stripped wooden floors, exposed stone walls and a log fire give this great country pub rustic appeal. Local ales and a good menu that will satisfy carnivores (steaks, beef stroganoff, burgers) as well as veggies (mushroom, cranberry and brie Wellington, vegetarian sausage and mash). Folk music nights on Thursdays.

20 Dryburn Moor & the Chimneys

Crossing the high moors between the East and West Allen valleys is a memorable journey by road or across country following old packhorse routes. A blanket of heather and windswept cotton grasses dominates the plateau and you can see for many miles around and down into the valleys. It's pretty desolate, which is Dryburn's greatest appeal, but it's not featureless or without wildlife. The skylark can always be relied upon up here and occasionally walkers may hear the plaintive 'pu-pee-oo' cry of the golden plover. Two prominent lead-mining chimneys punctuate the skyline 2½ miles southwest of Allendale (♀ NY807537) and below them, a raised turf mound shoots across the landscape – one of the old 'horizontal chimneys' or smelting mill flues so prevalent in these parts.

> *"A blanket of heather and windswept cotton grasses dominates the plateau… It's pretty desolate, which is Dryburn's greatest appeal, but it's not featureless or without wildlife."*

21 Allenheads

Strong veins of lead ore made Allenheads the most important lead-mining area in Britain at one time. Today, the village centre at least seems to hide away from the world in a hollow by the river, but those who take the slip road off the B6295 will find it's a welcoming place with much old-world character.

A sense of order pervades the buildings at Allenheads with its neat rows of miners' houses, workshops and estate offices, many of which were constructed under the instruction of Victorian engineer and mine agent, Thomas Sopwith, who was fixated with rules, punctuality and self-improvement. He built the school on the hillside in 1849 which he could see from his riverside house using a telescope. Any pupil caught arriving just a few seconds late would be reprimanded.

Allenheads Inn catches the eye with its little lead-mining train, stocks under the trees and old wagon wheels. Built in 1770, it was the

LEAD MINING

Evidence of lead mining in the North Pennines appears from medieval times, though it's very likely the Romans also mined here (land this rich in minerals so close to major Roman forts would surely not have gone unnoticed). Boom time came in the mid 18th century and lasted for over 100 years but the industry crashed quite suddenly in the 1870s when cheaper markets for lead opened on the continent. At its peak in the 1860s, the North Pennines produced a quarter of Britain's lead.

The two big lead-mining companies operating in the North Pennines (W B Lead in the Allendales and Weardale, and the London Lead Company in Teesdale and Alston area) had a profound impact on the character of settlements through their promotion of obedience, discipline and education, which is partly why you see so many chapels, schools, reading rooms and mine agents' houses in the mining communities.

Miners received paltry recompense for the lead ore they dug and for their reduced life expectancy due to breathing in dangerous dust, so it became commonplace in the 18th and 19th centuries for them to supplement their income by farming. Small houses and enclosed fields, known as 'allotments', are still seen on some North Pennine hillsides.

former home of the Beaumont family – one of the biggest mine owners in the North Pennines. Opposite is a small **Heritage Centre** – giving an introduction to the village, its mining heritage and community life.

¶¶ FOOD & DRINK

The **Allenheads Inn** (✐ 01434 685200) is fine for a pint of Black Sheep but for lunch you might want to try the cosy **Hemmel Café** (✐ 01434 685568 ☺ spring & summer, daily; winter Thu–Sun ♿ inside café; disabled toilet in the square). A favourite with cyclists on the Coast-to-Coast trail, the café serves sandwiches, coffees and Sunday lunches (prepared with local meats).

BLANCHLAND & THE DERWENT VALLEY

The upper Derwent Valley on the edge of Consett is well known to outdoor enthusiasts in Durham and Tyneside who come to fish, sail and cycle. Beyond the reservoir, the Derwent continues on its journey to the Tyne.

Here, we stay with the upper reaches of the valley and take in the moorland and woodland scenery, and the ancient settlement of Blanchland with its 12th-century abbey.

22 Derwent Gorge & Reservoir

The main car park where there's a shop and café is reached by turning off the B6278 a mile east of Edmundbyers

The River Derwent's journey from the Pennine moors to the Tyne is halted by the three-mile-long-**Derwent Reservoir** – the second-largest reservoir in Northumberland, frequented by birdwatchers, anglers, picnicking families, windsurfers and dinghy sailors. **Derwent Reservoir Sailing Club** (DH8 9PT ✆ 01434 675258 ◎ www.drsc. co.uk) offer sailing and windsurfing lessons. You can cycle along the mixed-use path that encircles the lake in 1½ hours or so, enjoying views of the moors, fields and woods rising

"The best place for woodland birds is the ancient oak woodland of Derwent Gorge and Muggleswick Woods."

above its shore; much of the route is wheelchair accessible, and there's a scattering of picnic tables. By the car park and loos near the dam, a well-stocked shop (and tuck shop) has everything you need to go fishing – you can also book fishing lessons here (✆ 01207 255250).

Mixed woodland and scrub along the southern shore of the reservoir attract finches and tits as well as the odd red squirrel, but the best place for woodland birds is the ancient oak woodland of **Derwent Gorge** and **Muggleswick Woods**, east of the reservoir, that cloaks the tightly ribboned River Derwent. Redstarts and wood warblers are recorded as breeding species here. Also look for plants associated with undisturbed woods such as sweet woodruff, wood sorrel and wild garlic in spring.

23 Blanchland

Seemingly unchanged for hundreds of years, Blanchland is more historically alluring than any village in the region. Walking over its humpbacked bridge on a summer's evening when the 18th-century sandstone houses are soaked in orange light is pretty hard to beat, but for me, Blanchland is at its most timeless in winter when the smell of coal seeps into the surrounding countryside, leading ramblers down off the heather slopes and towards the yellow glow from the Lord Crewe Arms.

The village almost certainly gets its name from the French white-robed Premonstratensian Canons who established an abbey here in 1165. Everything else you see grew around the abbey – and in some cases from its venerable walls, including the pub which was once the Abbot's lodge, kitchen and guesthouses and which still has its priest's hole.

St Mary's Church, hidden by trees just beyond the embattled gatehouse, is hugely atmospheric inside and clearly built out of the ruined abbey with a soaring archway and lancet windows of the Early English style; the rest was reconstructed in the 18th century. A medieval stained-glass panel near the altar shows a white-robed monk, the folds of his cloak still just visible.

According to folklore, during the turbulent centuries of cross-border fighting, the monastery almost evaded plundering by the Scots who had lost their way on the fells in heavy fog. Unfortunately, the untimely ringing of the bells announcing it was safe to come out of hiding, revealed the abbey's whereabouts to the invaders. Blanchland later suffered under Henry VIII and eventually came into the ownership of Lord Crewe, Bishop of Durham.

"St Mary's Church, hidden by trees just beyond the embattled gatehouse, is hugely atmospheric."

Once you've wandered around the centre and admired the stone square of cottages, visited the church, tea rooms and fetching post office (note the stone cheese press outside and the white post box), you might consider taking a stroll down to the wooded banks of the River Derwent (opposite).

A longer – and **more strenuous walk** – could take you up on to the heather moors that enclose Blanchland (take ✻ OS Explorer map 307 with you). A recommended route starts at the north end of the village by the car park. Follow the road that climbs out of Blanchland, passing Shildon's stone cottages on your right after half a mile or so. Note the evocative ruin of the **Shildon lead-mining engine house** on the wooded slope to your left. It dates to the early 19th century and once housed a steam-powered pump that drew water out of a nearby mine. After passing Pennypie House, continue straight ahead over grouse moors in the direction of Burntshield Haugh. Once you reach the brow of the hill, turn left along an old packhorse track (the **Carriers' Way**). Ponies once carried smelted lead along here to the River Tyne. Return to Blanchland via Birkside Fell, Newbiggin Fell, Newbiggin Hall and Baybridge (note the old chapel).

Blanchland's annual **agricultural show** is held over the August Bank Holiday. Earlier in the month is the **Slaley Show** (second Saturday in August; western end of Slaley village). Expect all the usual dog and sheep displays as well as vintage vehicles, live music, folk dancers, rides for children and so on.

¶¶ FOOD & DRINK

The old school facing down the main street is now the **White Monk Tearoom** (✆ 01434 675044 ☺ daily ♿) which serves sandwiches, soups, jacket potatoes and cakes.

Lord Crewe Arms The Sq, Blanchland DH8 9SP ✆ 01434 675469 ☺ daily ♿ eating areas downstairs only. Refurbished in recent years and now one of the most expensive hotels in Northumberland, the Lord Crewe Arms is becoming well known as a very good place to dine (and drink) as well as stay. Once associated with the abbey (monks used the gardens as a cloisters), the building has retained many of its medieval features including huge fireplaces and a stone vaulted crypt (now a bar serving Northumbrian ales). In the upstairs dining room, chicken is roasted over an open fire adding to the appeal of this upmarket restaurant. Expect a range of good-quality meat and fish dishes served with vegetables from the garden. Salmon, sardines, mackerel and pork are cured in the garden smokehouse.

Punch Bowl Edmundbyers DH8 9NL ✆ 01207 255545. Friendly, tastefully decorated country pub in an old hilltop village with a big green. Serves good pub dinners (steak and ale pie, sausage and mash, steaks, Sunday lunches, etc) and has a beer garden, three local ales on tap, an adjoining tea room and decent, average-priced B&B accommodation.

🚶 BLANCHLAND RIVERSIDE WALK

❋ OS Explorer map 307; start: north side of the bridge over the River Derwent (B6306), 📍 NY966502; 1½ miles; difficulty: easy; refreshments at Blanchland

Though muddy in places, this is an easy riverside trail through gentle wooded countryside. There's a lovely bathing pool with a shingle bank for children to play on not far after leaving Blanchland.

With your back to the village and just before the bridge over the River Derwent, turn right on to a lane and through an opening in the wall on your left, picking up a grassy footpath that leads to the water's edge. Turn right and walk with the bubbling Derwent on your left, looking out for dippers and goosanders and a little waterfall streaming down the opposite bank. You'll pass a dry stone wall with an eye-catching run of very large coping stones. After a boardwalk, cross a bridge on to the far side of the river and then continue a short way up the road before turning into woodland by the footpath sign (this may be hidden by trees). Follow the trail back to Blanchland through dark Sitka spruce and then brighter oak and birch woodland. The village appears quite wonderfully below as you emerge from the trees. Return to the village centre by crossing the humpbacked bridge.

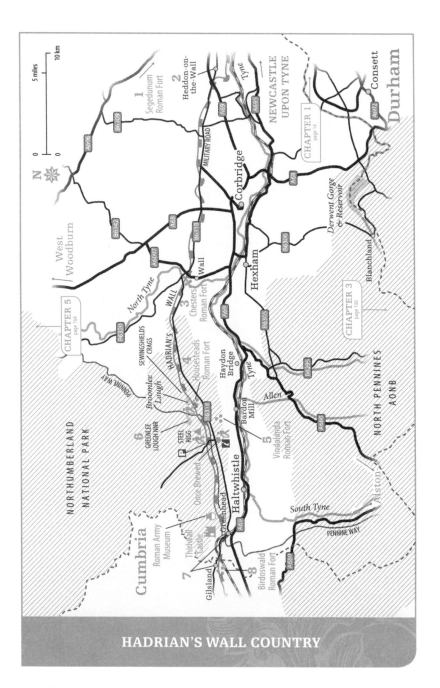

HADRIAN'S WALL COUNTRY

4
HADRIAN'S WALL COUNTRY

North of the Tyne Valley, the hills begin their gallop towards Scotland but are momentarily stopped dead in their tracks by a surge of igneous rock across the middle of Northumberland. This dramatic escarpment is made even more impassable by a ten-foot-high stone barricade ribboned along its uppermost lip. Built 2,000 years ago and spanning, in its entirety, 73 miles across the neck of England, Hadrian's Wall is the region's most famous attraction – and an awe-inspiring feature of the rugged Northumberland landscape. According to English Heritage it's 'the most important monument built by the Romans in Britain'. The best-preserved stretch, between Chesters and Brampton, rides the tops of the highest hills and rocky ridges where undulating grasslands roll far into Cumbria and down through the Tyne Valley. This is superb walking country indeed.

GETTING AROUND

In summer, by train from Newcastle then bus, you can pretty much reach every town and visitor attraction along Hadrian's Wall; in the low season there is no bus service, and visiting the Wall from **railway stations** along the Tyne is not always easy if travelling on foot. Most likely you'll need to take a taxi (eg: Hexham-based **Hadrian's Wall Taxis** ✆ 01434 606565). That said, Vindolanda is possible on foot from **Bardon Mill station** (two miles) along Chainley Burn, and you can also access the Wall in three miles from **Haltwhistle station** by following Haltwhistle Burn. Both routes are fiddly and you'll definitely need ❋ OS Explorer map OL43.

The dead-straight **Military Road** (B6318) is the usual access point for the major Roman forts if driving. It runs parallel to Hadrian's Wall and offers views of the Wall and surrounding upland landscape, but

---

ℹ️ TOURIST INFORMATION

Once Brewed National Park Centre Military Rd, NE47 7AN (near Vindolanda) ✆ 01434
344396 🕓 Easter–end Oct, daily; weekends only at other times ♿. Sells coffees and a small
selection of sandwiches; free internet access.

---

cars fly along this road and cyclists should be very cautious. The old
Roman road, the **Stanegate** (see box, page 152), is a mile or so south of
the Military Road and is a recommended alternative for cyclists – and
motorists who like to tootle along.

BUS

The **Hadrian's Wall Country Bus** (🖰 www.hadrians-wall.org), route
number AD122, stops at every popular jumping-off point for the Roman
ruins, including Chesters, Housesteads, Once Brewed, Vindolanda and
Birdoswald, and connects with trains and local buses (eg: the Arriva 685
bus) from Newcastle and Carlisle that stop at Hexham and Haltwhistle.
The AD122 operates seven times a day every day between Easter and
the end of August. In September it's a weekend-only service. However,
do check the website or call ahead because government cut backs
may affect the frequency of the service. **Multi-day Rover passes** allow
unlimited travel and can be bought from the driver. **Disabled badge
holders** travel for free (buses have low-floor easy access).

Unusually, the AD122 can take a couple of **bikes**: there's no charge, but
it's a first-come-first-served service.

TRAIN

Northern Rail (✆ 0845 000 0125 🖰 www.northernrail.org) operates
a regular daily service between Newcastle and Carlisle stopping at a
few stations of some use for Hadrian's Wall visitors, including Hexham,
Bardon Mill, Haltwhistle and Brampton. Hadrian's Wall Country Bus
(see below) connects with Hexham and Haltwhistle train stations.
Purchase combined bus and train tickets at Hexham railway station.

CYCLING

Hadrian's Cycleway is well signposted (National Cycle Network route 72)
on its 174-mile course from Ravenglass on the Cumbrian coast to South

Shields on the River Tyne. In Northumberland, mostly it runs south of Hadrian's Wall; the off-road stretch along the Tyne through Newcastle to the North Sea is shared with the Hadrian's Wall Path for walkers.

Cyclists can make good use of the Newcastle–Carlisle **railway** to access Hadrian's Wall (see opposite) which is never more than a few miles north of stations on the line. Bikes travel free; two per service; no need to book.

BICYCLE HIRE, REPAIRS, TRANSFERS & HOLIDAYS

Bicycle hire (and repairs) are offered at a couple of places close to the line of Hadrian's Wall, including **Edens Lawn Cycle Hire** (Haltwhistle NE49 0HH ✆ 01434 320443) and **The Cycle Hub** (Newcastle Quayside (on Hadrian's Cycleway) NE6 1BU ✆ 0191 2767250 ⌂ www. thecyclehub.org). Repairs are also undertaken at **ActivCycles** (17 Watling St, Corbridge NE45 5AH ✆ 01434 632950). A couple of adventure companies offer transfers for you and your bike, including **Pedalpushers Cycle Hire** (Brampton ✆ 016977 42387) and **Pedal Power** (Amble ✆ 01665 713448, 07790 596782 ⌂ www.pedal-power.co.uk) where you can also hire bikes and book cycling holidays in Hadrian's Wall country.

WALKING

Ramblers will find no shortage of excellent walks in and around Hadrian's Wall. The scenery doesn't really get going until your back is to Heddon-on-the-Wall, but from then on, the landscape becomes increasingly remote, rough, ascending and unbound. By the time you clear Chollerford and Chesters Roman Fort on heading west, you enter the most memorable countryside on the whole of the Wall: undulating farmland, some of the largest lakes in Northumberland, soaring craggy cliffs and far-reaching views north across Redesdale's heavy plantation forests. I've outlined a few half-day walks in these pages which take in some of the most popular stretches of Hadrian's Wall, but you may want to explore some less-visited parts such as the River Irthing (near Birdoswald Roman Fort) and around Thirlwall Castle (page 161).

WALKING HOLIDAYS, BAGGAGE TRANSFERS & TAXIS

Shepherds Walks (✆ 01669 621044 ⌂ www.shepherdswalks.co.uk) is a reputable local travel company based in Rothbury that offers self-guided and led trips along Hadrian's Wall (see box, pages 148–9). Also consider **Hadrian's Wall** (✆ 01434 344650 ⌂ www.hadrianswall. ltd.uk). They will also take your bags if you're walking independently, as will **The Walkers' Baggage Transfer Co** (✆ 0871 423 8803 ⌂ www.walkersbags.co.uk) and **Hadrian's Haul** (✆ 07967 564823 ⌂ www.hadrianshaul.com). For taxis, see *Chapter 3*, page 104.

HADRIAN'S WALL & ROMAN FORTS

When built on the orders of Emperor Hadrian in AD122, the **Wall** extended for 73 miles from coast to coast with a 25-mile extension south through Cumbria. It took three legions consisting of 5,000 men as little as, perhaps, a decade to build. But, they didn't just build a mighty wall with a deep channel on its north side: 16 **forts** were constructed, as well as the **vallum** – a 20-foot ditch with a mound either side running the length of the south side of the Wall. According to English Heritage, this immense earthwork likely functioned as 'the Roman equivalent of barbed wire'. Now, if it weren't for the colossal and visually more striking Wall, perhaps more would be made of the vallum in history books. It really is a remarkable feat in its own right.

Although the Wall had a defensive role, it mainly functioned as a barrier marking the northwest edge of the Roman Empire (Hadrian being more concerned with containing his kingdom than expanding it). It was, say English Heritage, a kind of Berlin Wall, and controlled the north–south flow of human traffic for some 250 years until the collapse of the Roman Empire in the 5th century.

To this end, a number of guarded posts were built along its length, one every Roman mile. Between these **milecastles** were two

WALKING THE HADRIAN'S WALL PATH

The 84-mile long-distance trail from Bowness-on-Solway on the Cumbrian coast to Wallsend in Newcastle is fully accessible to walkers and is well signposted. What many visitors would call 'the best bit' is the well-preserved section of Wall in the central area, roughly between Chollerford and Brampton. That said, just because the Wall breaks up and often vanishes altogether either side of these settlements isn't to say the walking is not scenic. The Solway Estuary is birdwatching heaven, and the tumbling farmland through the Tyne Valley is quite dreamy in parts. Even Wallsend has a certain appeal: it is as manmade as Sewingshields Crags is wild, but there is something very raw about the industrial scenery with its cranes and old shipbuilding yards at Swan Hunters.

But, back to 'the best bit'. Between Sewingshields and Greenhead, the hills rise for 12 spectacular, thigh-busting miles, holding the Wall to the sky and out of the reach of builders of past centuries.

On a misty morning when the clouds cover the roads and all signs of modern life, observation towers – or **turrets**. Some, like the Milecastle 37 west of Housesteads with its broken arched gate, are impressive to this day. Little kindles the imagination more than on a wet, misty morning when the Wall rises and falls through the fog and the walker is forced to seek shelter on the inside wall of a milecastle. One can only imagine what the Roman soldiers thought about being stationed up on this remote ridge.

Despite the 'recycling' of Wall stones in settlements and farm buildings in the Tyne Valley in the centuries that followed the retreat of the Romans, the central section, between Chesters and Brampton, where you'll find the most impressive Roman forts, is still very well preserved. Chesters, Vindolanda, Housesteads and Birdoswald all have their highlights and some have superb on-site museums housing Roman treasures unearthed over the last few centuries.

The preservation of the forts and Wall in this central section has been greatly assisted by the rough, inaccessible countryside. Of course, this is also what makes Hadrian's Wall exceptionally good walking and cycling country, and an increasing number of visitors come here to take on the 84-mile **Hadrian's Wall Path** or 160-mile **Hadrian's Cycleway**.

* * *

the Wall rollercoasters across the landscape peeking up through bowls of fog wherever the Whin Sill crags rise high enough – it's evocative moments like this that will stay with the walker.

At any time of year the weather can be foul in the uplands of Northumberland and, just like soldiers 2,000 years ago, you may find yourself huddled under the Wall sheltering from the wind. Chill-proof clothing is recommended throughout the year.

Most people walk east to west, usually because Newcastle is better connected than

the Cumbrian coast, but there are a few downsides: it's more likely that you'll have the wind and rain hitting your front and purists won't like starting a walk at a place called Walls*end*!

Make sure you set out with good **supplies**. You'll find plenty of villages to refuel at, but you may have to walk perhaps a couple of miles off the Wall in remote parts.

Even though the route is well signposted, you should take OS Explorer **maps** 314, 315, OL43 and 316. You'll be grateful when a weather front rolls in.

∦ CYCLING IN THE HEART OF HADRIAN'S WALL COUNTRY

※ OS Explorer map OL43; start from Once Brewed National Park Centre (Military Rd, NE47 7AN) or Bardon Mill train station; 15 miles; difficulty: moderate with some climbs; refreshments at Once Brewed, the Milecastle Inn (Military Rd, NE49 9NN ✐ 01434 321372 ⊙ daily for lunch & in the evening), Haltwhistle and Bardon Mill

Some of the very best Wall, hill and river valley scenery is experienced on this trail from Bardon Mill, which follows the lofty **Pennine Cycleway** (NCN Route 68) into Northumberland National Park. The long-distance trail, incidentally, also extends south from Haltwhistle making for a very ample day's jaunt into the North Pennines along a disused railway line to Alston (described on pages 127–9).

From **Once Brewed**, cycle north crossing Hadrian's Wall by Steel Rigg car park (♀ NY750676). Descend into the endless hill-farming country bordering Redesdale and continue as far as **Edges Green** (♀ NY722687). For the return, head west via **Whiteside** (♀ NY706690). An outstanding view of the Roman wall snaking across the backbone of the Whin Sill escarpment comes into sight as you pedal south to the Milecastle Inn where you can refuel. Continue due south up Shield Hill and then free-wheel into **Haltwhistle**. The final leg east dips in and out of some pretty settlements including Melkridge with its old stone cottages and green, and offers glorious views of pastures and farms in the South Tyne Valley.

✳ ✳ ✳

1 SEGEDUNUM ROMAN FORT

Buddle St, Wallsend NE28 6HR ✐ 0191 236 9347 ⧉ www.twmuseums.org.uk/segedunum
⊙ Apr–early Nov, daily; Mon–Fri 10.00–14.30 & occasional Sat at other times of the year; café; ♿

Segedunum (meaning 'strong fort') was built under the order of Emperor Hadrian and marks the end point of Hadrian's 73-mile wall across northern England (hence the town's name, 'Wallsend').

Inside the fort, a tall viewing platform, which looks like an airport control tower, rises over this industrial and archaeological site providing an amazing bird's-eye view of the garrison buildings (not that impressive in itself because hardly any stones remain *in situ*) and enhancing your appreciation of its scale. It provides an equally clear view of the Tyne above the famous Swan Hunter shipbuilding yards (you can still see the rectangular inlets where hulls including the *Mauretania* were constructed).

An indoor **museum** contains displays (many geared towards children) and some Roman objects including a rare stone toilet seat, and exhibits detailing the industrial heritage of the area in more recent centuries. Outside, the main attraction is a full-scale reconstruction of Europe's only fully working Roman **bath house** where part of the hot-room floor has been removed to show how the Romans engineered under-floor heating.

Other Roman buildings are marked out in lines of stones; they were only rediscovered when the terraces of Victorian housing running down to the shipyards were demolished.

2 HEDDON-ON-THE-WALL

As you approach Heddon, look out for the long stretch of Hadrian's Wall crossing a field on the left of the Hexham Road. Note too that on entering this pleasant village high above the Tyne Valley, locals greet you in the street. Welcome to Northumberland.

The friendly village centre is reached by turning left where the Wall ends. If you come for lunch at the Swan Inn on Towne Gate (see below), make sure you visit **St Andrew's Church** opposite, parts of which date to the Saxon period. A wide Norman arch spans the sanctuary and a large fragment of a Celtic cross rests to the left of the altar.

¶¶ FOOD & DRINK

Dingle Dell Deli and Tearoom 3 Taberna Close, NE15 0BW ✆ 01661 854325 ♿. This friendly little foodstore and café is close to the Hadrian's Wall Path and serves a lovely cup of tea and good scones. Walkers can pick up freshly made baps for a few pounds or a Hadrian's Lunch Box (sandwich, pie, cake and bottle of water) – a bargain at just £5.

Swan Inn The Towne Gate, NE15 0DR ✆ 01661 853161 ♿ ramp at side entrance. Popular, family-friendly gastro pub in the centre of Heddon serving traditional pub fare all day (best known for its daily carvery but also serving a range of dishes from scampi to lasagne). When the sun's out, sit in the beer garden and take in the expansive view of the Tyne Valley.

Wylam Brewery

South Houghton Farm, NE15 0EZ ✆ 01661 853377 ♿ www.wylambrewery.co.uk ♿

Go to any decent pub in Northumberland serving real ales, and chances are you will come across a favourite like the Rocket or Red Kite from the celebrated Wylam Brewery (based in Heddon-on-the-Wall). You can sample their beers at the Swan Inn (see above) or by going on a brewery

THE STANEGATE

In the years before the construction of Hadrian's Wall, the Romans built a military road linking settlements between Corbridge and Carlisle. The line of the Stanegate (a medieval name meaning 'Stone Road') is 1½ miles south of Hadrian's Wall but is not to be confused with the much busier B6318 Military Road that runs tight to the Wall.

The eight-mile stretch of the Stanegate from **Fourstones to Vindolanda** makes a very pleasant route to Hadrian's Wall from the Hexham area and offers views of upland meadows and pastures the whole way.

Between **Fourstones** and **Newbrough** the road is flanked by a scattering of stone cottages, a curious bright green clapboard chapel dating to the late 19th century, two pubs and a picturesque stone church. **The Red Lion** (NE47 5AR ℘ 01434 674226) at Newbrough is a decent enough place to refuel (also a reasonable B&B). The lane to the side of the pub heads north to **Carr Edge woodland** – the site of the **Lookwide Campsite**, the first

official Scout camp led by Lord Baden-Powell in 1908 (a year after the famous Brownsea Island experimental camp). To locate it, follow the road for 1½ miles, then turn off right along a footpath signed to Carr Edge; a memorial cairn in the woods marks the spot.

Climbing out of Newbrough on the Stanegate, the road flattens and the views of farmland become even more expansive. Lines of dry stone walls follow the sloping contours of the land towards Hadrian's Wall, sheep and cows graze in fields and, in spring, the sky is filled with the song of curlews and skylarks. This is very good cycling country.

Grindon Lough (♀ NY806677) is one of four natural lakes in the Hadrian's Wall area and is sometimes visited by migrant whooper swans and pink-footed geese in winter.

The last three-quarters-of-a-mile stretch of the Stanegate to **Vindolanda** is lost under grassland and re-emerges at the Roman site where it formed what was essentially a Roman high street.

tour lasting an hour or so. Tours cost £8 (includes up to three pints) and run on Fridays and Saturdays (depending on demand).

3 CHESTERS ROMAN FORT

🏠 **Carraw B&B** (page 274)

Chollerford NE46 4EU ℘ 01434 681379 ☉ Apr–early Nov as well as Feb school holidays & Easter, daily; weekends only at other times ♿ most of the site including the museum; English Heritage

If Housesteads is 'the fort with the loos' and Vindolanda the one with the high street and writing tablets, then Chesters is all about the bath house. At least that's what it has become known for. Chesters also boasts a **museum** which has been open to visitors since 1896 and is filled with an astonishing collection of Roman treasures amassed by John Clayton between 1840 and 1890. It is thanks to him that so many Roman artefacts and buildings in Northumberland survive at all.

Clayton bought a number of forts and stretches of the Wall to stop them being plundered for stone, and put the most precious objects in his 'Antiquity House' in the garden. Even if he had only saved a handful of the Roman stone plinths, altar stones, reliefs of gods, memorial stones, metal tools and jewellery on display in the museum created after his death, you would be impressed, but there are hundreds of Roman finds here.

The **fort** stands on a hill above the River North Tyne, near Chollerford, in parkland laid out by the Clayton family in the early 19th century. In the centre is the colonnaded courtyard of the headquarters building, still with its paved flooring and well (notice the phallic good luck symbol carved into the paving). Next door is the commanding officer's house, complete with its private bath house (by the tree). To the left are the remains of three barrack blocks.

A large **bath house** lies outside of the fort wall by the wooded riverside and represents the best example of its type in Britain, as well as being one of the most intact Roman

"A large bath house lies outside of the fort wall by the wooded riverside and represents the best example of its type in Britain."

structures on the whole of Hadrian's Wall. You gain an idea of how soldiers would have moved from the changing room (the large room with a row of arched 'cubby holes' which may have been used for hanging clothes or could even, an expert at English Heritage told me, have held statues of the seven days of the week) into progressively warmer chambers. Treatment rooms include a sauna, a steam room and hot and cold baths. Like all Roman bath houses, it was a place to wash (using oil, not soap) and socialise. Here soldiers had their skin cleansed, played board games and chatted. At Segedunum Roman Fort in Wallsend, a replica bath house has been created based on the ruins at Chesters.

By now you will have appreciated the view of the **North Tyne**, which forms rapids as it rushes on its way to join the South Tyne at Hexham. Note the stones on the other side of the river – these are the remains of the abutment of two Roman bridges. You can take a closer look by crossing the road bridge at Chollerford and taking the path immediately off to the right.

¶¶ FOOD & DRINK

A café within the grounds of **Chesters Roman Fort** with outside picnic tables is due to reopen in summer 2015. The **George Hotel** (NE46 4EW ✆ 01434 681611 ♿) by Chollerford Bridge is open for light lunches (paninis, soups) until 17.00 and then hot dinners (fish and chips, burgers and so on) later on. The restaurant overlooks pretty gardens and is one of the few places serving food close to Chesters Roman Fort. Much better still is the **Barrasford Arms** (NE48 4AA ✆ 01434 681237) a few miles north of Chollerford (page 208). Roman Wall walkers will be pleased to stumble upon **St Oswald's Tea Room** (NE46 4HB ✆ 01434 689010 ○ May–end Oct, Tue–Sun; variable opening at other times of the year) on the Military Road a couple of miles east of Chollerford where you can sit in a pretty garden in full sun with an inexpensive coffee, breakfast, baked potato, sandwich or bowl of soup.

4 HOUSESTEADS ROMAN FORT

🏠 **Grindon Farm** (page 273), **Once Brewed YHA** (page 274), ⛺ **Herding Hill Farm** (page 274), **Winshields Farm** (page 274)

Off the Military Rd, near Haydon Bridge NE47 6NN ✆ 01434 344363 ○ daily, year-round; café & small museum; ♿ disabled parking by the museum & paved path to the fort but most of the site is not accessible due to the grassy terrain & steep gradient; English Heritage

Housesteads is the most complete Roman fort in Britain and the most visited of the four main garrison stations in Northumberland owing in part to its dramatic position on the top of a cliff of igneous rock. Built in the years following the construction of Hadrian's Wall, the fort sits snug to the stone barricade, teetering on the edge of the Roman Empire.

CHARIOTS TO TRAINS

Take a close look at the stone floor in the east gate entranceway which reveals two heavily worn grooves created by Roman carts coming and going over the years. The distance between the channels shows that the Roman cart wheels were just shy of five feet apart – the same dimension adopted in the centuries thereafter. It is also, not coincidentally, the same width as standard railway gauges in Britain today (4 feet 8½ inches).

Before the invention of steam engines, horses pulled carts on wooden tracks so it is thought the same standardised axle length was applied when these wooden rails were replaced by metal ones and 'iron horses'. It's nice to think that the great Victorian railway engineers based at Wylam, some 20 miles away from Housesteads, developed the railway line based, by default, on the measurements of Roman carts.

As with other forts, Housesteads is typical in its arrangement of buildings with its centrally located headquarters building, granaries, hospital and commanding officer's residence. The last consists of rooms arranged around a courtyard and has an excellent example of Roman under-floor heating technology. The floor, now mostly removed, was raised on rows of pillars under which hot air circulated.

The well-preserved **latrine** in the southeast corner of the site often interests visitors most. The room is oblong with a raised central area and a gutter running around its perimeter. Two wooden benches with holes for around 30 bums once bridged the gap between the central stone plinth you see today and the outer walls. It is thought soldiers cleaned themselves using a kind of natural sponge made of moss attached to the end of a stick. The functions of the trough and bowl are not known for certain though plenty of people have made guesses.

The four **gates** around the curtain wall are of interest, particularly the west gate, still with its door pivot holes, and the east gate with its stone flooring deeply worn by the wheels of carts (see box, opposite).

✳ ✳ ✳

HADRIAN'S WALL WALKS
Steel Rigg: a classic Hadrian's Wall walk

OS Explorer map OL43; start: Steel Rigg car park, ♀ NY750676; 5 miles, or 6 miles to include Winshield Crags; difficulty: moderate walk on undulating ground; no refreshments unless you extend this route to Housesteads where there's a café

This well-trodden circular walk takes in some of the most photographed scenery in Hadrian's Wall country and gives you two perspectives of the Wall: from the Whin Sill looking north across farmland into 'barbarian' country, and from below the crags gazing up at the Wall ribboned along the edge of the spectacular escarpment. If you extend the route to Winshield Crags on your return, you'll also experience one of the most breath-taking views in the whole of the region from Cumbria to the east coast.

From the southeast corner of Steel Rigg car park, follow the footpath signs to the national trail. At the Wall, turn left through the gate. The next few miles are tough as you cross the Wall several times and make a series of steep ascents and drops, but the views of the dramatic Whin Sill escarpment and glinting Crag Lough below are tremendous. Your first challenge is the climb to the top of **Peel Crags** – one of the most photographed vantage points on the Wall. Just beyond Milecastle 39, you'll pass a prominent sycamore in a hollow (known as '**Sycamore Gap**').

Highshield Crags are traversed by way of a path through woodland and over a couple of stiles. Once past Hotbank Farm, take a deep breath for the stiff ascent to **Hotbank Crags** where a superb view westwards awaits.

The return leg begins where the Pennine Way parts company with the Wall by a ladder stile. Descending into grassland to the north of the Wall continue straight ahead, ignoring the Pennine Way path to your right. At a stone ruin (an old lime kiln), turn left and continue in a westerly direction across grassland until you meet a farm track. Turn left on this track, walking southwest until you reach a dry stone wall and a farm gate. Don't go through the gate but turn right and head due west crossing a couple of fields by way of stiles.

Eventually you join a farm track. Cross a stile and over the next field to an enclosure. With a dry stone wall on your right, follow the path which becomes a farm track until you meet a road. Exit the farmland by a ladder stile, turn left on to the road and walk uphill back to the car park.

For **Winshield Crags**, continue past the car park and turn into a field on your right by a gate (signed). Climb steadily on the grassy path ahead to a height of 1,132 feet – the highest point on the whole of the Hadrian's Wall Path. Return to Steel Rigg car park the way you came.

Round walk from Housesteads into 'barbarian' country

OS Explorer map OL43; start: Housesteads Roman Fort, NY788688; 4 miles; difficulty: moderate to strenuous walk on rough grasslands and with some climbs; café at Housesteads

A classic walk in Hadrian's land taking in sections of the Wall either side of Housesteads, tremendous countryside views and skylark-rich grasslands.

Woodland hides the first stretch that begins in the northwest corner of Housesteads Roman Fort. With the Wall to your right, walk through the copse noticing the Wall plant life as you go (masses of ferns, mosses and woodland plants sprout from the stones).

Exiting the woodland by a gate, you'll soon reach one of the most impressionable milecastles on the Wall: **Milecastle 37**, which stands over three feet high and retains parts of its arching north gate stones.

Continue across damp grassland. After a gate with a ladder stile, the path follows a dry stone wall marking the course of Hadrian's Wall before the familiar turf-topped muscley Roman stones reappear, rollercoasting across the grasslands ahead. From here, the Wall Country views are perhaps some of the best along the whole of the long-distance path. Glinting below towering cliffs below and enclosed by buttercup meadows in spring is glacial **Crag Lough**.

Passing a belt of conifer trees, descend to **Hotbank Farm**, which you enter by a kissing gate signed 'Milecastle 38'. Cross the farmyard, go through a farm gate and follow a stony track. Bear to the right after a farm gate with a ladder stile.

At a fork in the track, continue to the right along a grassy track towards a waymarker ahead. Ignore a turning by a stone ruin and continue straight on for 200 yards where there's a farm gate. Go over the ladder stile, crossing the Pennine Way footpath. The grasslands become increasingly muddy underfoot as you skirt **Broomlee Lough**, where cuckoo flowers dot the tussocks in spring. Note too the sheepfold on your right. The path is unclear but just head for the stand of conifers ahead which you enter and exit by gates.

Once back in open land, walk diagonally towards the Wall, aiming for a gap where there's a farm gate and ladder stile (about 500 yards away and not immediately in view). This is **King's Wicket**.

Now back into Roman territory, turn right and follow the Wall to a copse where there's a ladder stile. Go through the woods. A wide section of Hadrian's Wall leads you on an arrow-straight course all the way back to Housesteads passing a Roman **gateway** by Knag Burn – an unusual opening in the Wall, as the information panel explains. The official route into Housesteads is from the south.

✳ ✳ ✳

5 VINDOLANDA ROMAN FORT

⋏ Hadrian's Wall Camping (page 274)
Near Bardon Mill NE47 7JN ✆ 01434 344277 ⏚ www.vindolanda.com ◷ Apr–early Jan (closed only on Christmas Day), daily; café; ♿ steep slope to museum from fort but disabled parking at museum & main fort entrance

> Never before have we had the pleasure of seeing a surviving and perfectly preserved wooden [toilet] seat. As soon as we started to uncover it there was no doubt at all on what we had found. It is made from a very well worked piece of wood and looks pretty comfortable. Now we need to find the toilet that went with it as Roman loos are fascinating places to excavate – their drains often contain astonishing artefacts.

Dr Andrew Birley, Director of Excavations, Vindolanda, 2014

THE ROMAN WRITING TABLETS

I want you to know that I am in very good health, as I hope you are in turn, you neglectful man, who have sent me not even one letter ...

Are we to return with the standard ... to the crossroads all together or just half of us ...

My fellow-soldiers have no beer. Please order some to be sent ...

Thanks to the damp, anaerobic soil at Vindolanda, a large number of leather, textile and wooden items that would otherwise have quickly rotted away survived here for almost 2,000 years until first discovered by archaeologists in 1973.

What excited the team most were the hundreds of small writing tablets about the size of a postcard. At first archaeologists thought they were wood shavings until they noticed a script scrawled across the fragments of birch, alder and oak. Among the tablets are the quartermasters' book-keeping records listing supplies for the garrison, the correspondence of commanding officers, and messages of a more personal nature: letters to family members and notes accompanying parcels. Perhaps the most treasured card is the famous birthday party invitation from Claudia Severa to Sulpicia Lepidina; it is the earliest record of female correspondence and Latin handwriting in western Europe.

It was probably only a matter of time before archaeologists at Vindolanda came across a message that would disclose a derogatory term Romans used to refer to native Brits. Tablet 164 revealed the slang word *Brittunculi*, meaning 'wretched Britons'.

A mile upstream from Bardon Mill where the land is green and bumpy all around is this Roman military station and museum housing some of the most important Roman finds ever recovered (see box, above). Discoveries are still being made today by experts and volunteers involved in Vindolanda's active archaeological research programme that began in the 1970s. Recent finds include a rare wooden toilet seat (see quote on page 157) and a gold coin dating to AD64–65 that bears the image of the Emperor Nero. Its value to a Roman soldier was over half a year's salary.

The Roman military **fort** and **village** were built in AD85, several decades before the construction of Hadrian's Wall a mile north. Over the following centuries the site was rebuilt several times and continued as a settlement with shops and domestic dwellings after the retreat of the Roman Empire.

Inside the **fort** walls, which would have once been at least 16 feet high, are the remains of the commanding officer's quarters, a granary and the headquarters building. Equally as fascinating are the food and textile **shops**, domestic dwellings, tavern and workshops that face each other along a main street outside the western fort gate. Drains line either side of the road and are covered with stone slabs at intervals marking the entrances to individual buildings. One even has the name of the 5th- or 6th-century owner crudely engraved into the stone: 'RIACVS' is clearly visible on the left as you enter the fort and could be a post-Roman name. With a little imagination you can imagine the smells, bustle and noise along what was essentially a high street.

After exploring the ruins and the convincing **replica stone tower** (climb to the top to gain a bird's-eye view of the site and wider countryside), take the path that leads downhill to a wooded ravine and excellent museum. A stream runs through the gardens where there is outdoor seating for the café.

The most treasured artefacts at the **Vindolanda museum** are the **Roman writing tablets** (see box, page opposite) discovered on site beneath a protective layer of clay in 1973. They are the earliest collection of written material in Britain and provide a glimpse of life in Roman Britain. Most of the 1,400 tablets recovered thus far are stored in the British Museum in London but nine are on display at Vindolanda. A short film tells the fascinating story of their discovery.

"Inside the fort walls, which would have once been at least 16 feet high, are the remains of the commanding officer's quarters, a granary and the headquarters building."

The rest of the museum is devoted to the remarkable array of other objects excavated at Vindolanda, including many ceramic vessels, tools, animal bones and weapons as well as intriguing domestic items such as a brush made from pig hair, basketware, a lady's wig, jewellery, leather shoes and a child's textile sock. One of the most exciting finds of recent years is a fragment of a bronze blade-like instrument which has holes punched along its length and the word 'SEPTEMBER'. It is thought to be a Roman calendar or a water clock and is the only example ever found in Britain.

Excavations are ongoing at Vindolanda and adults over the age of 16 can join the team on an **archaeological dig** for one week or longer. Applications open in early November each year for the following season.

Taking the footpath from the back entrance of the museum, you can **walk** to the stables at Low Fogrigg and back in under an hour by following the bubbling **Chainley Burn** through woodland and across grassland. Extend this route to Bardon Mill by continuing along the river (a good way of reaching Vindolanda if you've come by train from Newcastle, Carlisle or Hexham).

On returning to the museum, continue uphill to the Roman road (the Stanegate) where you will see a stone pillar, the only **Roman milestone** in its original location.

6 GREENLEE LOUGH NATIONAL NATURE RESERVE

Access from Gibbs Hill farm parking area, 2 miles north of the tourist information centre at Once Brewed, ♀ NY747690

Walking through the reed beds in summer with dragonflies and damselflies coming in and out of view, you may hear the song of sedge and grasshopper warblers or spot reed buntings (like a sparrow with a prominent white collar and drooping moustache) on the top of a stem of sedge. Stepping off the boardwalk, you'll soon come to a bird hide overlooking Northumberland's largest

"A footpath leads walkers through meadowland full of yellow rattle, clovers, knapweeds, vetches and butterflies."

freshwater lake – the most interesting, biologically, of all the glacial lakes in Hadrian's Wall country on account of its aquatic plant life and diversity of wetland habitats. Otters, rare white-clawed crayfish, eels and plenty of trout and other fish inhabit these waters alongside common ducks, herons and mute swans. With the exception of ospreys, which are occasionally spotted in summer, winter birds on the lake are more interesting with goldeneye appearing among wigeon and teal, and whopper swans – their sociable honking calls loudly announcing their presence.

North of the lake, a footpath leads walkers through meadowland full of yellow rattle, clovers, knapweeds, vetches and butterflies which marks the half way point on a four-mile circular **walk** from Gibbs Hill. It's signposted some of the way and pretty easy to follow using ❇ OS Explorer map OL43. The western bulge of the lough is the only side of the lake you'll see on this walk which otherwise crosses farmland and hay meadows and offers a wonderful view of the Whin Sill crags.

GAIL JOHNSON/S

CASTLES & GARDENS

Northumberland has more castles than any other county in England, the most staggering of which are found along the Heritage Coast. Gardens open to the public include Howick, Alnwick and Belsay.

1 Chillingham Castle is full of curiosities. **2** Alnwick Castle is known as the 'Windsor Castle of the North'. **3** The wooded quarry gardens at Belsay Hall. **4** Dunstanburgh Castle lies on a spectacular headland between Craster and Embleton.

BELSAY HALL/EH

KEVIN TATE/S

BARTER BOOKS

TYNE VALLEY VIEWS/A

SS

TOWNS & VILLAGES

Hexham, Alnwick and Rothbury are some of the most appealing market towns in the region boasting vibrant communities and many historical buildings, but we highly recommend taking a few back roads and visiting some of Northumberland's less well-known villages described in these pages.

STUART FORSTER/A

DAVID TAYLOR PHOTOGRAPHY/A

1 Barter Books is a characterful secondhand bookshop in a former Victorian railway station.
2 Hexham Abbey in the spring. 3 The historic town of Berwick-upon-Tweed. 4 New Year's Eve
Ba'al celebrations in Allendale. 5 The town of Wooler against the Cheviot Hills. 6 Corbridge's
sandstone terraces. 7 Unlike Scottish bagpipes, Northumbrian pipes are bellows blown.
8 Narrow-gauge steam locos at Alston can be a handy way of exploring the South Tyne Valley.

VN

GEMMA HALL

GEMMA HALL

HUNTING HALL

Experience a very special green holiday at an award-winning Northumbrian family farm

Hunting Hall
Beal, Berwick upon Tweed
Northumberland

www.huntinghall.co.uk
Tel: 01289 388652
Email: info@huntinghall.co.uk

Something different for the weekend

Whether **wild camping** or **watching wildlife**, these Bradt guides reveal how to make the most of your weekend. Visit **www.bradtguides.com** and use the code **52WW** to get a **40% discount** on each title.

Bradt

7 GREENHEAD & GILSLAND

🏠 **Chapelburn House** (page 274), **Willowford Farm** (page 274)

On your way out of Northumberland and into Cumbria, you come to two pleasant villages in quick succession. **Greenhead's** riverside setting, stone terraces, church and village hall make it a welcome stop for ramblers, cyclists and motorists.

On a hillside a half-mile north of the village is the ruin of **Thirlwall Castle** – a 14th-century ruin reached by following the riverside footpath (go up Station Road by the phone box and turn right at the gate signposted to the castle). The fortress is soon upon you – all bitten and crumbling now – but clearly once a mighty edifice. It was built to defend the wealthy inhabitants from raiding Scots and was abandoned in the 1700s. The walls are nine-feet thick in places and were constructed using masonry from Hadrian's Wall. The same stones were robbed and recycled a second time for use in nearby houses.

Gilsland is a quiet Cumbrian stone village, which sits in a dip in the hills and is reached from Greenhead by following a road high up over hilly farmland or on foot along the Hadrian's Wall Path. The village was popular in Victorian times with visitors who came by train to enjoy the sulphur-rich waters just north of the settlement.

Gilsland Spa (CA8 7AR ✆ 016977 47203; refreshments) is an 18th-century mansion and hotel above the River Irthing where it is said that Sir Walter Scott met his future bride when he visited in 1797. The wooded grounds are particularly scenic and are accessible along a public footpath. A few hundred yards north of the footbridge is a large boulder and two small rounded ones by the river: the **Popping Stone** (presumably the large one) is said to be where Scott 'popped' the question to his lover, though the tale is without evidence.

WALKS AROUND GILSLAND

The landscape around Gilsland and Walltown is varied and offers good day walks. You'll experience some of the best Roman Wall scenery: open farmland, wooded rivers, ruins and one of the tallest sections of Hadrian's Wall, while avoiding the crowds.

The crumbling 14th-century Thirlwall Castle marks the centre point of two great circular walks: east to Walltown along Hadrian's Wall and return via the vallum; and west to Gilsland village following the vallum, returning via Gilsland Spa, the River Irthing and farmland.

Opposite Gilsland Green, on Hall Terrace, is a 17th-century cottage – and former hostelry – known as Mumps Hall which is now the **House of Meg Tea Rooms** (see below). It is famed for the legend of a notorious landlady nicknamed Meg of Mumps Hall who was said to have murdered and robbed many passing travellers in the 18th century.

A good stretch of **Hadrian's Wall** can be found by continuing uphill from the House of Meg Tea Rooms, passing the Methodist church on your right.

South of the railway line, **Milecastle 48** (also known as the Poltress Burn Milecastle after the river it watches over) is said to be one of the most intact of all on the Wall. Though its walls are not particularly high, you can see the foundations of rooms. The up and down route, which takes about 15 minutes to walk from Gilsland, is signposted from the start and takes you via a playground (children: note the extremely long, high slide) and under a viaduct where the Poltress Burn makes its merry way.

Roman Army Museum

Carvoran, Greenhead CA8 7JB ✆ 016977 47485 🖥 www.vindolanda.com/Roman-Army-Museum ◷ Apr–end Oct, daily; Nov–21 Dec, weekends only; buy a 'joint site ticket' which includes admission to Vindolanda & a saving of 20%; café; ♿

Vindolanda's sister museum delves into the world of the fierce and unstoppable Roman army in all its spear-thrusting, shield-bearing magnificence. Different aspects of the Roman military are detailed across three galleries and include the daily lives of legionnaires and auxiliaries. You'll learn about the life of Hadrian and the wider context of the army in relation to the Roman Empire and see life-size models of soldiers.

Everyone raves about the museum's 3D film, *Edge of Empire*. Re-enactments of ambushes and clashes with native Britons and the life of soldiers are brought to life in a Hollywood blockbuster-style format.

Outside, children can indulge in their own Roman re-enactments in the shadow of one of the tallest sections of Hadrian's Wall (**Walltown Crags**) and the fort at Carvoran (now largely an outline).

▌ FOOD & DRINK

Both Greenhead and Gilsland offer a couple of choices for light lunches, coffees and cakes. There's the cheerful **Greenhead Tea Room** (CA8 7HE ✆ 016977 47400) on the main road through the village and, in Gilsland, the **House of Meg Tea Rooms** (4 Hall Terrace, CA8 7BW ✆ 016977 47777).

Samson Inn Gilsland CA8 7DR ℘ 016977 47880 ☺ daily for lunch & evening meals ♿.
For a substantial meal your best bet is this old coaching inn which is much improved in
recent years and now serves very good restaurant food. There are usually a couple of meat,
fish and vegetarian options, some made with regional produce. A roaring fire is a welcome
sight for rain-soaked cyclists and walkers.

8 BIRDOSWALD ROMAN FORT

Gilsland CA8 7DD ℘ 016977 47602 ☺ Apr–end Oct & Feb school holidays, daily; weekends
only rest of year; tea room & a small museum; ♿ English Heritage

Compared with Housesteads and Vindolanda, the fort at Birdoswald is
more of a ruin and has fewer buildings, but its curtain wall, granaries
and gates are worthy of note – and, wow, what a view! Situated at the top
of a steep, wooded escarpment, the military station and the centuries-
old farmhouse look across several miles of undulating fields and
Roman Wall. The two granaries date to the early 3rd century but were
demolished and rebuilt in the following century. The wooden posts you
see show where a later timber hall once stood.

The 30 miles of Hadrian's Wall to the west of Birdoswald was originally
a turf construction but was later replaced with stone. You can see this
older **turf wall** by exiting the fort through the south gate and following
the footpath heading west. Plunging views of the **River Irthing**.

¶¶ FOOD & DRINK

Slack House Farm Scypen Café Gilsland CA8 7DB (half a mile north of Birdoswald
Roman Fort & 1½ miles west of Gilsland on the B6318) ℘ 016977 47351 ⌨ www.
slackhousefarm.co.uk ☺ Thu–Mon but phone ahead to check, especially during winter
♿. Cosy organic café on a tumbledown working farm and serving light lunches (soups,
scones, quiches), and a couple of evening dishes at 19.30. The cheese and yoghurt are
made on site to a 1688 recipe: the milk is taken straight from the herd of brown and
white Ayrshire cows in the nearby fields and immediately worked for up to five hours. The
cheese is then left to mature for up to six months. You can try a glass of the farm's creamy
unpasteurised milk or buy fresh dairy produce and organic meats to take away.

UPDATES WEBSITE

For additional online content, photos, accommodation reviews and more on Northumberland,
visit ⌨ www.bradtguides.com/northumberland.

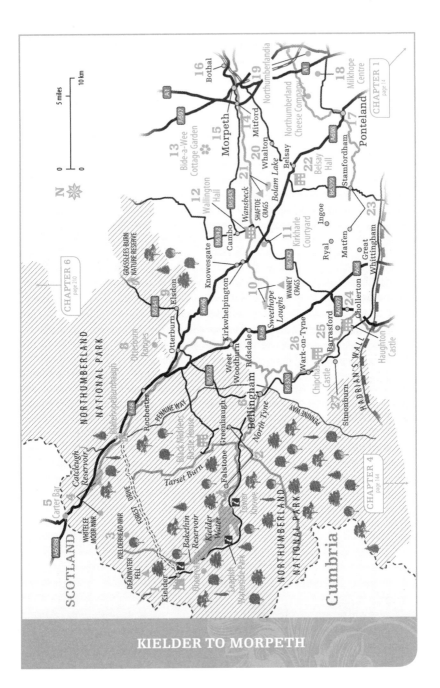

KIELDER TO MORPETH

5
KIELDER TO MORPETH

Five hundred years of cross-border warfare and clan fighting made this stretch of upland countryside a very dangerous place to live. Those lawless years ended after James I came to the English throne in 1603, but parts of **Redesdale** (from Kielder to Otterburn and as far north as Carter Bar on the Scottish border) still have a wild edge. Dark forests, lonely fells, rough farmland and Cheviot moors dominate the landscape, enticing ramblers and cyclists who savour solitude.

Kielder, England's largest forest, is a vast uninhabited expanse of conifer trees and moorland that merges with the Cheviot Hills on the western edge of Northumberland. Its remote location, hilly terrain and large reservoir make the area popular with mountain bikers, watersport enthusiasts, walkers and wildlife watchers.

"Northumberland's gentle corner is well known to Tynesiders, but less so to visitors."

Travelling east out of Redesdale, the hills collapse into the lowland farmland around **Ponteland** and **Morpeth** and you'll find yourself dipping in and out of well-to-do villages, tootling along green lanes and glimpsing country houses between the trees and hedgerows. Northumberland's gentle corner is well known to Tynesiders, but less so to visitors. Here you'll find two of the region's finest manor houses (Wallington and Belsay) and a number of picturesque villages and gardens. Cyclists will enjoy the country lanes connecting all these places.

GETTING AROUND

Unless you're on two wheels or don't mind tightly planning your holiday around the infrequent buses, you're going to need a **car** to access much of the countryside covered in this chapter. The only **train** station of help is at Morpeth (under 15 minutes from Newcastle).

i TOURIST INFORMATION

Bellingham TIC & Heritage Centre Hillside, NE48 2GR ✆ 01434 220616 ☺ end Mar–end Oct, daily (opens on Sun at 11.00) ♿. There's a café in an old train carriage here, and a small museum (pages 181–2).

Morpeth Chantry Bridge St, NE61 1PD ✆ 01670 623455 ☺ all year, Mon–Sat; Aug & Dec, daily ♿. Also houses a craft shop and Bagpipe Museum (pages 195–6).

Tower Knowe Kielder NE48 1BX ✆ 01434 240436 ☺ Easter–end Oct, daily ♿. Large lakeside visitor centre with a café and a shop stocked with crafts, walking maps and local books.

BUS

Reaching Morpeth is no problem as there are fairly regular services from Newcastle every day; accessing the likes of Kielder, Bellingham or the countryside around Ponteland and Otterburn is more difficult – but not impossible. For some services, you'll first need to get to Hexham or Morpeth by train or bus which is fairly straightforward from Newcastle.

Spirit Buses (⌂ www.spiritbuses.co.uk) reach the countryside around Morpeth and Rothbury (Rothbury–Elsdon (17) and Rothbury–Wallington Hall (18), for example), but buses run only a handful of times a week.

Newcastle–Morpeth (X14) At least five services a day Monday to Saturday
Newcastle–Hexham via Ponteland, Stamfordham and Matfen (74/74A) At least six services Monday to Sunday
Hexham–Kielder via Bellingham (880) Two services a day on Tuesday, Friday and Saturday, and eight services a day Monday to Saturday as far as Bellingham

CYCLING

Cycling in the countryside covered by this chapter is a joy: there are plenty of quiet back roads around the likes of Ponteland, Matfen and Belsay, and high passes with far-reaching views of moors and dense forest in Redesdale and Kielder. The **Rievers Route** (NCN Route 10) takes in the best of both landscapes on its 172-mile coast-to-coast journey from Whitehaven to Tynemouth, traversing Kielder Forest and stringing Bellingham together with Matfen, Stamfordham and Ponteland.

An exhilarating stretch of the **Pennine Cycleway** (NCN Route 68) links Elsdon, Bellingham and Wark Forest before continuing to Hadrian's Wall. Expect dense forests, remote farmland and river scenery.

An extensive network of bike-friendly trails, graded according to difficulty, criss-cross the whole of the **Kielder** area.

 CYCLE HIRE & REPAIRS

The Bike Place shops in Kielder village (NE48 1ER ℘ 01434 250457 ⊝ Apr–end Oct, daily; closed Tue & Wed at other times unless you've pre-booked bike hire) and Bellingham (1 King St, NE48 2AX ℘ 01434 220210 ⊝ Mon–Sat) ⬥ www.thebikeplace.co.uk. Mountain bike hire and repairs.

Kirkley Cycles Kirkley, Ponteland NE20 0AJ ℘ 01661 871094, 07734 471969 ⊝ daily. Repairs and bicycle equipment. Café (⊝ closed Mon).

Sims Cycle Workshop 7b Old Queens Head Yard, Morpeth NE61 1PY ℘ 01670 504376 ⊝ Mon–Sat. Repairs and equipment.

WALKING

As you travel from east to west through the central belt of Northumberland, the landscape changes considerably, from gentle farmland cosying up to stone villages in the lowlands to the remote moors, upland meadows and forests encountered further west around Redesdale. Walking in Redesdale is not all challenging though and there are a number of easy woodland and waterfall walks, some of which are described in these pages (see *Hindhope Linn* on page 175 and *Hareshaw Linn* on page 182). But if you really want to get away from it all, wax your boots and set off for **Kielderhead National Nature Reserve** (pages 178–9). Come prepared, as it is pretty wild, boggy and lonesome in a lot of places. You'll definitely need ✳ OS Explorer map OL42 to plot your route across the open – and often featureless – moors (there are few footpaths). If you don't want to hike out into the wilderness, you could scale **Deadwater Fell** from the Kielder Castle area, which is signed. A good set of lungs is essential for this climb to the top at 571 metres from where you can see all the way to the North Sea and even to Edinburgh's outlying hills.

The Pennine Way travels over remote moors on its course through the Cheviots and Redesdale, and skirts the eastern edge of Kielder before continuing south to Bellingham.

TAXIS

Bellingham Taxi ℘ 01434 220570
Broadway Cabs Ponteland ℘ 01661 822200
Just Taxis Morpeth ℘ 07957 495503

KIELDER'S FORESTS & LAKES

Solitude is not difficult to find in England's largest forest, which covers 230 square miles of upland terrain. As you drive into Kielder along the lakeside road, the tall Sitka spruce trees gather around you, and for a while the landscape takes on the appearance of the great Highland forests. The scenery is made all the more Scottish in character by vast areas of open moorland and the presence of ospreys and red squirrels.

Kielder is no untouched wilderness, however, this being a plantation forest surrounding the largest reservoir in northern Europe and supplying 25% of England's domestic timber. It may be a young landscape, created in the aftermath of World War I to replenish timber supplies, but it is still astonishingly scenic. The Campaign to Protect Rural England described Kielder as the most tranquil place in the country with the darkest night skies. If you'd like to be convinced of this, I recommend a dusk walk to the observatory. Halfway up is a large boulder by the Skyspace sculpture where you can sit looking out over the trees and reservoir. The chorus of song thrushes on spring and early summer evenings is quite something. As the light fades and only the silhouette of the hills and tree tops can be seen, the first planets appear. Stay here long enough and you will see more stars than you have seen anywhere else in England.

1 AROUND KIELDER WATER

🏠 **Kielder Water Lodges** (page 274)

Kielder's activity centres, information points, lodge accommodation and camp/caravan sites are dotted along the southern shores of the reservoir. The main hubs are Leaplish Waterside Park and Kielder Castle and village where you'll find a bike-hire station as well as the start of many walks and cycle rides.

BEFORE YOU SET OFF

Kielder is a remote place with very limited mobile phone signal, few places to eat and only one petrol station (at Kielder village). The only place to pick up food supplies is the Kielder Village Store (page 174), which also doubles as a post office and has Wi-Fi and a cash machine. Opening times of visitor centres are variable and limited in winter, so phone ahead to check (see opposite). Also see ⊘ www.visitkielder.com.

KIELDER'S TOURIST INFORMATION SITES

All three of Kielder's tourist information sites are on the south side of Kielder Water; the main centre is at **Tower Knowe** (page 166), which is staffed.

Leaplish Waterside Park (NE48 1BT ✆ 01434 251000 ☉ closed in Jan) is halfway along the lake. Many visitors stay here (it has a caravan park and lodges) and make use of the watersports on offer. Also here is the **Boat Inn Restaurant** (page 174), a **bird of**

prey centre (page 171), crazy golf, a small indoor swimming pool, and a shop selling outdoor clothes. Information point only.

Kielder Castle is the Duke of Northumberland's former hunting lodge and found at the western end of the reservoir. It is a popular starting point for trips into the forest and has an information point and a tea room (page 174). A bike-hire station, campsite and Kielder village are all nearby.

Outdoor activities at Kielder

A superb network of trails for cyclists, walkers, horseriders and wheelchair users is maintained by the Forestry Commission. One of the most accessible (and beautiful) is the **Lakeside Way**, which circumnavigates the reservoir in 27 miles. It lends itself well to **marathons** for obvious reasons (⊘ www.kieldermarathon.com). If you don't want to walk (eight to ten hours) or cycle (three to four hours) the whole way round, you can return using the Osprey Ferry (see box, page 171).

Off-road **cycling** and **mountain bike trails** range from family-friendly green routes such as the loop of the Bull Crag peninsula, to red routes like the Deadwater Trail (and its black route extension) that climbs to the summit of Deadwater at 1,900 feet. At the top you can see the Pentland Hills just south of Edinburgh and the Lake District. **Hire bicycles** at The Bike Place (page 167). Download routes from ⊘ www.forestry.gov.uk/kielder.

For **watersports**, contact the **Calvert Trust** (✆ 01434 250232 ⊘ www.calvert-trust.org.uk/kielder ☉ early Feb–end Nov) between Tower Knowe and Leaplish. This charity works closely with disabled children and their families but anyone can hire their canoes (instructor-led sessions only). The Merlin Brae Water Ski Club near Tower Knowe (✆ 01434 250037 ⊘ www.merlinbraewaterski.co.uk ☉ May–Sep, weekends only) offers waterskiing and wakeboarding lessons.

Fishing permits and basic equipment for novices are available to hire at Leaplish.

FOREST ART

Dotted around the reservoir and forest are over 20 unique sculptures inspired by Kielder's landscapes. A giant timber head, stone maze, huge rotating metal seats and a 'forest' of twinkling silver disks should give you an idea of what to expect. Pick up a printed guide at information centres or see ⊘ www.kielderartandarchitecture.com for locations.

Wave Chamber is a conical stone hut and camera obscura a mile west of the Hawkhope car park on the north side of Kielder Water (best visited in the afternoon and/or on a sunny day). Inside it's pitch black at first, but when your eyes adjust you'll see a real-time image of the reservoir projected on the floor. The building echoes the sound of the waves on the shore outside, adding to the experience.

Skyspace is reached on the track to the observatory and would not be out of place in a retreat centre. It's another round chamber (♿ wheelchair accessible) with a hole in the roof which draws your eye to the clouds (or stars) above; outside, a rock ledge provides a far-reaching view of the forests, moors and lakes.

Architecture as art is a reoccurring theme at Kielder but nowhere more so than at the **Kielder Observatory** (pages 172–3), and **Sky Den** – a tree house in the Calvert Trust complex, designed by TV's George Clarke. You can stay here if you book far enough in advance (⊘ www.canopyandstars.co.uk). Built above a wooded ravine, this hut is full of imaginative uses of space; most impressive is the eye-catching triangular bedroom that also doubles as a platform for star gazing when you open two side walls to reveal the night sky.

Gentle **walks** are plentiful around the reservoir and many routes encompass Kielder's public art works. A couple of recommended trails include the lakeside path to the Belling peninsula on the north shore of Kielder Water and the riverside walk from the picnic area at Matthew's Linn. For hills and remote scenery, visit Kielderhead NNR (pages 178–9).

"Gentle walks are plentiful around the reservoir and many routes encompass Kielder's public art works."

Back-country camping is permitted by the Forestry Commission on 17 sites around Kielder. There are no facilities; just a rough patch of grass to pitch up for a night. Campers must dig latrines. Those requiring more facilities should try the campsite near Kielder village (page 275). There are also eight **bothies**. For locations and to book the wild campsites or bothies, call the Forestry Commission (⊘ 01434 221012).

Birds of Prey Centre
Leaplish Waterside Park, NE48 1AX ✆ 01434 250400 ⌂ www.kwbopc.com ☺ closed
Christmas Day; demonstrations in summer, daily at 13.30 & 15.00; winter at 14.00 ♿

Right by the reservoir at Leaplish is this large centre with an impressive
collection of owls, vultures, hawks and, quite randomly, a couple of
pelicans. Outside flying demonstrations are held every day. Courses
include a two-hour session for children under 14 to learn about (and
try) flying a bird of prey. Private Hawk Walks last 1½ hours.

Kielder viaduct
Northumberland has an impressive number of viaducts owing to the
railway network that once ribboned across the region. Crossing over
the North Tyne near Bakethin Reservoir is this castellated viaduct
dating to 1862 that is well used by cyclists and walkers today but was
originally built to carry the now defunct Border Counties Railway on
its journey from the Tyne Valley to Scotland. It was engineered with
seven 'skew arches' that were individually shaped so the viaduct aligned
with the river.

Kielder Salmon Centre
Close to Kielder Castle, NE48 1HX ✆ 01434 250269 ☺ Apr–end Sep, daily ♿

Run by the Environment Agency, this salmon hatchery is the largest of
its type in England and Wales. Close to a million fish every year are
reared here to restock waterways in the north of England including the
Tyne – the top salmon river in England and Wales. Displays explain the
lifecycle of the fish and conservation of the rare freshwater pearl mussel,
also grown at the centre. In autumn you may be able to see the salmon
being 'stripped' of their eggs if you phone in advance.

OSPREY FERRY
✆ 01434 251000 ⌂ www.visitkielder.com ☺ end Mar–end Oct

Kielder Water's motor cruiser operates a 'hop on, hop off' service four times a day, roughly from 10.00 to 16.00 (phone or go to one of the visitor centres to check times). It's useful if you're doing a linear walk or cycle ride on the Lakeside Way (the ferry takes a limited number of bicycles, pushchairs and wheelchairs). It stops at the Belvedere art installation, Leaplish and Tower Knowe (buy your ticket at either of the latter two places).

WILDLIFE WATCHING

Ospreys, goshawks and tawny owls breed successfully at Kielder because of the remoteness of the forest and the protection from persecution afforded by the Forestry Commission. There's an organised **osprey viewing station at** Leaplish (see opposite) but to see one fishing try Bakethin Reservoir at the north end of Kielder Reservoir.

A large extent of Kielder is open **moorland** dominated by heather and sphagnum mosses and inhabited by waders and grouse. Dragonflies and damselflies are easily spotted hovering over damp ground where you may also see cranberry, bog asphodel, sundew and bog rosemary. One of the most accessible moorland wildlife habitats at Kielder is behind Tower Knowe. From the road, a trail climbs to the lake at **Falstone Moss Nature Reserve** (♀ NY707860).

In the conifer-dominated forests, look out for **crossbills** perched on the uppermost branches of trees, **roe deer** and **red squirrels**. At Kielder, our native squirrel has the upper hand over greys, making this their last stronghold (60% of the red squirrel population in England). They are not infrequently seen around the Kielder Castle entrance to Forest Drive and at Leaplish where there are hides. Chewed pine cones on footpaths are a sign that squirrels are about.

The Forestry Commission rangers and wildlife experts lead a number of **wildlife-watching trips** throughout the year, including dawn deer safaris, owl hunts, fungi forays, goshawk walks and badger watching (✆ 01434 250209 🖥 www.forestry.gov.uk/kielder).

Kielder Observatory

Signposted off the main road, a third of a mile south of Kielder Castle from the turn-off it's 2 miles uphill to the observatory ✆ 07805 638469 🖥 www.kielderobservatory.org; parking; toilets ♿

No need to be an astronomy buff to come here: the enthusiasm of the staff and volunteers at the observatory will soon have you hooked. Even without the astronomy bit, the experience of travelling to this remote place, the hilltop views at dusk and the building itself are worthy of the trek alone.

The striking timber structure juts out of the hillside on stilts; inside there are no windows, except for two roof shutters that become 'your eye into the universe' when they open to reveal a dark sky dusted with millions of stars. Two huge telescopes crank into gear as soon as the shutters open. They turn automatically on a room-sized circular track like sunflowers searching for the sun, except they are seeking planets of course.

Gary Fildes, the director of the observatory, gives gripping evening talks. He began the event I attended with this taster: 'We grow ambivalent to how violent the universe can be. About half an hour ago, a meteor the size of a double decker bus passed us just 45,000 miles away.' That was followed by a fascinating talk about the Northern Lights, peppered with facts and awe-inspiring stories about the solar system. About 30 of us (mostly people with no knowledge of astronomy) packed into the cosy lecture room ooh-ed and ah-ed at slides depicting various phenomenal astro events while Gary talked enthusiastically of solar winds, sun spots and chromal mass ejections. At one point he showed a film clip of the sun emitting flares. He paused it on a particularly violent burst and said casually: 'There's enough energy in that flare to power the USA for 100 million years.'

For all the latest on solar activity at Kielder and for information on talks and the hugely popular **Aurora nights** in autumn, visit the website.

Osprey Watch
Leaplish Waterside Park ☉ end May–early Aug, weekends

After a 200-year absence, ospreys nested at Kielder in 2009 and have continued to raise chicks in the tree tops ever since. Catching sight of one of these magnificent birds of prey pulling a trout from the lake is quite something. Volunteers at the Osprey Watch are equipped with telescopes to allow visitors to get close-up views of the birds on their nests.

THE NORTHERN LIGHTS

'When can you see the Northern Lights?' is a question the director of Kielder Observatory, Gary Fildes, is asked a lot. 'It all depends what ingredients you put into the mix – and having an active sun,' he responds. Kielder is the best place in England to watch the phenomenon because of the dark skies and its relative closeness to the North Pole. The A69 corridor is also good, says Gary, as long as you can see the northern horizon and you're away from city lights. If the conditions are right (clear skies and a strong solar storm) you may see curtains of flickering green light. Powerful storms peak every 11 years.

The strength of the sun's flares are indicated by something called the KP index: the higher the number, the more spectacular the light show will be. Go to ⬿ www.spaceweather. com to find out the KP index for a given night. 'KP5 and above is what you're looking for,' advises Gary. 'If you get a KP9,' he says animatedly, 'drop the baby'.

An informative blog (🖉 www.kielderospreys.wordpress.com) is full with information about the Kielder birds and their migratory routes.

Forest Drive

This pot-holed track traverses the upland landscape north of Kielder Water from Kielder Castle to Blakehopeburnhaugh in 12 slow-going miles. If you're in a hurry to reach the A68, this is not the best route; but if you're happy to trundle along enjoying the moorland and forest scenery and perhaps stopping for lunch or a walk, Forest Drive is for you. Halfway along, the Sitka spruce trees open up, permitting a long view into the hills with Kielderhead to the north and Emblehope Moor to the south.

On reaching **Blakehopeburnhaugh**, not the longest place name in England in case you are wondering (that is Cottonshopeburnfoot a mile north), there's a parking area where you'll find the starting points to a couple of lovely **woodland walks** (as well as access to the Pennine Way). **Hindhope Linn** is a magical waterfall in secluded woodland and is easily reached in just over a mile by following Blakehope Burn (see opposite).

Walking north from the car park, you can make a circuit to **The Three Kings**, a stone circle thought to be between 3,000 and 4,000 years old. Return by following the Pennine Way along the River Rede.

ℍ FOOD & DRINK

The café at **Tower Knowe** information centre (page 169) sells scones, sandwiches, soups and strong coffee, and has a lovely terrace overlooking the reservoir which catches the afternoon sun. **Duke's Pantry** at Kielder Castle (NE48 1ER 🖉 01434 250100 ☉ daily 🕭) serves breakfast and lunch (soups, quiches, sandwiches, lasagne, etc) and **The Boat Inn Restaurant** (NE48 1BT 🖉 01434 251000 ☉ closed Jan 🕭) at Leaplish Waterside Park serves standard pub lunches and dinners and caters to holiday makers. **The Angler's Arms** (Kielder village, NE48 1ER 🖉 01434 250072 ☉ daily 🕭), however, is more of a locals' pub.

There's a small **grocery and general store** in Kielder village (🖉 01434 250245 ☉ Mon–Sat & Sun mornings) but it's not particularly well stocked with fresh foods (you're better off shopping in Bellingham).

Without doubt, the best place for a hot lunch or dinner in the Kielder area is **The Pheasant Inn** at Stannersburn, east of Kielder Water (page 176).

✳ ✳ ✳

🚶 WATERFALL WALK: HINDHOPE LINN

❋ OS Explorer map OL42; start: car park at Blakehopeburnhaugh, ♀ NT784001; 2 miles return; difficulty: easy trail on a well-marked woodland path

Walk through the car park passing the toilet block on your right, go over a bridge and past a house and continue up a rough gravel track for almost no distance until you reach a signpost off to the right for Hindhope Linn.

From here it only takes 15 minutes or so to walk to the waterfall which is reached along a well-trodden woodland path above a gorge and through trees, bilberry and bracken.

Hindhope Linn's long spout plummets into a pool enclosed by trees and luxuriant ferns. It's a most enchanting setting. Return the same way.

* * *

2 FALSTONE, GREENHAUGH & THE TARSET VALLEY

🏠 **The Pheasant Inn** (page 274), **Tarset Tor Bunkhouse** (page 275), **Wild Northumbrian** (page 275), ▲ **Kielder Campsite** (page 275)

Kielder village is largely a modern settlement and of little appeal to visitors, but at the eastern end of the reservoir there are a couple of hamlets with good pubs, eateries and guesthouses, including **Falstone** which stands out for its tea room, peaceful setting by the North Tyne and children's playground. The enclosed green by the river is a tranquil spot with picnic benches. If you wander along its banks (see route description on page 177), you'll come to a contemporary sculpture called **Stell** (a local word for sheepfold) where you can take a seat on one of two stone 'sofas'.

SCENIC ROAD: GREENHAUGH TO OTTERBURN

If heading east out of Kielder in the direction of Otterburn, you could take the road signed for 'High Green' on approaching the junction at Gatehouse Farm (1½ miles north of Greenhaugh). Sheep frequently stray into the quiet single-track road which ascends quickly into remote countryside making for a spectacular journey across moorland. It's perfect for cycling, but you'll need good leg and lung muscles for the climb to 1,000 feet. Once you're at the highest point, roughly where the Pennine Way crosses the road, the terrain flattens out allowing you to enjoy the view of the Cheviots before free-wheeling into lowland farmland around Otterburn.

In the sheep-grazed hills a couple of miles northeast of Falstone, you come to **Greenhaugh**. It's not really on the way to anywhere, unless you're visiting nearby Black Middens bastle, so generally this hamlet, consisting of a stone street, friendly pub and farm selling fresh eggs by the roadside, goes unappreciated by visitors.

"There are some lovely walks around Greenhaugh including a three-mile-long circular trail which passes an upland hay meadow stuffed with great burnet, sweet-vernal grass, wood crane's-bill, eyebright, pignut and self-heal."

There are some lovely **walks** around Greenhaugh and the **Tarset Valley**, including a three-mile-long circular trail to Thorneyburn Lodge and church via the Tarset Burn which passes an upland hay meadow stuffed with great burnet, sweet-vernal grass, wood crane's-bill, eyebright, pignut and self-heal. To get there, head south of the village on the main road and take a track off to your right signed for Boughthill (♀ NY796870).

Nearby **Sidwood** (northwest of Greenhaugh) is a mixed woodland inhabited by red squirrels. In the same vicinity is a superb example of a **bastle house** (see box, page 181).

¶¶ FOOD & DRINK

Holly Bush Inn Greenhaugh NE48 1PW ♪ 01434 240391. This 300-year-old former drovers' inn (also providing B&B accommodation), is always full of friendly locals drinking real ale and having a good chinwag. Even in summer, the range fire burns strong. Food is served every evening from 17.00 (selection of meat and fish dishes; all pretty standard pub fare such as steak and ale pie). Folk musicians sometimes play in the small front room.

Old School Tearoom Falstone NE48 1AA ♪ 01434 240459 ◯ Easter–end Oct ♿ outside toilet & a low step into café. Former Victorian school selling cold and hot lunches. The tea room has free Wi-Fi and doubles as a small shop selling crafts and homemade jams, etc.

The Pheasant Inn Stannersburn NE48 1DD ♪ 01434 240382 ◯ daily, early afternoon for lunch & from 18.00 for dinner; Nov–Mar, closed Mon & Tue. One of the best pubs for Sunday lunch or dinner in Northumberland. Hearty traditional British mains and puddings made with local produce (the roast Northumberland lamb is particularly good). Great selection of local ales served in an unpretentious 400-year-old farmhouse with much rustic appeal (low beams, wooden furniture and old photographs of Redesdale life hanging on the walls). Be sure to book in advance.

✳ ✳ ✳

🚶 SHORT CIRCULAR WALK FROM FALSTONE

❋ OS Explorer map OL42; start: Old School Tearoom, ♀ NY723874; ¾ of a mile; difficulty: easy, flat trail along the river; refreshments at the Old School Tearoom & Blackcock Inn

This is an exceptionally easy family trail that takes in a lovely, shallow stretch of the River North Tyne where there are a few places for throwing pebbles and having a paddle.

From the tea room in the old school (opposite the Blackcock Inn), walk along the residential street until you meet the river. Turn left and follow a woodland path with the lazy River North Tyne on your right. When you emerge from the trees, the Stell sculpture is ahead (page 175).

Continue along the riverside, as far as a stone crossing. The path veers left along the edge of a meadow with Falstone in view dead ahead. Re-enter the village by a gate on to the road where a footpath leads to the tea room in about 200 yards.

✳ ✳ ✳

OTTERBURN, BELLINGHAM & THE HILLS

Rough are Redesdale's fells, rough are the grasslands and old fortified farmhouses, and rough is Redesdale's history. The scenery is desolate at times with only the occasional farm surrounded by fells and tussocky grasslands, a scattering of towns and hamlets and a few settlements guarding the Roman road into Scotland (the A68). As you head north towards the Scottish border at Carter Bar, the landscape becomes particularly moody and typically Cheviot-like with bulky hills muscling into one another and views for many miles around. Snow posts appear on roadside verges.

Further south around the Woodburns and Ridsdale, the sheep-grazed grasslands are interspersed with the odd heather slope, field of buttercups and Forestry Commission woodland. Lapwings tumble above damp meadows and the pitiful cry of curlews is always in earshot in spring. I once broke down on the road between Bellingham and West Woodburn and spent a very enjoyable hour watching a meadow filled with courting curlews. Other good places to break down on a sunny day in spring would be the lanes around Ridsdale and Elsdon and the high road over Whitley Pike from Greenhaugh to Otterburn (see box, page 175). Cyclists and Pennine Way walkers will enjoy many a bird-filled sky hereabouts.

REDESDALE'S BASTLES

Some of Northumberland's historic fortified farmhouses – or 'bastles' – have been converted into barns or more cheerful-looking cottages; a few stand on the loneliest of fells all ragged and ruinous and instilling a tremendous sense of the region's lawless past. Many of the best examples are found in Redesdale, an area made even more atmospheric by the occasional sound of artillery fire from Otterburn's army training camp.

If you are prepared to hunt around a bit with a map, there are several clusters of bastles in the countryside between Kielder and Elsdon. Two of the best preserved are **Woodhouses** (page 218) and **Black Middens** (♥ NY772900). The latter stands near Kielder's Tarset Burn (signposted off the quiet lane from Greenhaugh to Comb). Black Middens is memorable for its external stone steps leading to the first floor entrance and holes in the doorway where a drawbar used to secure the opening. You'll find a good few bastles around here (an English Heritage board by the roadsides shows you their locations). Continuing north up the Tarset Burn, you come to **Boghead Bastle** (♥ NY761910) at the bottom of a slope by Highfield Burn, which has a duct above the doorway that enabled those sheltering on the first floor to douse the entrance in water if it was set alight by raiders.

On the road between Bellingham and West Woodburn, there are a couple of restored bastles among farm buildings at **Hole** and **Low Leam**. A pull-in area just east of Low Leam farm promotes access to the isolated bastle of the same name.

The striking ruin of **Shittleheugh Bastle** (♥ NY869950) stands in open countryside marked by medieval ridge and furrow fields a couple of miles northwest of Otterburn (reached by public right of way 400 yards south of Elishaw on the A696). Only the original ground-floor doorway and striking gable ends remain intact. The walls stand to full height and look sculptural against the sky.

3 KIELDERHEAD NATIONAL NATURE RESERVE

A wide, black upland region, which looks wintry even in the sunshine ... The song of the lark would be out of place here; the curlew's cry harmonises with the scene.

Walter White *Northumberland and the Border*, 1859

North of Kielder Reservoir, an extensive area of moorland stretches north to the Scottish border. Thigh-high heather, bracken and dwarf shrubs like bilberry cover the slopes, but as with the Cheviot landscape elsewhere, there are also plenty of peat bogs, gullies and squelching moss-covered hummocks to trip up, over and down. I once read a description of a 13-mile hike across those moors likened to 'a week in the Burmese jungle'. I wouldn't say the walking was quite that arduous, but you'll certainly want sturdy waterproof boots and gaiters.

I should add that the terrain, while rough underfoot, is also dramatic and beautiful: all those swelling hills creating endless coloured folds, clouds rolling fast across big skies and the sun picking out individual slopes to bathe in light.

"Much of Kielderhead is designated a Site of Special Scientific Interest (SSSI) for its moorland flora and breeding birds."

Though undeniably lonesome (don't expect to meet many – if any – fellow walkers up here), these moors are full of **wildlife** surprises: the sudden appearance of a merlin pursuing a meadow pipit, a wild Cheviot goat, exquisite day-flying emperor moths skimming the heather, and an expanse of cloudberries, their orange fruits ripe to eat.

Much of Kielderhead is designated a Site of Special Scientific Interest (SSSI) for its moorland flora and breeding birds which include golden plover, dunlin, red grouse, curlew and even ring ouzel. Cottongrasses, sphagnum mosses, bog asphodel and mountainous shrubs like bilberry grow in abundance. Also look out for the insectivorous sundew (see box, page 216) where it's mossy and wet. Downy birch and rowan trees crowd the sides of secluded waterways hidden in ravines.

4 WHITELEE MOOR NATIONAL NATURE RESERVE & CATCLEUGH RESERVOIR

Heather slopes, wooded cleughs, peat bogs and tussocky pastures characterise the hilly ground all the way to the Scottish border. Burns run off the fells feeding Catcleugh Reservoir and the River Rede that winds its way through the grasslands. Otters swim here as they do in most rivers within Northumberland National Park.

Catcleugh's sheet of water enclosed by trees provides an eye-catching vista. The reservoir was created in the late 19th century to supply water to Tyneside and, as with Sweethope Loughs further south, ospreys sometimes help themselves to trout. There is public access across the dam: from the southern end, you can follow Chattlehope Burn up to Girdle Fell and Chattlehope Spout. It's hard-going with so much wiry heather underfoot, but the view of Catcleugh Reservoir and surrounding forests at the top will stay in the memory.

5 CARTER BAR

Scotland bursts upon the traveller coming over the brow of the hill at Carter Bar. From the lofty vantage point at 1,400 feet above sea level you can see the Lammermuir Hills to the north. There's a large parking area where many people stop to take in the view and stretch their legs. A path to the west winds up boggy Carter Fell and into Whitelee Moor National Nature Reserve. From here, Catcleugh Reservoir comes into sight.

6 BELLINGHAM

🏠 **Boat Farm** (page 274) ⛺ **Demesne Farm** (page 275), **Boe Rigg Campsite & Bunkhouse** (page 275)

Land Rovers parked outside Bellingham's (pronounced 'Belling-jum') Country Store and wagons passing with livestock should tell you that this small, unassuming town cradled by hills caters for the farming community. It's a pleasant enough place to stop for lunch and a good base for exploring Kielder Forest (ten miles away) and Redesdale's lonesome hills (behind you).

St Cuthbert's Church is hidden somewhat at the western end of the High Street past the town hall (the building with a distinctive green clock tower) and behind the Black Bull Hotel. It dates in part from the 13th century and has a highly unusual stone roof. It survived the lawless centuries that followed its construction unlike many other medieval buildings that burned down when reivers were in town. Inside, you'll see the impressive barrel vaulted roof spanning the nave in 15 stone ribs.

"St Cuthbert's Church survived the lawless centuries that followed its construction unlike many other medieval buildings that burned down when reivers were in town."

On exiting the church, a few steps to your right is a curious curved tomb called the **Lang Pack** which is associated with a legend set in nearby Lee Hall. One night in 1723 the manor was left in the charge of servants who were visited by a pedlar who wanted to stay overnight. Permission was refused but the servants agreed that he could store his large, heavy pack inside. After the pedlar left, they were alarmed to see the bag moving so they shot at it with a pistol (as was the way in Redesdale back then). On opening the bag they found the body of a man wearing a whistle. Suspecting a raid, the servants armed themselves before blowing the whistle to lure the dead man's accomplices. Sure enough, the gang appeared and were swiftly shot dead. Come morning their bodies had disappeared. The body in the pack is buried in the churchyard.

Outside the churchyard and reached via a path to the east of the Black Bull, is **St Cuthbert's Well** – a stout pant – that is not as old as it looks (probably 18th century) though the cover may be medieval.

One of the oldest and largest **agricultural shows** (⊘ www.bellinghamshow.co.uk) in Northumberland is held just outside Bellingham on the bank holiday at the end of August. Expect all the usual traditional sheep and dog shows, folk music, food tents and plenty of activities for children including pony rides, face-painting and so on.

Bellingham Heritage Centre

Woodburn Rd, NE48 2DG ✆ 01434 220050 ⊘ www.bellingham-heritage.org.uk ◷ end Mar–end Oct, daily; café (page 182); ♿

In Bellingham's old train station yard is this unexpected museum (adjoined to the **tourist information centre**) that chronicles the upland industries and communities of bygone years. It houses displays on the Border Reivers and relics from the days of coal mining and traditional upland farming. There's also a photographic exhibition and large display of old cameras (quite random but intriguing nonetheless). The old smithy dates to 1834 and comes from nearby Stannersburn. It was formerly

BASTLES HOUSES & TOWERS

Murder, theft and arson were enough of a persistent threat in the borderlands during the 16th and 17th centuries to necessitate the construction of defensive farmhouses. These bastle houses are dotted all over Northumbria and the Scottish Borders, providing a visual reminder of the centuries of reiver raids.

Bastles are essentially two-storey dwellings with hugely thick walls and tiny upstairs windows. If an attack was feared, livestock was rounded up and locked in the ground floor before families climbed on to the second storey, sometimes by ladder or rope which was then pulled inside. See page 178 for details of some of Redesdale's prominent bastle houses.

Tower houses (sometimes called pele towers) are generally understood in Northumberland to be tall, fortified structures of several storeys and often with a battlement. Unlike bastle houses they are associated with the estates of prominent landowners. As well as protecting inhabitants, towers served as lookout points and warning stations where beacons would be lit to alert locals of approaching invaders.

the workshop of an elderly man who had worked as a blacksmith for many decades. One afternoon in the 1970s, he locked up and decided not to return. Those who run the museum did a commendable job of rebuilding it exactly how he left it, still with a couple of unopened bottles of beer among his tools of which there are around 500.

¶¶ FOOD & DRINK

A couple of tea rooms and pubs serving food dot Bellingham's centre, including the **Cheviot Hotel** (Front St, NE48 2AU ℘ 01434 220696), which is a popular inn with a town-facing beer garden serving pub food and real ales. Between Bellingham and Kielder, there's a pleasant bistro off the main road at **Boe Rigg Campsite** (page 275).

Carriage Tea Room Woodburn Rd, NE48 2DG (next to the tourist information and heritage centre, ¼ mile east of Bellingham town centre) ℘ 01434 221151 ⊙ closed Christmas Day ♿ on entering the carriage you must be able to transfer into a special narrow wheelchair, otherwise there's an outside table for disabled customers. Take a seat in the 1957 maroon and yellow carriage and enjoy an inexpensive sandwich or scone and a cup of tea.

Fountain Cottage Tea Room Front St, NE48 2DE ⊙ daily ♿. At the far north end of Bellingham's main street (B6320) is an old workhouse converted into a cheerful café with outside tables serving a good selection of cakes and savoury lunches. Friday evening is fish and chips night. The small building next door, incidentally, was once a mortuary.

Hareshaw Linn

Bellingham town centre, reached by following the riverside path/road opposite the police station; car park at the trail entrance

The **walk** to this 30-foot-high waterfall in Bellingham is one of the most picturesque in Northumberland National Park. After an unremarkable first half mile to a picnic spot by the river (passing an old ironworks dam), the trail delves deeper into woodland, criss-crossing Hareshaw Burn many times. Continuing upriver, the trees become older and more heavily clothed in luxuriant mosses, jingling streams fall off the steep-sided gorge and huge boulders pile in the river. When I last walked this trail in spring, all the usual woodland plants including primroses, wood sorrel and dense patches of wild garlic were in flower. Nuthatches, wrens and tree-creepers hid behind the trunks of oaks as I passed and I caught sight of a buzzard through the trees.

The waterfall is one of the most pleasing kind, not a tunnel of water but a cascade spraying in every direction on hitting rocks before entering a dark plunge pool.

It takes a couple of hours to walk to Hareshaw Linn and back but it's easy to navigate (no map needed) and very family friendly. You can't walk beyond the falls, so no chance of going too far. Children can be willed onwards by the promise of a money tree. Perhaps that's building it up too much: it's actually a stump decorated with coins, guarded by a huge fir next to one of the bridges.

7 OTTERBURN

Otterburn's medieval tower, coaching inns, historic mill and convenient location near the junction of two major roads (the A696 and A68) should make it an obvious stopping place for travellers

THE BATTLE OF OTTERBURN

Cowards had no place there, but heroism reigned with goodly feats of arms; for knights and squires were so joined together at hand strokes, that archers had no place on either party.

J Froissart *The Ancient Chronicles*, 1388

One of the most well recorded of all the Anglo–clashes in Northumberland is the Battle of Otterburn, famously fought by moonlight on 19 August 1388. It ended with a victory for the Scottish army, despite the death of their leader, the Earl of Douglas, and the capture of the legendary Henry 'Hotspur' Percy of Alnwick Castle and his sibling. The battle is immortalised in a couple of ballads: one English, *The Ballad of Chevy Chase*, the other Scottish. *The Battle of Otterbourne* contains the following verses:

It fell about the Lammas tide,
When the muir-men win their hay,
The doughty Douglas bound him to ride
Into England, to drive a prey ...
When Percy wi' the Douglas met,
I wat he was fu' fain;
They swakked their swords till sair they swat,
And the blood ran down like rain.

The location of the battlefield is not precisely known but the best consensus is that it took place just west of Otterburn, an area that still retains its open character. **Percy's Cross** stands in a small plantation by the side of the A696 and is thought to mark the spot where the Earl of Douglas was killed. It was already of some age when it was moved a couple of hundred yards in 1777.

BORDER REIVERS

They were cruel, coarse savages, slaying each other as the beasts of the forest; and yet they were also poets who could express in the grand style the inexorable fate of the individual man and woman, and infinite pity for all the cruel things which they none the less perpetually inflicted upon one another. It was not one ballad-maker alone, but the whole cut-throat population who felt this magnanimous sorrow, and the consoling charm of the highest poetry.

G M Trevelyan *The Middle Marches*, 1914

The border country from the late medieval period until the mid 17th century was the Wild West of Britain: a violent place marked by clashes between rival kinship groups in Scotland, Northumbria and parts of Cumbria who had greater ties to family groups than to country. These allegiances provided a level of security to the border people who had suffered centuries of Anglo-Scottish warfare.

Some of the most notorious families were the Armstrongs, Elliots, Forsters, Dodds, Milburns and Robsons – surnames which remain some of the most common in the North East today. Reivers rode on horseback wearing steel bonnets and armed with swords, and travelled across the Cheviot Hills raiding farmsteads, stealing livestock from one another and seeking retribution.

Incidentally, it is because of the Border Reivers that we have the words 'bereaved' and 'blackmail'. The former speaks for itself but the etymology of 'blackmail' is not as clear. The word is thought to originate in the border region (also used further north) where payments and goods were offered in return for immunity from raids.

A culture of story-telling developed in the hills in which tragic love stories, raids and clashes were recalled in song. Recital of melancholic border ballads died out during more peaceful times in the latter half of the 17th century, but some were recorded before they were lost completely; most famously by Sir Walter Scott in his *The Minstrelsy of the Scottish Border*. There's an extract of *The Battle of Otterbourne* in the box on page 183.

heading into the national park, but if I'm honest, it's one of those places that sounds a bit better than it actually is. Certainly Otterburn has seen brighter days now that the pubs have closed and the village festival is no more.

The most prominent historic attraction is **Otterburn Tower**, now the (questionable) four-star Otterburn Castle Country House Hotel, a hugely impressive castellated manor house in landscaped grounds founded in the years after the Norman Conquest. The oldest part is the

14th-century tower which is incorporated into the 19th-century manor and is now an elegant wood-panelled dining room.

The Otterburn Trail (pick up a leaflet in the Otterburn Mill) is a fairly easy **walk** (just a few miles) that takes you in a loop around the hills north of the village and encompasses the **Iron Age hillfort** at Fawdon Hill. You'll enter the wooded banks of Otter Burn, which is indeed home to otters.

Otterburn Mill

Otterburn NE19 1JT ✆ 01830 521002 ◈ www.otterburnmill.co.uk ◷ daily ♿

'The Queen has now made a selection from the patterns of Otterburn Tweed, which you kindly sent ... '. So began a letter from Buckingham Palace penned to the Otterburn Mill in 1939 pertaining to blankets for the young princesses, Margaret and Elizabeth. Since then orders for Otterburn Pram Rugs from the 18th-century mill have not stopped. The main difference now is that the chequered fabric (pastel pink, yellow and blue) is no longer produced at Otterburn, production having ceased in 1976. Today, alongside woollen goods for sale, you'll find budget outdoor clothing in the large former weaving sheds, a café and displays of old machinery.

🍴 FOOD & DRINK

There's not a great choice in Otterburn; your best bet is probably the café/restaurant at **Otterburn Mill** (see above) or the **Border Reiver newsagents** (NE19 1NP ✆ 01830 520682 ◷ daily until 15.00) which doubles as a café selling all-day breakfasts, soups, quiches and scones.

8 OTTERBURN RANGES

Forget for a moment that this open moorland is England's second-largest live firing range and focus instead on the fact that it is also one of the most unspoiled stretches of countryside in Northumberland covering 90 square miles and one-fifth of the national park. The ranges are often closed to the public (during training exercises) but the rest of the time (when red flags are not flying) you can enjoy some of the most remote moors and roads in England (access permitted for cars). This is great cycling country with open views all around and dead quiet roads.

It's fitting that this military training camp should be sited in an area once well known to Roman soldiers. There are no longer Roman forts

ACCESS ON THE OTTERBURN RANGES

The Controlled Access Area is roughly southwest of the River Coquet to the River Rede/A68 at Byrness & as far south as Otterburn; when red flags are flying it means you must not enter the zone ☺ Firing Times are published on the Ministry of Defence's website (✆ 01830 520569 ✎ www.gov.uk/ government/publications/otterburn-firing-times) & when red flags are not flying (usually 1 weekend every 6 weeks & every day between mid-Apr & mid-May), visitors must keep to the military roads & waymarked paths; there are no access restrictions on Ministry of Defence land north of the River Coquet.

here but you can visit the earthworks which mark where **Roman camps** housed squads during the construction of the Roman road, Dere Street. The most easily accessible is **Brigantium** at High Rochester (take a track from Rochester, on the A68) where Roman masonry remains *in situ*. The earthen walls of **Chew Green camp** (♀ NT787084) are seen where the Roman road crosses the Scottish border.

Archaeological remains also include prehistoric burial cairns, lost medieval villages, bastle houses and lime kilns. One of the most interesting of the 75 Scheduled Monuments on the ranges is the **World War I practice trench** near Silloans, which brings to mind those at Ypres and the Somme (♀ NT836027; site not marked on OS Explorer maps). Access is from Bushman's Road but you must be escorted to the site (groups should speak to the Ministry of Defence on the number above to arrange a visit). Armchair travellers may like to take a trip on Google Earth to see a birds-eye view of the trenches which appear as deep zig-zagging fissures in the ground.

This vast area has not been improved or farmed since it came under the management of the Ministry of Defence in 1911, which explains why the waterways and grassland habitats are in such good condition and **wildlife** thrives. Otters, black grouse and merlin are some of the more unusual upland inhabitants. Curlews, lapwings and skylarks will certainly accompany walkers in spring.

9 ELSDON

It's hard to find in Redesdale, or anywhere in Northumberland National Park, a more appealing village with such an intriguing past. Descending into Elsdon, your first impression is of a very old settlement hiding away below hills rippled with the tell-tale signs of medieval farming. At its centre, Elsdon boasts a large open green surrounded by 18th-century cottages, three inns and a church of great antiquity. Two of the pubs have changed use but still retain interesting features like the rustic sculpture of Bacchus sitting on a barrel above the doorway of the old Bacchus Inn (east side of the green).

Guarding the village to the north is one of Northumberland's most intact medieval **towers**, once the residence of successive church vicars. It dates from the 14th century. There's no public access, but visitors are permitted to walk some way up the drive to inspect its mighty walls.

The other notable defensive structure in Elsdon is a Norman **motte and bailey castle** consisting of two large earthen ramparts that rear over the northeast corner of the village. Architectural writer Pevsner describes it as the best example of its type in Northumberland.

St Cuthbert's Church

There are two churches really worth visiting in Redesdale: one at Bellingham (page 180), the other at Elsdon. Both reflect in their walls those unstable times of cross-border fighting. As you enter Elsdon's 14th-century church, notice the deep grooves in the pillar on the left; they are said by Tomlinson in his aforementioned guide to have been

COCK-FIGHTING, BULL-BAITING & PAGAN TRADITIONS

'In consequence of the long isolation of the village amid moors and morasses, remote from the enlightening influences of civilisation', wrote Tomlinson in his 1888 *Comprehensive Guide to Northumberland*, 'many pagan customs and superstitions were observed till within a very short time ago. The Midsummer bonfires, through which cattle were driven to protect them from disease were burning only a few years ago on Elsdon green – their origin, in the worship of Baal, being forgotten.'

Other bygone traditions include cock-fighting and bull-baiting. At the southern end of the green is a pinfold which looks similar to a sheepfold but was used to house stray livestock until their owners paid a fee for their release. My Victorian guidebook notes that Elsdon's **village fête** at the end of August has 'long been obsolete'. Well, the tradition has been revived since 1888; it's once again a popular family event drawing crowds to the bunting-decorated green during the August Bank Holiday.

made 'by the fierce bowmen of Redesdale in sharpening their arrows before leaving church'. It's an evocative image and an intriguing tale that seems to have endured. At least, the church-going locals I spoke to had heard the story.

A more shocking discovery was made in the 19th century when a **mass grave** containing a large number of human skeletons was unearthed by the north wall of the nave. They were all young men and boys and were thought to be Englishmen who fell during in the notorious Battle of Otterburn in 1388 (see box, page 183).

Look in the vestry and you'll see a cabinet containing **three horse skulls** discovered in the spire above the bell turret during restoration work in the late 19th century. The animals may have been sacrificed as part of a Pagan ceremony during the construction of an early sacred building, but whatever the reason they ended up in the belfry, they are certainly a very unusual feature in an English church.

Elsdon's grim side

Besides horses' heads, bull-baiting, cock-fighting and a mass grave of fallen warriors, Elsdon's darker past is revealed just outside of the village on a lonely hillside by the side of an unclassified road to Morpeth. At Steng Cross stands **Winter's Gibbet** (or 'Winter's Stob' as Northumbrians used to call it) – a gibbet with a wooden head hanging from its post. My aunt, who lives nearby, tells me that the head periodically goes missing. It marks the spot (the gibbet is not original) where the body of William Winter was hanged in chains following his execution in Newcastle in 1791 for the murder of a local woman.

SCENIC ROAD: KIRKWHELPINGTON TO ELSDON

If travelling into Redesdale from the south by car, you'll probably take the A68 or the A696. The latter is initially unremarkable – a straight passage north with green fields all around – but after Kirkwhelpington, you gain altitude and the scenery becomes more typical of the Northumberland uplands with heather moors, forests and a sense of remoteness.

Five miles on and the road reaches its highest point at around 1,000 feet. From here, you gain an unbeatable view of the Simonside Hills and distant Cheviots. If making this journey in August, you will be blown away by the colour of the hills when the heather comes into flower, transforming the landscape from green and yellow to shocking pink.

Incidentally, she was killed at The Raw, an unmistakable bastle house on a farm three miles north of Elsdon (visible from the farm track).

The superstitious folk of Elsdon are said to have rubbed wood chips from the gibbet on their teeth as a cure for toothache in the 19th century.

⅋ FOOD & DRINK

Impromptu Café NE19 1AA ✐ 01830 520389 ☉ closed Thu. You can be sure of a cheerful welcome in this great little cyclists' café (also a visitor information point) that has been run by the same couple since 1980. It's housed in the old school house near the pele tower and is identified by the bicycles stacked outside.

❋ ❋ ❋

⅍ HIKE & A DIP IN DARDEN LOUGH

❋ OS Explorer map OL42; start: layby at Grasslees Burn Nature Reserve, 3 miles northeast of Elsdon on the B6341, ♥ NY958981; 4 miles; difficulty: fairly strenuous climb over rough terrain; refreshments at Elsdon

Choose a hot day in August to do this circular hill walk and enjoy the heather slopes in flower and a plunge in the mountain tarn at the top. The key is to strip off (there's rarely anyone around) as soon as you reach the lough and before you've cooled down, which doesn't take long on this exposed hillside. On the hike you'll be accompanied by mountain bumblebees (black with a red bum), meadow pipits and red grouse the whole way. It's a stiff ascent but the route is fairly easy to navigate by following wooden marker posts. Allow around 2½ hours. You'll need stout waterproof boots as the terrain is very uneven and boggy in parts.

Set foot from the Grasslees layby and follow the signpost downhill to Grasslees Burn and then begin your climb through bracken and heather. There are a couple of sections where the path leads away from the fence line, but for the most part, follow it continuously to Darden Lough. Squelch on through Miller's Moss, about halfway to the lough, with its large cushion mosses and head for the post on top of a hillock to your right. The heather is deep and bushy and reached the top of my thighs in places.

The ground flattens as you approach the dark, remote mountain lake. Roughly 500 yards to the east is a smaller tarn which also makes a good plunge pool.

After your swim and with the tarn on your left, follow a fence line uphill to Darden Pike cairn where you can see the craggy Simonside Hills and the distant Cheviots. Follow the marker posts downhill. The trail swings eastwards before rejoining the path you climbed on the outward walk.

❋ ❋ ❋

10 SWEETHOPE LOUGHS & THE WANNEY CRAGS

Sweethope Loughs (NE19 2PN, west of Knowesgate, signed off the A68 ✆ 01434 618579), essentially one large trout-filled lake, is largely hidden out of sight by a ring of conifer trees, but a public right of way around the lake's southern edge affords views of the blue expanse. Ospreys occasionally help themselves to fish on their way to Africa in September but humans must obtain a **fishing** permit to take advantage of one of the best trout lakes in Northumberland.

Of most interest to walkers, climbers and birdwatchers will be the nearby **Wanney Crags** rising above Sweethope Loughs to the north (reached by a footpath from the single-track road along the northern edge of Sweethope Loughs (♀ NY944829), or by rough track connecting to the A68, a half-mile south of Ridsdale (♀ NY907836); look out for the Forestry Commission sign '**Fourlaws**' at both entrances). At the top of Great Wanney, find yourself a rock to sit on and enjoy Redesdale's countryside unfolded before you with the Simonsides and Cheviots both in sight.

'High o'er wild Wanny's lofty crest, where the raven cleaves the cloud', begins an old local ballad. Ravens inhabit the crags here to this day. They try and nest every year but often give up when rock climbers take advantage of the first fine days of the year in early spring. For this reason, choose where you sit carefully so as not to disturb the birds (and wait until later on in summer to go climbing if you can). You may see their acrobatic courtship display during which the male rolls on to his back mid-flight to impress his mate. Peregrines sometimes swoop by, and goshawks and other birds of prey are not uncommon.

North of Great Wanney, a wide track winds through heather and woodlands towards the A68. Keep to the track as it passes between Aid Moss and Aid Crag and avoid the rough public footpaths from March to August so as not to disturb nesting birds. On summer evenings you might be fortunate enough to hear nightjars close to this track (try the area around ♀ NY918836).

ALONG THE RIVER WANSBECK: KIRKWHELPINGTON TO MORPETH

Welcome to Capability Brown country. The celebrated garden designer was born at Kirkharle and lived here until he was 23. The landscape for miles around is at times like a vignette of an 18th-century country estate where undulating meadows, waterways, ponds and ancient broad-leaved trees come together to picturesque effect as if planned by Brown himself.

The River Wansbeck flows off Redesdale's craggy hills and into lowland farmland around the rose-filled village of **Kirkwhelpington** before passing through the National Trust's **Wallington** estate. Good cycling lanes thronged with wildflowers lead to **Middleton** and **Hartburn**. The former has a pub, the Ox Inn; the latter is just a very picturesque hamlet of stone about a cross and church.

From **Mitford** to **Morpeth**, road and river intertwine through woodland making for a memorable journey with the Wansbeck dancing through the trees. The B6343 crosses the river several times by way of old stone bridges, the last being particularly eye-catching with its huge sandstone blocks.

11 KIRKHARLE COURTYARD

NE19 2PE, midway between Ponteland and Otterburn and just off the A696 ℘ 01830 540362 🖉 www.kirkharlecourtyard.co.uk ◷ daily; café; ♿

You'll find jewellery and furniture makers, sculptors and painters based in a clutch of converted stone barns here, as well as displays relating to Capability Brown's garden designs (this being his birthplace), a bakery and a children's playground. It's worth coming here just for the **café** (cream teas, cakes, sandwiches, soups, etc) situated in a peaceful corner of the site where sparrows chatter about the outside tables.

It's a short ten-minute **walk** along the road from Kirkharle's main car park to the 14th-century **St Wilfrid's Church** where Brown was baptised. If you want to walk further, take the cross-country route to Kirkwhelpington, a pretty village two miles north. The walk starts from the **Loraine Monument** next to Kirkharle Courtyard and is described on a nearby board. The memorial stone and information panel will tell you everything you might (not) want to know about how Robert Loraine met his death in this field in 1483.

12 WALLINGTON HALL

🏠 **Shieldhall** (page 274)

Cambo NE61 4AR ℘ 01670 773600 ◷ gardens & cafés open all year, house open early Mar–early Nov (closed Tue) ♿ National Trust

Four grinning dragon heads greet you on the approach to Wallington – one of the great country houses of Northumberland. You could easily spend most of a day at this National Trust property exploring the rooms,

LANCELOT 'CAPABILITY' BROWN (1716–83)

The great 18th-century landscape gardener lived at Kirkharle until he was in his twenties, and went to school in nearby Cambo. A plan for the landscaping of Kirkharle was found in the 1980s and is almost certainly Brown's work. The design was never realised – until 2010. It will be some years before the trees around the pond mature, but already the lakeside trail is a pleasant place for a wander where you can watch house martins catching airborne insects. Brown went on to create many of the great country estates in England, including Hulne Park at Alnwick Castle.

gardens and woodlands, and playing games in the grassy courtyard. Next to the Palladian clock tower is a café with outside tables, a shop selling plants and herbs and a large enclosed green where children can freely run around while parents watch from the terrace.

The late 17th-century house has many memorable rooms and features: the Italianate plasterwork of the drawing and dining rooms, the fine collection of Victorian dolls' houses, a cabinet containing 3,000 toy soldiers, wall tapestries and a complete kitchen dating to the 1900s with the largest dresser you'll see anywhere.

The **Central Hall** was styled on an Italian Renaissance *palazzo* and is arranged over two levels with arcades painted with ferns and flowers. Guests used to enjoy high tea here. They were surrounded by eight large pre-Raphaelite paintings still hanging today and which were all created by William Bell Scott in the mid 19th century. His brief was to 'illuminate the history and worthies of Northumbria' and so we see depictions of the Industrial Revolution on Tyneside, the construction of Hadrian's Wall, and Danes invading from the sea. In some, the action in the background tells the story, as in the *Grace Darling* painting.

"The Central Hall was styled on an Italian Renaissance palazzo *and is arranged over two levels with arcades painted with ferns and flowers."*

Today, if you want to enjoy a cream tea in the house, follow the sound of gramophone music to a quaint **tea room** (☺ Wed–Mon afternoons) furnished with 1940s chairs and tables to reflect Wallington's wartime links when evacuees lived in the house.

Wallington's **walled garden** is reached at the end of a short walk through woodland and past an ornamental pond. A thin stream trickles through the green oasis landscaped with terraces of plants and shrubs. A kiosk serves ice cream and drinks at the far end of the garden.

A longer **walk** is enjoyed by descending through woodland to the River Wansbeck (native white-clawed crayfish live in the water and red squirrels in the trees). The river eventually flows under Northumberland's most elegant **bridge** – a Palladian crossing on the southern edge of the estate. Wait until you see it bathed in evening light.

Cambo

Cambo, the old estate village of Wallington, lies a short distance north of the Hall, whiling away the years at the top of a hill. It boasts nothing more than a couple of rows of stone houses, a 16th-century pele tower, a church and a hilltop view of tumbling farmland, but a hamlet quainter than this is hard to find. Ox-eye daisies, roses and sweet peas fill the cottage gardens and herbs drape over the stone walls adding to Cambo's English country village appeal.

At the north end of the village is the 19th-century parish **church** which overlooks open countryside. A young Lancelot 'Capability' Brown used to walk across these fields (those to the west of the village) every day on his three-mile journey from Kirkharle to Cambo's school house. Apparently one former schoolmaster (after Brown's time) kept an annotated record of former alumni which is decoded by the following rhyme:

> The names distinguish'd by a star
> Were the most docile by far;
> And those with equi-distant strokes
> Were secondhanded sort of folks;
> But where you find the letter B
> A humdrum booby you will see;
> And where an exclamation's set,
> The rascals went away in debt.

Herterton Gardens

Cambo NE61 4BN ✆ 01670 774278 🖉 www.herterton.co.uk ☉ early Apr–end Sep; occasionally at other times

In 1976, Marjorie and Frank Lawley began creating out of derelict farmland five distinctive gardens in the one-acre grounds of their 16th-century house. They have not stopped digging, cultivating and clipping topiary bushes since. Interestingly, the Lawleys decided to bring back the formal gardens once seen in many country estates before the trend for open landscaped parklands. To that end, they consulted Elizabethan gardening books including William Lawson's *A Country Housewife's Garden* (1619), written with domestic gardeners in the North East in mind.

Among the five plots are a formal, physic, flower and nursery garden. Memorable stone features include a huge urn thought to be Roman and the old arches of a granary which shelter two statues (a falconer and a Viking) said to have come from Alnwick Castle.

13 BIDE-A-WEE COTTAGE GARDEN & NURSERY

Stanton, near Netherwitton NE65 8PR ℰ 01670 772238 ℰ www.bideawee.co.uk ☺ mid-Apr–end Aug, Wed & Sat 13.30–17.00 ♿ partial access

Bide-a-Wee is hidden away off a road to nowhere roughly between Morpeth and Longhorsley. Undulating meadows grazed by sheep surround the gardens which were formed out of an old sandstone quarry over two decades ago. Paths snake up and down and through the quarry where ferns drape from rock walls and over ponds crowded with more shade-loving, moisture-licking plants. Elsewhere, you will find colourful herbaceous borders, swathes of cornflowers (this being the home of the national collection of *Centaurea*), and a row of beehives.

14 MITFORD

Mitford is nestled in woodland by the River Wansbeck a few miles west of Morpeth. For those staying in Morpeth, I'd recommend taking the car along the B6343, simply to enjoy the scenery along the riverside and all the humpback bridges crossed *en route*. A mile or so from Morpeth you'll come to a sharp bend in the road where **Lowford Bridge** carries the B6343 over the Wansbeck. Though not magnificent, the early 19th-century crossing is memorable for its huge square blocks of honey-coloured sandstone and wooded surroundings.

Mitford itself is nothing hugely special though it does have a pub, old mill and a lone thatched cottage (one of only a handful of thatched buildings remaining in Northumberland). Undoubtedly, the hamlet's greatest appeal is the pastoral setting, church and ruined castle.

St Mary Magdalene Church (☺ Jun–Aug, Tue & Thu 14.00–16.00) faces the ruin of Mitford Castle about half a mile west of Mitford. Both are reached by way of a lane off the main Mitford to Morpeth road (signed for Mitford Church). You can also **walk** here from Morpeth (just a few miles) across meadows and along the wooded riverside. The church's oldest stonework dates from the 12th century and includes the priest's door and south arcade, but for the most part it has the appearance of a solidly Victorian edifice with a steeple and tall spire. Like the castle opposite, the church was destroyed by fire several times, notably in 1216 during King John's northern rampage.

Mitford Castle appears in a field guarded by crows and jackdaws and looks arresting on its green knoll even in its crumbling state. As you can believe, it has been ransacked many times since its construction in the mid 12th century.

15 MORPETH & CARLISLE PARK

This busy working town off the A1 is cocooned in a loop of the River Wansbeck. South of the waterway is Carlisle Park, which is easily one of the town's most attractive features with its gardens, castle and riverside footpath. To the north is Morpeth's centre. A steady stream of cars continually passing through the market town detracts somewhat from Morpeth's appeal; but overlook the traffic and you'll find a number of historic streets and buildings.

Bridges & bagpipes

The dainty **Chantry Footbridge** dates from 1869 and rests on the hefty piers of a 13th-century crossing. The three-arched **road bridge** opposite was designed by Thomas Telford and built in 1831.

On the north side of the river, the 13th-century **All Saints Chantry** (see box, page 166) crouches between the footbridge and the road bridge, where it once operated as a toll house for the crossing. It's now the **tourist information centre** and home to a wonderful **Bagpipe Museum** that also serves as a meeting place for bagpipe players and enthusiasts,

ALLEYWAYS & YARDS

As you slowly wander around Morpeth's streets, you'll notice a number of narrow passageways between buildings. They take us back to the days when the town was a stopping point for horse-drawn coaches travelling from Edinburgh to London on the Great North Road. Inns provided shelter to travellers, and adjoining blacksmiths and stables (reached via alleys) took care of the coach horses.

so you may well find local musicians playing the distinctive soft notes of the Northumbrian smallpipes as you wander around the instrument displays. Unlike Scottish bagpipes, the Northumbrian pipes are bellows blown. The instrument requires much concentration to play; hence musicians often have a far-away look as they perform.

Market Place

At the western end of Bridge Street, you'll hit the Market Place by a small roundabout and crossroads. Vanbrugh designed the Town Hall which was built in 1714 and rebuilt following a fire in the late 1800s. The reception is in the old butter market. If you're passing, have a peek inside, especially to see the grand staircase, which the receptionist may allow you to view if you ask.

Morpeth's landmark **clock tower** stands alone at the entrance to Oldgate on the other side of the roundabout. Its irregular-shaped stones (recycled from a medieval building) give the appearance of a building much older than its early 17th-century construction. Note the two figures at the top: they are known as Clarence and Cuddy and are said to do a commendable job of keeping an eye on the town. A curfew bell is tolled every day at 20.00 except on Wednesdays when the bell ringers are practising. Richard Major, the Tower Captain (how's that for a job title?) told me the tradition goes back to 1706.

"Vanbrugh designed the Town Hall which was built in 1714 and rebuilt following a fire in the late 1800s."

Carlisle Park, Morpeth Castle & the riverside

Rowing boats and swans glide along the River Wansbeck, enhancing the setting of **Carlisle Park** on the southern edge of Morpeth. There's a paved riverside towpath here (suitable for wheelchairs), a bowling green and a paddling pool. Near the park's formal flowerbeds is the **William Turner Garden** (✎ 01670 623509 ☉ daily until dusk) which celebrates the 'father of English botany' in a series of eye-catching gardens containing medicinal herbs.

It's a bit of a steep hike up **Ha' Hill**, where once stood an 11th-century motte and bailey castle until it was destroyed by King John in 1216. The reward for the climb is a view over Morpeth's red-tiled rooftops, the imposing early 19th-century **Court House** (once the old gaol and

GREAT MORPETHIANS

Collingwood is a name you hear a lot in the North East: on street signs, monuments and pubs from Tynemouth to the Scottish Borders. The Admiral is largely unheard of outside of the north despite leading the British armada to victory in the Battle of Trafalgar after Nelson was killed. Before the famous 1805 battle, Collingwood lived with his wife in the Georgian brick house bearing his name on Oldgate. For more about Collingwood, see box, page 237.

If you wander through Carlisle Park, you'll likely come across gardens celebrating one of the country's greatest botanists, **William Turner**, who was born in Morpeth in the early 16th century. In his most celebrated work, *A New Herball*, Turner provided the first systematic account of plants and their medicinal properties in English which helped to popularise common names such as daffodil and primrose.

On the southern outskirts of Morpeth is the medieval parish church of St Mary where the suffragette, **Emily Davison**, is buried. She famously stepped out in front of George V's racehorse during the Epsom Derby in 1913 and later died of her injuries. Huge crowds gathered for her funeral. Her gravestone bears the epitaph of the Women's Social and Political Union slogan: 'deeds not words'.

sometimes mistaken for the castle) and the surrounding countryside. When the Ha' Hill castle was razed, it was replaced by **Morpeth Castle** (now a Landmark Trust holiday property) to the south above Postern Burn. Although not a complete castle (only the old 14th-century gatehouse survives), it is nonetheless impressive.

FOOD & DRINK

Picknickers will find plenty of places in **Carlisle Park** to enjoy sandwiches. In the town centre, try the tranquil **Millennium Green** – a pretty garden tucked away down an alley (Old Bakehouse Yard) off Newgate Street. Morpeth has plenty of reasonable cafés, including the pretty **Café des Amis** (52 Newgate St, NE61 1BQ ☎ 07585 614156) that specialises in cakes and has a sheltered outdoor seating area.

The Cheese Shop 6 Oldgate, NE61 1LX ☎ 01670 459579 ⬚ www. thecheeseshopmorpeth.co.uk ⬚. Facing the clock tower is this fine specialist shop stocking over 150 varieties of cheese from Northumberland and further afield.

PepperPot 5 Oldgate, NE61 1PY ☎ 01670 514666. This cosy, friendly Italian by the clock tower uses many local ingredients in its pizza and pasta dishes, including some regional cheeses from Morpeth's Cheese Shop across the road (eg: goats cheese from Elsdon), Northumbrian meats and seafood from the North Sea. Good value, laid-back and child friendly.

16 BOTHAL

The River Wansbeck continues merrily from Morpeth, becoming more wooded and dreamy on its final coast-bound journey. About 3½ miles east of Morpeth, it meanders past Bothal Castle and its neat 19th-century estate village which ranks as one of the most pristine in Northumberland. You can make this journey on foot by following the riverbank trail the whole way.

Bothal's medieval church and uniform honey-coloured houses with their distinctive metal-patterned windows and maroon paintwork are hidden in a hollow, and the village as a whole feels very much cut off. Mature broadleaved trees (stunning in autumn) rise on a steep bank above Bothal, increasing this sense of seclusion. There's no visual link from the village to the **river**, but it is easily accessed by following a grassy lane from the memorial cross and St Andrew's Church (note the distinctive bell cote). Those wishing to cross the Wansbeck have the choice of stepping stones or a wire bridge. It's beautiful down here and a nice spot for a swim.

"The River Wansbeck continues merrily from Morpeth, becoming more wooded and dreamy on its final coast-bound journey."

Bothal Castle, which dates from 1343, is a beast with huge curtain walls, a tower and gateway, but because of its isolation few people seek it out – or even know of its existence. Unfortunately, it's not open to the public, but striking views are had when approached from the west by road (also from the riverside and the aforementioned track).

AROUND PONTELAND

Well-to-do villages dot the countryside around Ponteland, including Matfen, Great Whittington, Whalton and Stamfordham which have a Cotswolds-like appeal. Like the countryside around Kirkwhelpington and Morpeth, this area continues the sheep-grazed, rolling grassland theme where a potter around a stately home followed by a cream tea or pub lunch are the order of the day. The quieter country lanes are similarly popular with cyclists and those enjoying a motor in the countryside. I've spent some very memorable afternoons with my grandmother around here, dawdling along byways, getting in the way of tractors, stopping to chat to cyclists, drinking cups of tea, going to fêtes and so on.

17 PONTELAND & DARRAS HALL

Ponteland was once a quaint old village and it still retains some of its old roots by the ornamental bridge over the River Pont. Here stands **St Mary's Church** with its Norman tower, and the Blackbird Inn, a manor house which started life as a fortified tower built in the 14th century before it became incorporated into the 17th-century manor. There's also a **vicar's pele tower** on Main Street (opposite Waitrose) but there's not much else of interest in Ponteland (which feels more like a small town these days than a village) to warrant stopping for long.

Mention must be made of the wealthy residential estate, **Darras Hall**, where many Newcastle United footballers live. Today there are plenty of 'Dallas' mansions to gawp at, but the original 1930s–60s dwellings you'll also come across formed part of this early 20th-century utopian suburb dubbed the 'Garden City of the North'. Cherry trees, ornamental conifers and rose bushes edge the manicured lawns and driveways of homes which all have features that distinguish them from the house next door. Think *Stepford Wives* … in rural Northumberland. Parklands and Avondale Road have some interesting 1960s houses with severely sloping roofs and almost floor-to-ceiling windows. They are not listed and gaping holes appear every few hundred yards on some streets where buyers have demolished the original houses in order to build the above-mentioned lavish mansions from scratch.

FOOD & DRINK

Ponteland's choice of cafés and restaurants is fairly varied with a pizzeria, a couple of pubs and a scattering of coffee shops. For a pub dinner, you could try the refurbished **Black Bird** (North Rd, NE20 9UH ℰ 01661 822684 ⛾), but your best bet is probably to head north out of Ponteland on the A696 to the **Highlander** (page 204).
New Rendezvous 3–5 Bell Villas (opposite the Diamond Inn), NE20 9BD ℰ 01661 821775. Decent Chinese food and attentive service in the old Blacksmiths; popular with locals including Newcastle United footballers and former striker, Alan Shearer (staff will tell you of after hours' games of poker with players).

18 MILKHOPE CENTRE

Blagdon NE13 6DA (just off the A1, 9 miles north of Newcastle) ☉ daily ⛾

This rural retail 'park' shares similarities with Kirkharle further north. The concept is similar: small local businesses brought together in converted 19th-century farm buildings in a rural setting. You'll find a

BELLASIS BRIDGE

1 mile north of Horton Grange on Green Lane, Ponteland

It comes as quite a treat to chance upon this medieval two-arched crossing humped over the River Blyth. You're most likely to find it if travelling on the back roads to the cheese farm. I once met a couple of cyclists here who told me the grouting was made with sand from around Tynemouth Priory, hence the fragments of shells between its stone blocks. Not the most enthralling discovery, I'll admit, but a curious one. Look over the left-hand side of the bridge as you approach the crossing from the south and you'll see shell fragments between the stones.

few furniture shops, an art gallery and a busy **coffee shop** – good luck getting a table on a Saturday lunchtime.

The **Blagdon Farm Shop** (☎ 01670 789924 ☼ Tue–Sun ♿) is superbly well stocked with local produce. The meat and cheese counters are particularly generous and they only stock meat from the Blagdon Farm estate or from local farms. 'I can tell you which farm every piece of meat you see came from,' the helpful lady behind the counter told me. All the big-name regional producers are represented; vegetables are grown in the estate's walled garden.

Northumberland Cheese Company farm

Green Lane, Blagdon (near Horton Grange) NE13 6BZ ☎ 01670 789798 ✎ www.northumberland-cheese.co.uk ☼ daily

If you take the car for a walk around the country lanes northeast of Ponteland, you may stumble upon this cheese farm and café. A more direct route would be to turn off the A1 at Seaton Burn.

"Foodies will have spotted Cheviot, Kielder and Hadrian cheeses in pretty much every good deli in the North East."

Foodies will have spotted Cheviot, Kielder and Hadrian cheeses in pretty much every good deli in the North East; well, this is where they are made. The stone farm buildings include a viewing window where you can see the cheese-making machinery at work.

Upstairs, a café offers quiches, cheese flans, cheese scones, cheese soup and, of course, the full range of Blagdon's cheeses. The nettle and Cheviot varieties are very popular (the latter is mouth-tingling sharp).

19 NORTHUMBERLANDIA

Fisher Lane, Cramlington NE23 8AU (just off the A1) ☺ dawn to dusk daily; visitor centre & modern café; ♿

An outdoor recreational area created from a former industrial site is not novel in the North East but this large complex of paths and hillocks on the outskirts of Cramlington is also an impressive landscape sculpture. On the ground it's hard to make out that all the undulating grassy slopes form an image of a woman, a quarter of a mile in length, lying face up. 'The Lady of the North', or, as locals prefer to call her, 'Slag Alice' (why 'Alice', I do not know) makes a worthwhile stopping point if travelling along the A1, especially if the kids need a run around. From Alice's breasts you can see Northumberland's hills and the North Sea.

20 WHALTON

Well-to-do Whalton is considered a very desirable village: a broad sweep of neat stone cottages with a manor house, pub, ancient church and community spirit in bucket loads.

Expect all the usual gala attractions at the annual **Whalton fête** in September (birds of prey demonstrations, Morris dancing, local craft stalls, vintage cars, traditional Northumbrian music and so on), as well as extremely entertaining sheep races, in which the animals compete with a doll made out of a pair of stuffed tights strapped to their backs.

Traditional festivals also include the **Ba'al Fire** on old Midsummer's evening (4 July) during which school children dance around a bonfire lit next to the Beresford Arms. At one time people used to leap through the flames. The event has Pagan origins and is historically a sun-worshipping festival.

As with many churches, it's not until you step inside that they reveal their antiquity. This is true of **St Mary Magdalene Church** which externally has the appearance of a 19th-century place of worship, but is almost solidly 13th century inside.

At the eastern end of the village just before you head back out into the open countryside, you'll come to **Whalton Manor** (NE61 3UT ✆ 01670 775205 ♂ www.whaltonmanor.co.uk ☺ gardens: mid-Apr–Oct for groups), which looks like a continuation of the fine stone houses it follows. It is claimed that the mansion is the longest manor house in England, but it is really just four dwellings merged into one. Parts date from the 17th century but most of what you see today was altered by

Sir Edwin Lutyens in the early 20th century. The archway seen from the road is his doing. If you get the chance to wander through the arch, you'll see the old stable (still in use) about a cobbled courtyard. It's wonderfully unchanged. Most people who book a tour come to see the **gardens** which were laid out by Gertrude Jekyll in 1908 and contain beautiful herbaceous borders set around a lawn.

Country lanes around Belsay

The unclassified roads winding through Whalton, Ogle, Berwick Hill and Bolam Lake are a cyclist's delight. You'll see the odd car and tractor, but mostly it's quiet enough to dawdle along, do a spot of birdwatching, stop for sandwiches and so on. There are no dramatic vistas – just fields and paddocks bound by hedgerows, the odd farm and a couple of old hogback bridges including **Bellasis Bridge** (see box, page 200).

You could make a trip to **Kirkley Hall** (NE20 0AQ, north of Berwick Hill ✆ 01670 841235 ⌂ www.kirkleyhallzoo.co.uk ♿), an agricultural college surrounded by farmland that also houses a small zoo with emus, marmosets, meerkats, reptiles, wallabies and farm animals. Peacocks and children wander freely. Picnickers will find a few spots to eat sandwiches near the playground; alternatively there is an uninspiring café offering sandwiches and baked potatoes.

21 BOLAM LAKE & SHAFTOE CRAGS

Near Belsay NE20 0EU ✆ 01661 881234 ⊙ year-round; café & visitor centre open at weekends, bank holidays & during school holidays ♿ the lakeside path is supposedly fully accessible but the ground is quite muddy & rough in places

Bolam Lake and woods are conveniently situated next to a couple of country lanes popular with cyclists and day trippers, making it a good stopping point for picnickers and those dreaming of a soft drink and a slice of cake (there's a café here and another up the road; see opposite).

The **lakeside path** (three-quarters of a mile; partly on a boardwalk) is very pleasant with views of swans and ducks in the large manmade lagoon crowded by mature trees. Red squirrels are sometimes seen in the woods around the café and visitor centre.

A very different **walk** to nearby **Shaftoe Crags** begins from the crossroads at Bolam West Houses (♀ NZ070823; reached by taking the road signed for Rothbury on the west side of Bolam Lake for about a mile north). You'll see a footpath sign on your left. Farm and grassy tracks eventually lead on to open moorland featuring impressive sandstone outcrops and a prominent standing stone. There are great views of Northumberland from here. You'll need ✳ OS Explorer map OL42.

⫻ FOOD & DRINK

Stable Coffee Shop Bolam West House Farm NE61 4DZ ✐ 01661 881244 ☺ Fri–Mon. Pleasant café in a farmland setting near Bolam Lake; popular with cyclists. Most food baked on site. Tables outside next to a hay barn.

22 BELSAY HALL

Belsay NE20 0DX ✐ 01661 881636 ☺ Apr–end Oct & during school holidays, daily; weekends only at other times; café; ♿ gardens & ground floor of hall & castle; English Heritage

Work began on Belsay Hall in 1806 when the owners returned from a year-and-a-half-long honeymoon travelling around Europe. The design of the **villa** is what architectural historians call Classical Greek Revival. Belsay is raised like a Grecian temple on a platform above three steps and is distinguished by its plain façade with almost no decorative masonry except for two huge Doric columns either side of the doorway. Some would say it's austere; others see beauty in those clean lines and smooth sandstone blocks. Incidentally, the stone was quarried from the garden. The Greek temple theme continues in the Pillar Hall – a square reception room surrounded by colonnades on two storeys.

The absence of furniture, ornaments and paintings might come as a disappointment to antiques enthusiasts, but others will find it enjoyable enough just to wander around the light-filled rooms, take in the view of the open parkland and imagine what the interior might have once looked like. Note the faded original William Morris wallpaper in the upstairs rooms. English Heritage has staged some superb contemporary art exhibitions here in the past (check online for upcoming events).

"You enter a series of green walkways that lead past magnolia trees, a croquet lawn and the winter garden."

Garden lovers are in for a treat. Formal terraces planted with shrubs and perennials fall away from the south side of the Hall. Walking away from the house with the terraces on your left, you enter a series of green walkways that lead past magnolia trees, a croquet lawn (you can watch matches here in summer) and the winter garden until you reach the wooded **quarry gardens**. This is the most distinctive and romantic of all the gardens at Belsay and clearly fashioned in the Picturesque style with plenty of intentionally rustic features. The air is cool and fresh and all around exotic ferns, rhododendrons, trees and creepers hang, sprout and climb over the roughly cut rock faces. At one point you pass under a giant rock arch. After the darkness and seclusion of the quarry, the path opens into the sun-filled parkland around the castle.

Some visitors don't make it past the Hall and gardens and so miss out on one of the finest fortified towers in Northumberland. As with many of Northumberland's embattled manors, **Belsay Castle** is formed of a mansion house (built in 1614 and now largely in ruins) with an earlier tower at one corner. As far as children are concerned, the 14th-century tower is an all-singing, all-dancing 'proper castle' with parapets, arrow slits and heavy, castellated stonework.

¶¶ FOOD & DRINK

You have two choices for lunch at Belsay, either the **English Heritage café** inside the grounds of the Hall, or the **Blacksmiths Coffee Shop** (NE20 0DU ✆ 01661 881024 ☉ daily) at the estate entrance. An outdoor table at the Blacksmiths is just the ticket on a sunny day. You can watch swallows flying around the surrounding meadow as you enjoy a bowl of soup or a cream tea.

If you're looking for a pub lunch (steaks, game pie, fish and chips, etc), the **Highlander** (NE20 0DN ✆ 01661 881220) on the Ponteland to Belsay road (A696) is a popular choice, especially on Sundays.

23 MATFEN, STAMFORDHAM & AROUND

A jaunt into the hinterlands west of Ponteland reveals more old villages and tranquil lanes suitable for touring by bicycle. It's hilly in places, especially as you climb northwards to Ryal. Cyclists can expect some exhilarating downward plunges, but plenty of stiff ascents, too. Around Stamfordham, the countryside is pretty tame and most walking routes make good use of footpaths across fields, bridleways and country lanes.

Stamfordham looks pretty ordinary at first as you head up Grange Road but you'll soon reach a large open green with its 1735 market cross (the covered building with four open arches) and two neat terraces, mostly in stone. **St Mary's Church** dates from the 13th century and though it was largely rebuilt in the mid 1800s plenty of old features survive, including the chancel arch.

If you're approaching Matfen from the south, be sure to look out for Hope Lane where there's a prominent castellated house and prehistoric **standing stone**.

Matfen Hall (NE20 0RH ✆ 01661 886500 ♿) is glimpsed between trees on your way to Matfen village. The early 19th-century country mansion is now a spa hotel with a large golf course. A bistro in the conservatory, where non-guests can indulge in cream teas, overlooks the 300-acre landscaped parkland; the grand Library Restaurant is open for evening dinners and Sunday lunches.

Matfen is what many people would call a perfect English village with its unaltered stone terraces set around a broad green lined with mature trees. A burn traverses the length of the village, passing under a couple of sweet bridges in its own time. The church dates from the mid 1800s and is not of huge architectural interest, but its 117-foot-tall spire rises above the rooftops completing the model village scene (that and the red telephone box).

"Matfen is what many people would call a perfect English village with its unaltered stone terraces set around a broad green lined with mature trees."

Ramblers, cyclists and Sunday day trippers make good use of the welcoming green and **village store** which doubles as a **café** serving light lunches.

Continuing westwards across fields dotted with hay bales and tractors, **Great Whittingham** is soon upon you. The village rises on a sloping hill and by now you should be aware that the terrain is becoming rather more undulating than around Stamfordham.

A plaque in the village reads: 'Best kept village 1977'. Not that it has gone downhill since then: the gardens of Great Whittingham's stone cottages are quite a sight in summer and the village has won various Britain in Bloom awards (in recent decades).

There's not a lot to see in the hamlet of **Ryal**, due north of Great Whittingham, but it does have wonderful views and a lovely little hilltop church, originally built in the 12th century but much changed since. Two hands are needed to turn the door ring. Inside, you'll find a large number of medieval cross slabs built into the wall. As is commonplace, they are carved with shears representing a woman and a sword for a man. Beyond the churchyard walls, lemon and green fields bound by hedgerows and blocks of forests stretch far into the distance.

Cyclists heading west on NCN Route 10 can expect a few thrilling rollercoaster miles ahead through a beautiful pastoral landscape. A mile east in the other direction, **Ingoe** sits amid prehistoric monuments including a burial mound and the **Warrior Stone**, a similar standing stone to the one at Matfen.

¶¶ FOOD & DRINK

Most of the aforementioned villages have old inns serving food. They include the **Black Bull** at Matfen (NE20 0RP ℘ 01661 855395 ☉ Thu, Fri & Sat evenings & Sun for lunch), which serves steaks, fish and chips and real ales), Stamfordham's **Bay Horse Inn** (NE18 0PB ℘ 01661 855469), and the **Queens Head** Chinese in Great Whittingham (NE19 2HP ℘ 01434 672516). Non-guests can dine at **Matfen Hall** (page 205).

High Farm House Brewery Southeast of Matfen NE20 0RG ℘ 01661 886192 ♂ www. highhousefarmbrewery.co.uk ☉ every day for lunch except Wed; evening meals offered on Thu, Fri & Sat evenings ☍. This is a good middle-of-nowhere place to eat and drink (there's a bar with four beers on tap). The owners of the 200-acre 19th-century working farm branched out into beer making in 2003 and now offer brewery tours. The café serves hot food, Sunday lunches (with Northumbrian meat), substantial sandwiches and lighter bites. Outside, tables in an open hay barn are just the ticket on a nice day. Walk off your lunch on a gentle three-mile stroll devised by the farm; children can burn some energy in the play area.

Vallum Military Rd, East Wallhouses NE18 0LL ℘ 01434 672652 (tea room), 01434 672406 (restaurant), 01434 672406 (shop) ♂ www.vallumfarm.co.uk ☍ except the restaurant. As its name suggests this working farm stands very close to the earthen ditch associated with Hadrian's Wall. Fields surround the café, shop and restaurant run by 'a community of artisan producers who share a passion for traditionally produced food, drink and craft'. Many items for sale in the shop and restaurants are produced on site. The café serves decent lunches and coffees and has a pleasant outdoor decking area with a view of a children's playground, beyond which is a tranquil lake fringed by reeds and young trees where swallows and house martins feast on airborne insects. Former North East Chef of the Year, David Kennedy, runs the restaurant (upmarket lunches and evening dishes served in an unpretentious upstairs room with countryside views).

24 CHOLLERTON

Many visitors on their way to Hexham must have put on their brakes at Chollerton on seeing its old church and scenic position overlooking a lush vale. One of the first features you'll notice about **St Giles's Church** is its irregular shape. The stone horse mount by the doorway is a clue as to its former use. It dates from the 19th century and is the old stable and hearse house.

Inside the church, the most intriguing stones are the pillars: round on one side of the nave; octagonal on the other. The former are Roman and no doubt came from one of the nearby forts. Also dating to this period is the old font on the right as you enter the church, which was a Roman altar in a previous life.

Uphill from Chollerton is a wonderfully complete and unchanged **19th-century farm**. It still retains its old windmill, blacksmith's forge, carriage house, farmhouse, and a row of cottages (described by English Heritage as an important example of industrial farm housing). There's no public access but you can take in the assemblage of buildings by pulling over at the side of the A6079.

25 BARRASFORD & NEARBY CASTLES

⚐ **The Hytte** (page 274)

Haughton Castle hides behind a bank of mature trees only revealing itself for the briefest of moments as you pass through the quiet settlement of **Barrasford**, a couple of miles north of Chesters Roman Fort. The village has a very good pub that draws in Sunday lunch parties, and a pleasant riverside **walk** offering a rare glimpse of Haughton Castle's exposed turrets.

"Haughton Castle hides behind a bank of mature trees only revealing itself for the briefest of moments as you pass through the quiet settlement of Barrasford."

To reach the river and see the medieval manor house, cross the stile by the bridge at the eastern end of the village and follow the merry burn to the River North Tyne. It's a bit brambly and the long dew-laden grasses tend to be trouser-dampening, but it's worth the tramp along the footpath for the views when you reach the wide, rapid-surfing North Tyne. At the riverbank, turn right by an old oak and follow the trail until you reach a cottage. The best view of the castle is from this point.

Haughton Castle (a right of way goes through the grounds) stands on the west side of the River North Tyne not far from Humshaugh looking rather stern with its formidable embattlements and small cheerless windows. It was fortified in the 14th century and survived the next few hundred years of cross-border conflict before being altered somewhat to become a more comfortable 19th-century country house.

If you continue northwest of Barrasford on the road to Wark, you'll come to **Chipchase Castle** (NE48 3NT ✆ 01434 230203 ✆ www. chipchasecastle.com ☺ house: Jun only; gardens: Easter–end Aug), next in the line of great Northumbrian country houses in the North Tyne Valley. Chipchase is a hugely impressive part-Jacobean, part-Georgian manor house with a medieval tower set within landscaped parkland. It forms the centrepiece of an estate that encompasses a stretch of the best salmon river in England and Wales (**fly-fishing** can be arranged through the castle). A small chapel stands alone in the grounds, and on the other side of the manor is a walled garden and nursery.

"Chipchase is a hugely impressive part-Jacobean, part-Georgian manor house."

⫴ FOOD & DRINK

Barrasford Arms Barrasford NE48 4AA ✆ 01434 681237 ☺ Nov–Apr, closed Mon; food served 12.00–14.00 & in the evenings. Hunting paraphernalia fills the bar of this 19th-century inn that has built up a very good reputation for its food. It's always busy at weekends so book in advance (you can also eat outside in a sunny garden). Local beers, and meats sourced from Northumbrian farms.

26 WARK-ON-TYNE

🏠 **Battlesteads Hotel & Restaurant** (page 274), **Southlands Farm Cottages** (page 275)

Wark is a large village facing the verdant banks of the North Tyne and is most memorably approached from the east across a slim metal bridge. It's pleasant enough with a green bound by well-kept stone cottages and a pub. The inn everyone talks about (Battlesteads; see below) is a short walk south of the village on the Hexham Road (B6320).

⫴ FOOD & DRINK

Battlesteads Hotel & Restaurant Wark NE48 3LS ✆ 01434 230209 ♿. Many people visit Wark just to come to this excellent-value 18th-century farmhouse restaurant, which has won numerous national awards, mainly on account of its green ethos, home-grown produce and dinner menu. Most ingredients are sourced within a 25-mile radius including most of the meats and veg (grown in polytunnels on site). Even their inexpensive sandwiches are that little bit special (crayfish tails with lemon mayonnaise, for example). It's hard to find steak and fish dishes as good and reasonably priced as this in Northumberland. You'll definitely want to book ahead, particularly for the Sunday carvery. On the downside, the restaurant is a bit characterless and gloomy (except for the tables in the conservatory).

27 SIMONBURN

The last time I visited this quaint hamlet, the roads were unusually jammed with cars shuttling locals to a special service to mark the retirement of the vicar. A lot of rural settlements must have once had a community like this. For visitors, there's not a lot here of course; just some rustic terraced cottages facing a large green, a tea room and 19th-century **St Mungo's Church**, but if your idea of a pleasant Sunday out is tootling through tranquil Northumbrian countryside on quiet lanes to an old-world hamlet with the promise of a cream tea, Simonburn is for you.

Simonburn Castle sits on a wooded mound half a mile northwest of the hamlet. Only fragments of masonry remain from the castle which was built in 1766 as an eye-catcher from Nunwick Hall to replace an earlier 13th-century tower.

The same distance in the other direction (northeast), you'll reach **Nunwick** – another flower-filled hamlet. **Nunwick Hall** dates from 1760.

¶¶ FOOD & DRINK

Simonburn Tea Room The Mains, NE48 3AW ✆ 01434 681321. This cosy tea room's biggest selling points are that it's in Simonburn and has a sunny garden. On the food front, don't expect anything special but the scones and sandwiches are decent enough.

FOLLOW BRADT

For the latest news, special offers and competitions, subscribe to the Bradt newsletter via the website ⬡ www.bradtguides.com and follow Bradt on:

 www.facebook.com/BradtTravelGuides   @BradtGuides

 @bradtguides   www.pinterest.com/bradtguides

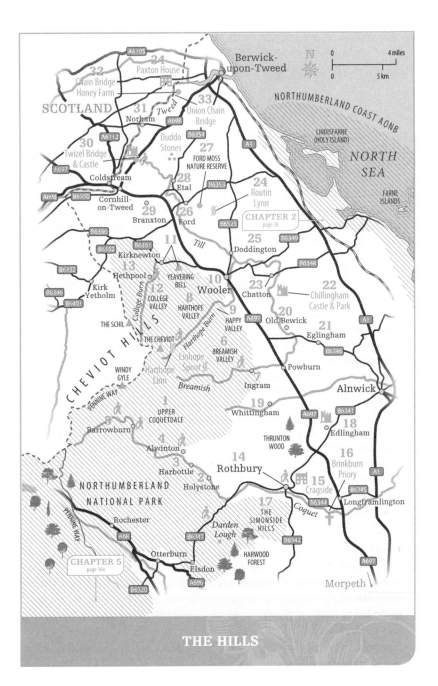

THE HILLS

6
THE HILLS

Solitude and big landscapes are guaranteed in the northern reaches of **Northumberland National Park**. There's a lot to pack in: hiking through valleys to waterfalls, watching the salmon run, searching for prehistoric rock art, cycling old drovers' trails, climbing heather-covered crags and exploring ruined castles.

The **Cheviots** can seem desolate with their largely tree-less slopes and covering of sub-montane grasses and shrubs, but between their folds are deep glacial valleys, trout-filled rivers, waterfalls and remote farmsteads. On many summits are remains of ancient **hillforts** and **Bronze Age cairns**.

Between the coast and Cheviot foothills, and extending for almost the entire length of Northumberland, is a long arc of craggy hills and moors hiding prehistoric rock carvings, castles, hillforts and an ancient wild cattle park. The best-known area is the **Simonside Hills** near Rothbury which should not be missed in August when the heather flowers turn the ridge deep pink.

The **River Tweed** marks the boundary with Scotland and is explored here along with places along its tributary, the **River Till**. Those who take a leisurely jaunt along these rivers will find a scattering of ruined castles and towers, and a couple of old-world villages.

"The Cheviots can seem desolate, with their largely tree-less slopes, but between their folds are glacial valleys, trout-filled rivers, waterfalls and remote farmsteads."

To access the national park and its hinterlands you can either shoot along the A697 or take a more meandering route (as described in this chapter) on old drovers' trackways and unclassified roads that criss-cross the moors and hills and hug the courses of rivers. By tooting along country lanes you encounter quite a few hamlets, farms and 19th-century villages.

GETTING AROUND

A car or touring bicycle is going to really help you explore the hills. Some towns and villages on the eastern edge of Northumberland National Park, notably Rothbury, and the border area can be reached by bus, but if you're heading deeper into the Cheviots without a car, you'll need to cycle, saddle up on horseback or hitch a ride along one of the tracks that runs through the larger Cheviot valleys. The only **train stations** of help are at Morpeth and Berwick-upon-Tweed.

BUS

Alnwick–Wooler via Chillingham and Chatton (470) and **via Whittingham and Powburn** (473); at least five services a day Monday to Saturday

Berwick-upon-Tweed–Galashiels Stopping at places on the Scottish border including Norham and Cornhill (67); eight services a day Monday to Saturday, fewer on Sunday

Berwick-upon-Tweed–Wooler via Ford and Etal (267); six services a day Monday to Saturday

Newcastle–Rothbury via Morpeth (X14 from Newcastle and 14 from Morpeth); at least five services a day Monday to Saturday

CYCLING

All the major **Cheviot valleys** (Breamish, Harthope, College and Upper Coquetdale) have paved tracks that follow their respective rivers through the brooding hills. Also consider the old **drove roads** that cross the Cheviot Hills, especially Salter's Road from Alnham, which is paved. Destinations on the edge of the Cheviot range including Alwinton, Harbottle and around Wooler hold great appeal on account of the quiet roads and undulating upland farmland scenery.

Cycling in **Coquetdale** using Rothbury as your base is highly recommended. You have the choice of off-road forest tracks maintained by the Forestry Commission and some fabulous B-roads that will appeal to the freewheeling-cyclist. Expect long views of the Simonside and

---

i TOURIST INFORMATION

Wooler Cheviot Centre, 12 Padgepool Pl, NE71 6BL ✆ 01668 282123 🕓 May–Oct, daily (on Sun until 14.00); Nov–Apr, Mon–Sat ♿

Cheviot hills at most high passes if pedalling to the likes of Whittingham and Harbottle, for example.

The **sandstone hills** on the eastern edge of the national park (roughly the area between the A697 and A1) have much to lure the road cyclist with a fondness for steep ascents. Around Doddington, Chillingham, Chatton and Eglingham there are some thrilling stretches which offer wide countryside views framed by the distant Cheviots. At some high points you can see the hills and the coast with just a turn of the head.

Mountain bikers are particularly well-catered for in the Rothbury and Upper Coquetdale area thanks to the Forestry Commission-managed conifer woods, including Harbottle, Thrunton and Harwood (collectively known as the Rothbury Forests).

Also consider touring the **River Till** countryside. The roads around here are fairly quiet and you'll dip in and out of a string of old villages with pubs and cafés.

The **Pennine Cycleway** (355 miles from Berwick-upon-Tweed to the Peak District) follows the River Tweed before turning south along the eastern edge of the National Park via Alwinton and Elsdon and onwards to Hadrian's Wall.

WALKING

With remote scenery and the highest summits in Northumberland, The **Cheviot range** is an obvious destination for the hill walker. Four major valleys (Upper Coquetdale, Breamish, Harthope and College) are all equally beautiful and have similar appeal with smooth-sided slopes folding into each other for as far as the eye can see, eager whisky-tinted burns, waterfalls here and there and a tremendous sense of remoteness and space. The rivers that run through each valley are a destination in themselves and many visitors come just to picnic by the water's edge or paddle among the rocks. There are few villages and hardly anywhere to buy food or pick up supplies so you might want to make a stop in the likes of Wooler and Rothbury beforehand. For that reason, both towns make popular bases for walkers. Rothbury is also well situated for the walker wishing to explore the rugged heather-clad **Simonside Hills** (pretty much on the doorstep of the town) and even the coast, which is under an hour's drive away.

Further north towards the Scottish border, the landscape is more agricultural in character, but what the area lacks in outstanding hill

LONG-DISTANCE PATHS

The **Pennine Way** and **St Cuthbert's Way** are the most popular long-distance routes in Northumberland. They both encompass the Cheviot Hills and cross some of the finest upland landscapes in the county. St Cuthbert's Way (62½ miles from Melrose in Scotland to Lindisfarne) is a favourite multi-day hike because it takes in the best of Northumberland's outstanding scenery from the remote Cheviots to the white sands and bird reserves at Lindisfarne. At one point (close to St Cuthbert's Cave) you can see both the hills and the sea.

walks, it makes up for with its riverside paths. You can hike along the Rivers **Till** and **Tweed** for much of their length.

Recommended walks in and around Northumberland National Park are suggested throughout this chapter. You'll need ✳ OS Explorer maps 339 Kelso, Coldstream & Lower Tweed Valley, OL16 The Cheviot Hills and OL42 Kielder Water & Forest. The Northumberland National Park website (⌖ www.northumberlandnationalpark.org.uk) has a comprehensive walking section which includes the excellent '**Rangers' Favourite Walks**' leaflet, available at tourist information centres and to download. Free **guided ranger walks** (summer only; no booking required) are also listed online and in leaflet format.

For **walking holidays** and guided and self-guided walks, Shepherds Walks (page 147), based in Rothbury, is recommended. They also run a well-stocked shop.

HORSERIDING

Bridleways (many of which are on ancient drove roads) cross the Cheviots linking the valleys and making this a superb place to visit on horseback. Northumberland National Park has a few maps detailing circular routes by horse on their website.

For guided horseriding trips in the Cheviots, try **Kimmerston Riding Centre** at Wooler (✆ 01668 216283 ⌖ www.kimmerston.com).

TAXIS

Coquetdale Taxis Rothbury ✆ 01669 620820, 078237 76109. Collect from in and around Rothbury, including the Simonside Hills.

Ron's Taxis Wooler ✆ 01668 281281, 0777 8543907. A journey from Wooler to Hethpool in College Valley, for example, costs around £14.

THE CHEVIOT VALLEYS & HILLS

Wherever you wander in north Northumberland, the Cheviots are almost always brooding in the distance, guarding the frontier with Scotland. There's no mistaking this stonking corridor of smooth humps down the western edge of the county, which are strikingly rounded and unlike all the other hill ranges in northern England.

The slopes of these long-extinct volcanoes are dominated by dwarf shrubs and grasses and, except for a few plantation woodlands, the Cheviots appear at first quite featureless. It's not until you set foot that the character of individual hills and valleys becomes apparent with their wooded ravines, ancient trackways, Iron Age hillforts and waterfalls. In terms of altitude, you'll find some of the highest hills in England here with six summits over 2,000 feet.

Though seemingly desolate, the vegetation covering the Cheviot plateaux forms an internationally important habitat characterised by sphagnum mosses, cotton grasses, sedges, cloudberry, bilberry and heather. In ravines, you may see alpine flowering plants including rose root, dwarf cornel and alpine willow herb.

Deep valleys radiate away from the highest peak, **The Cheviot**, which marks roughly the centre of the range. **Upper Coquetdale**, **Breamish**,

LOCAL WORDS

burn stream

bleugh gully (pronounced 'clook')

cuddy small horse or pony

haar sea mist (sometimes called 'fret')

haugh flat land by water (pronounced 'hoff')

heugh jagged hill

hope sheltered valley eg: Linhope, Harthope

kirk often seen in place names eg: Kirknewton, Kirk Yetholm (Old Norse origins, meaning 'church')

knowe small hill

law hill

linn waterfall

lonnen lane

lough mountain lake (Northumbrian equivalent of 'loch', pronounced 'loff')

muckle big

Northumbrian 'burr' used to describe the local pronunciation of 'r'

shiel shepherds' or fishermen's huts

stell sheepfold (round, stone enclosure)

tup ram

whaup curlew (somewhat onomatopoeic if you've ever heard curlews in the breeding season)

yon that

yow ewe (sheep)

SUNDEWS

On open ground where there's a covering of moss and it's squelchy underfoot, look out for the meat-eating round-leaved sundew – a tiny insectivorous plant about the size of a baby's hand with disk-like projections covered in pink hairs. In really wet bogs, you may see the great sundew (long, tapered leaves but otherwise similar to its more widespread relative). On the tip of each hair is a drop of what looks like dew which is sugary and irresistible to insects, but also sticky. Once stuck, the plant digests its prey over a couple of days.

Harthope and **College** valleys are named after their respective rivers which rush eagerly off the hillsides. In glacial valleys like College and Harthope, the burns form wide, straight channels through the hills; other rivers, like the Coquet, are of the meandering, oxbow-lake-forming type. For the most part, they are all rocky and fairly shallow with shingle banks and rapids and the odd pool suitable for bathing.

Horseriders, cyclists, walkers and back-country hikers will find miles of lonely footpaths and bridleways in the Cheviots and a handful of quiet paved tracks that will take you deep into remote countryside, with no through roads. This is not the Cotswolds and you won't find quaint villages strung along valley basins or many places to pick up supplies, so you'll need to come prepared. Isolation and remoteness is what will draw you here. Those day trippers who come looking for cream teas and gift shops quickly turn around and head back out.

1 UPPER COQUETDALE

Seasoned travellers to Northumberland National Park go dreamy-eyed when you mention Coquetdale. It's a much-sung valley that oozes lush scenery and has parts that feel wonderfully remote. I'm talking really about Upper Coquetdale – roughly the extent of the River Coquet from its jingly beginnings in the southwestern corner of the Cheviots at Chew Green, past Barrowburn, Alwinton, Harbottle and on to Rothbury, 30 miles from its source.

The upper reaches are classically Cheviot-like: big heavy moors, sparkling burns, flower-filled hay meadows and the occasional stand of conifer trees; but further south around Holystone, the landscape becomes wooded (now with ancient broadleaved trees) before entering the open flood plains at Hepple.

Accessing Upper Coquetdale

A paved road extends for 12 lonely miles from Alwinton to the Roman camp, Chew Green, on the Scottish border, making for a memorable **cycling** trip. For much of the way it follows the River Coquet through the valley passing farmsteads like Barrowburn.

Walkers who have come by car will find several parking areas off this main track which mark the start point of popular hikes into the hills, including to Windy Gyle (page 238) and a number of trails from Alwinton. You don't have to walk far before you feel the swelling moors enclosing you; every time you turn back, the hills seem to have shuffled in that bit closer.

The River Coquet forms the northern boundary of the **Otterburn military training area** (pages 185–6), which covers the southern moors in the Cheviot range. Countryside and hills north of the river are yours to explore at any time; south of the river, there are restrictions. Red flags indicate the ranges are closed to the public. In reality, most visitors explore the hills to the north anyway because the signed walking trails are on that side. If you want to experience the desolate moors to the south, you'll need to check access restrictions first (see box, page 186).

2 HOLYSTONE'S WOODS, MOORS & WELL

Plantation forest dominates the hilly ground between the hamlets of Holystone and Harbottle, but amid the conifer trees is a remnant patch of ancient oak woodland. The dawn chorus here in spring is quite something. As well as all the common woodland birds, you may hear wood warblers or see flycatchers; look out, too, for red squirrels.

In the early noughties, an astonishing discovery was made on **Holystone Common** (just south of Holystone Burn): a six-foot skyscraper ants' nest

NORTHUMBERLAND NATIONAL PARK

With some 2,200 residents in total, Northumberland National Park is the least populated of all the national parks here in the UK by quite some way. It borders Scotland in the west, while in the south it extends as far as Hadrian's Wall, encompassing the whole of the Cheviot range and the Simonside Hills.

You'll find a huge amount of information online (www.northumberlandnationalpark. org.uk), and at the Cheviot Centre in Wooler (page 213) and National Park Centre at Hadrian's Wall (page 146).

inhabited by half a million insects. The conical mound is made of pine and spruce needles and constructed by the uncommon hairy northern wood ant. There are some 70 nests around here; just be careful not to disturb them – they are rare and take years to build.

You can explore Holystone Woods from the Forestry Commission car park and picnic area west of the village. A longer hike could incorporate **Harbottle Crags** (open heather moorland northwest of the forested slopes).

Closer to the village centre is **Lady's Well** (signed) – a secluded pool with a cross in the middle. The rectangular stone basin is thought to be Roman. There are no obvious remains of the Augustinian nunnery that once stood in Holystone.

Woodhouses Bastle

Some two miles south of Holystone, reached by a grassy track from the Hepple to Harbottle road is one of the best examples of a border fortified farmhouse. It stands at the top of a grassy vale keeping watch over the Coquet River basin and distant Simonside Hills, and probably dates from the 16th century but has been reroofed in relatively recent times. As is typical of bastle houses (see box, page 181), the walls are hugely thick and the windows are small holes and slits. You can see into the ground floor which has a stone vaulted ceiling.

"Some two miles south of Holystone, is one of the best examples of a border fortified farmhouse."

3 HARBOTTLE

This sleepy hamlet along the River Coquet is best known for its 12th-century **castle** (originally a motte and bailey) which teeters on the edge of a grassy summit above the main street. Built as a defence against the Scots, it now lies completely ruined, with crumbling walls and scattered stones everywhere; the view of the forests, craggy hills, houses and church below makes the climb to the top worthwhile.

A small **village show** (⌀ www.harbottleshow.com) on the first Saturday in September brings together the finest sheep, veg, cut flowers, jams and crafts produced in the local area.

For a short, stiff **walk**, take the footpath from the car park at the western end of Harbottle (beyond the parking area for the castle) and climb for half a mile up the craggy, heather-covered hills opposite the village to **Drake Stone** – a huge rock (said to have healing properties) near an icy tarn. You can return in a loop via West Wood by following the trail along the northern shore of the lake. The circular route is around two miles. Pick up refreshments at the Star Inn ($\mathscr{O}$ 01669 650221) on the main road through Harbottle (opening times are a bit variable but you can usually get a drink on weekend afternoons and after 19.00 during the week).

4 ALWINTON

Alwinton lies at the meeting of two good trout rivers – the Coquet and Alwin – and route of the ancient drove road, Clennell Street, which once extended from Morpeth to Kelso. Like Harbottle, Alwinton is another quiet hamlet of stone, but the scenery is more open and you feel as though you are at the doorway to the Cheviots rather than at the garden gate.

Several highly worthwhile **walks** start from Alwinton, including two circular routes that take you deep into the hills. One follows the Usway

OLD DROVE ROADS

Footpaths, cart-tracks, packhorse routes and livestock trails have crossed the Cheviots for as long as these moors and valleys have been farmed. The Romans created highways through Northumberland's hills, notably Dere Street that crosses high ground in the southwest corner of the Cheviot range. Drove routes expanded in the late medieval period and especially after the Union of the Crowns when relatively peaceful times promoted cross-border trade. During the 18th and early 19th centuries, tens of thousands of animals (mainly cattle) were seasonally driven across the border.

Some drovers travelling from Scotland also traded in illicit goods, especially whisky (duties on the liquor were higher in England thus promoting an illicit trade).

Whisky stills were hidden in rocky outcrops in a number of places. A mile or so west of Barrowburn, where Rowhope Burn meets the Coquet, there was once an 18th-century inn (evocatively named Slymefoot) that was notorious for receiving smuggled spirits.

Clennell Street, Salter's Road and The Street are some of the best-known drove routes that are still used by farmers. Nowadays, ramblers and horseriders also make good use of them. They are largely wide tracks (grassy, dirt or paved) that tend to take a drier route over the hills, avoiding bogs.

Popular **walks** include the stretch of Clennell Street that runs north of Alwinton above the River Alwin, and The Street to Windy Gyle (page 224).

NORTHUMBERLAND DARK SKY PARK

Come nightfall, much of Northumberland is bathed in pitch-black skies owing to the remoteness of the region and large expanses of uninhabited forests, hills and moorland – something that was recognised by the International Dark Skies Association who awarded 'Gold Tier' status to Northumberland National Park and Kielder Water Forest Park in 2013. The county shares the accolade with the likes of Death Valley in North America and is the only Dark Sky Park in England. Within the new zone, which covers 572 square miles of Northumberland, the Cheviot valleys and hills offer some of the best spots for star gazing. See the 'Dark Sky Park' pages at ⊘ www.northumberlandnationalpark.org.uk for events.

Burn and the other goes via Copper Snout; both return to Alwinton along Clennell Street. I've described a shorter river and hill route on page 221.

St Michael and All Angels Church is half a mile south of the village. It dates from the Norman period and is curious for two reasons: the footpath made from old gravestones (including one with a prominent skull and crossbones carving), and the flight of steps from the nave to the chancel. Not much masonry survives from the 11th and 12th centuries, but you will find some Early English features dating from the 13th century; the rest is Victorian.

"The Alwinton Border Shepherds' Show is one of the largest (and oldest) fairs in the county."

The annual **Alwinton Border Shepherds' Show** (⊘ www.alwintonshow.co.uk) in October is traditionally the last of the season in Northumberland. It's also one of the largest (and oldest) fairs in the county. Expect all the usual displays: sheepdog trials, craft tents, food stalls, Cumberland and Westmorland Wrestling and bagpipe music.

ᵞ FOOD & DRINK

Rose and Thistle NE65 7BQ ⊘ 01669 650226 ⊙ closed on Mon until 19.00. Hot dishes and sandwiches in an old stone pub said to be where Sir Walter Scott researched material for *Rob Roy*. Nothing fancy (baked potatoes, pasta dishes, pies) but the location is great for weary hikers coming down off the hills. Currently food is served early afternoon and early evening.

✳ ✳ ✳

A SHORT HILLSIDE WALK FROM ALWINTON

OS Explorer map OL16; start: Alwinton car park, NT919063; 5 miles; difficulty: moderate walk with an initial climb; refreshments at the Rose and Thistle in Alwinton (page 220) & the Clennell Hall Country House Hotel

Shepherds and traders of bygone centuries once used the wide, time-worn drovers' track you follow on the first leg of this walk to travel to and from Scotland. The return is along an unpaved track which follows the lively River Alwin to Clennell Hall.

From Alwinton's car park walk back through the village until you reach the green by the river. Cross Hosedon Burn by way of a footbridge and turn left. You'll see a fingerpost signed for **Clennell Street**. Once you've passed a farm on your left, the track continues steeply uphill by the side of buttercup meadows. Many low summits are now in sight. It's very peaceful up here with only the song of skylarks, bleating sheep and the occasional 'tuk, tuk' of a distant tractor carried in the wind. Ignore the footpath to your right and continue uphill and over a stone wall by a farm gate using a ladder stile. Follow the path to the left as it skirts Castle Hills.

Where the main track bears left a little further ahead, strike off right to a gate about 50 yards away. Once through this gate, bear left across the field, through another gate and then follow the path to the right along the side of the hill. Note the old sheepfold below on your right. Enjoy the view of the silvery River Alwin below and perhaps the odd hare sprinting through the grasses.

After a junction with a track, the path descends towards the corner of a forest. At the bottom of the hill, begin the return leg by passing through a gate and turning right. Follow the River Alwin for 1½ miles to Clennell Hall, crossing the water by way of footbridges. Now a hotel with a bar open to non-guests, **Clennell Hall** (01669 650377) goes back many centuries and still retains its ancient defensive tower. When you come to a crossroads, follow the track to the right. Go through a farm gate and keep to the dry stone wall. On crossing a cattle grid, turn right and cross the river via a footbridge (signed to Alwinton). Turn left and head up the path and then cross the field in front to reach Clennell Street. Retrace your steps to Alwinton.

* * *

MIDGES

Midges can be a bother in summer in the national park, but they are not as vicious as the infamous Highland midges. You'll probably still want to take repellent, though, especially if camping. The best I've tried is Avon's Skin So Soft – dry oil body spray. Yes, it's a beauty product but midges hate this stuff. It's occasionally stocked in some campsites and outdoor shops; otherwise order it online (www.avonshop.co.uk).

5 BARROWBURN

🏕 Barrowburn Camping Barn, Cottage and B&B (page 276)

Barrowburn farmstead stands by the River Coquet deep within the valley, six miles upriver from Alwinton and reached along a paved road. The hills and flower meadows hereabouts are some of the most beautiful in the whole of the Cheviot range and walkers will find plenty of options for hikes, which are made all the more enjoyable by the promise of a cuppa and slice of cake at the tea room (surely one of the most remote cafés in England). Barrowburn's fascinating history is best recounted by Ian Tait, a sheep farmer who has lived here all his life (see box, opposite).

"The meadow is a blaze of yellow, green and purple in June and July."

The meadow behind the farm is a blaze of yellow, green and purple in June and July when yellow rattle, buttercups, eyebright, clovers, wood

GYPSY KINGS & PRESIDENTS

The following tale was told to me one winter's afternoon at the Barrowburn Tea Room. It concerns a poacher in the mid 19th century who was chased by a couple of gamekeepers to his home. The story goes that the poacher hid his shotgun in his son's crib but that the gun accidentally went off, shooting the child through the arm. On hearing the story – and realising the child would never be able to work on the land – the landlord's wife rather kindly paid for the child to receive an education. His name was Andrew Blythe (the Blythes were a famous gypsy family in Kirk Yetholm just over the Scottish border) and he eventually made a living travelling the Cheviot Hills teaching shepherds' children how to read and write. He opened the school house at Barrowburn and was the schoolmaster there for 50 years, as his gravestone in Kirk Yetholm describes.

If that wasn't a good enough story in itself, there's another tale about the Blythes which sounds a bit too good to be true but is intriguing nonetheless. The Blythes were related to the gypsy royal family, whose kings and queens lived in the Gypsy Palace at Kirk Yetholm (a cottage with a fascinating history). The last king was Charles Faa Blythe, whose coronation in 1898 was watched by 10,000 spectators.

Back in 1752, 18 gypsies from Northumberland (including members of the illustrious Blythe clan) were transported to South Carolina from Morpeth Jail. Two centuries later, a man named William Blythe, who was said to be a relative of one of these Northumberland gypsies in South Carolina, died in a car crash in 1946, three months before the birth of his son, William Jefferson Blythe. After his mother remarried, the boy changed his name to William Jefferson Clinton, better known as Bill Clinton.

HILL FARMING & COMMUNITY LIFE IN BARROWBURN

Ian Tait is a fifth-generation hill farmer at Barrowburn and has lived here since birth. His flocks of Cheviot sheep are the white-faced ewes you'll see in the hills around the farm. 'They're the wildest domestic sheep in the world,' says Ian. 'Skittish, but intelligent and very protective of their young.' Their mothering instinct is so strong in fact that they sometimes 'steal' another ewe's lamb. 'It's not unusual to see two ewes claiming one lamb as their own.'

There are not many buildings at Barrowburn except for the farm, old school house and community hall. Over a cup of tea and scone one winter's day, Ian told me about how the community once centred around these scattered buildings. 'The building downriver used to be a dance hall. It's used for storage now and is full of hay, but if you were to look under the hay, you'd see a beautiful sprung wooden floor.' It was here that the local farmers and their families used to dance to border folk songs, including the Barrowburn Reel.

'The school was the focus of the community,' Ian says. It was opened by a gypsy in the late 19th century (see box, opposite) and closed in the 1970s. Ian now runs the old school house as a camping barn but he remembers how farmers' children (including himself) used to travel from all around to the simple stone building on the hillside. 'There was only one teacher and all ages were taught in the same room: big kids at the back and younger kids at the front. If the weather was bad in winter and most children couldn't get to school, we used to sit in front of the fire in the teacher's house next door, drinking hot Ribena and doing our maths.'

'School trips were not just for the children,' Ian recalls. 'The whole community would join us and we'd all go off to the beach at Tynemouth for the day.'

crane's-bill and knapweed come into flower. Mountain bumblebees (see box, page 248) also like this field. Heading up the track, perhaps on a walk to Murder Cleugh (pages 224–5), are two buildings that can be hired: the Deer Hut and a camping barn. The latter is the old school which was opened by one of the famous Kirk Yetholm gypsies in the late 19th century.

¶ FOOD & DRINK

Barrowburn Tea Room NE65 7BP ✆ 01669 621176. A real fire (lit most of the year), a friendly welcome by the Tait family and inexpensive tea, cakes, scones and sandwiches lure walkers and cyclists off the hills. Up the farm track is a camping barn and basic self-catering cottage run by the farm (page 276).

Walks around Barrowburn

You can head straight into the hills from parking areas along the paved track through the valley. The walks outlined here are just a taster and can easily be completed in a few hours. A more strenuous and longer route is the eight-mile **circuit of Windy Gyle** that begins and ends a mile west of Barrowburn where Rowhope Burn meets the Coquet. This is a superb route offering some of the most memorable views in the whole of the Cheviot range, but it's a tough old climb. It begins on the historic drove route, The Street, which meets the Pennine Way on the Scottish border for the eastward hike to Windy Gyle. The return is made by following a track high above Trows Burn and then tracing Rowhope Burn back to the main road.

✳ ✳ ✳

A SHORT CIRCULAR WALK FROM BUCKHAM'S BRIDGE TO DEEL'S HILL

✵ OS Explorer map OL16; start: Buckham's Bridge car park, ♀ NT824107; 3 miles; difficulty: 1 steep climb; the rest is mostly on flat, damp ground; refreshments at the Barrowburn Tea Room (page 223)

This straightforward short hike with hilltop views begins from Buckham's Bridge, four miles up the Coquet from Barrowburn. Within a few hundred yards of following Buckham's Walls Burn northwest, you'll come to the first pool where you could take a dip. They become more generous as you press on. On reaching a junction of two burns by a sheepfold, you change course and head west, though still following the same burn. A few hundred boggy yards later, there's another sheepfold and a track leading up **Deel's Hill**. The view at the top of hills sloping into one another deserves a few moments to be taken in before you descend back to the car park.

A CLASSIC BARROWBURN HIKE TO MURDER CLEUGH

✵ OS Explorer map OL16; start: Wedder Leap car park, ♀ NT866103; 5 miles; difficulty: moderate hike on grassland & through woods with some strenuous inclines; refreshments at the Barrowburn Tea Room (page 223)

It's a short walk from Wedder Leap car park along the River Coquet to the remote Barrowburn farmstead and tea room from where this hill and forest walk begins. Take the uphill track passing a meadow stuffed with buttercups, clovers and yellow rattle, and the green Deer Hut and old school house (marked as a bunkhouse on Ordnance Survey maps). Follow an uphill gravel track before descending towards Hepden Burn. After a short stiff climb the path levels out to the entrance of **Middle Hill Forest** which you enter via a ladder stile. Go through the dark woods and then, on stepping back into the open landscape, keep to a narrow path that hugs the side of a steep hill with views of the Usway Burn below and Yarnspath Law opposite. **Murder Cleugh** is not far ahead and is approached from the northeast after crossing the burn. The perimeter fence leads all the way to the southwest corner of Murder Cleugh where you pass through a farm gate. Just around the corner on the left, a memorial stone in the copse reads: 'Here in 1610 Robert Lumsden killed Isabella Sudden.' The return route over **Barrow Law** is special, with the humps of several summits all around and a far-reaching view of the River Coquet channelling a silvery course through the valley.

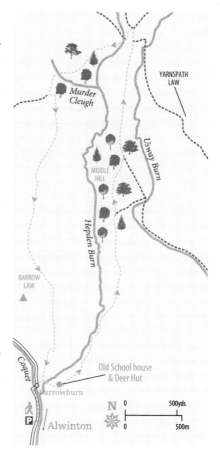

* * *

6 BREAMISH VALLEY

One of the big four valleys in the English Cheviots, Breamish Valley is quite different from the U-shaped Harthope and College valleys further north in that its shallow river takes a more roundabout route through the landscape on its way east. For that reason it doesn't have quite the same tunnel views, but the walker will instead feel embraced in an amphitheatre of hills. A major draw for many day trippers are the hillforts, and Linhope's waterfall which are fairly easy to access from the paved road running through the valley.

A paved track takes you up and down the hills and alongside the river for several miles into the core of the valley. You can drive as far as Hartside; thereafter the road to Linhope is just for residents.

As you hike or take the car for a walk through the valley, you will notice ancient cultivation terraces on many slopes. This whole area has been farmed for thousands of years; the evidence of which is all about you. There are Bronze Age burial cairns dotted in a number of places, the odd abandoned medieval village and an impressive concentration of hillforts built some 2,300 years ago. At Wether Hill and Brough Law near Ingram you can even see the outlines of Iron Age roundhouses.

Linhope Spout waterfall

Tucked below conical Ritto Hill and surrounded by some hefty summits is the secluded hamlet of **Linhope**, which hides under trees by the meeting of the River Breamish and Linhope Burn. The **walk** to the waterfall, a mile or so from Linhope, is straightforward with a short ascent and descent at either end but nothing that should put off families. Follow the farm track along the edge of a stand of conifers and then a well-trodden path round the side of a hill and down into a wooded ravine where Linhope Spout plunges 60 feet through a secluded rock cleft into a dark pool. A visit in freezing conditions is highly recommended when icicles the size of swords hang from the rocks.

7 INGRAM

🏠 **Ingram House** (page 275), **Cheviot Holiday Cottages** (page 276)

This sweet hamlet is the first you come to on taking the paved track through Breamish Valley. Tucked away at the end of a side lane, it is worth seeking out for the **church** which dates in part to the early Norman period. The tower and tower arch are some of the oldest structures. Look out for a small headstone a few feet high which has a stone carving of a man and woman holding hands, and a couple of headstones with skull and crossbones near the porch door.

The National Park Centre has closed and is now a useful café (see opposite), but an **archaeological exhibition** in an adjoining room is still open. It focuses on the valley's human history over several millennia, and features earthenware discovered during digs at the Iron Age hillforts in the valley.

Ingram and nearby Powburn each put on **country shows** in the summer. Ingram's (second Saturday in September) is more intimate with

WILDLIFE IN THE VALLEYS

Classic upland bird species like ring ouzel (also known as the 'mountain blackbird'), wheatear and whinchat inhabit the sheltered slopes of burns. Higher up, particularly where there are crags, look out for peregrine falcons and ravens (the Hen Hole in College Valley is a good place). Red grouse are frequently seen (and heard) flying out of heather, particularly in the Simonsides.

Along the fast-flowing rivers, dippers are easy to spot on rocks (like a plump blackbird with a prominent white 'bib'). The other bobbing bird you are likely to see on the shinglebanks is the grey wagtail (slate-coloured back and yellow chest). Look out for rarer yellow wagtails as well (almost completely yellow), particularly around meadows. Breeding waders include common sandpipers, oystercatchers, redshank, lapwing and curlew – or 'whaup' to give it its local name.

Northumberland boasts some of the best salmon and trout rivers in England, notably the rivers Tweed, Till and Tyne. Salmon and sea trout spawn in Cheviot burns. Find a bridge in autumn from which to watch them leaping over rapids.

Good places to look out for goosanders and otters are in the lower reaches of some rivers such as the Coquet (in the Rothbury and Brinkburn Priory area, for example) and the River Breamish around Ingram. Otters are famously elusive but you never know where you might spot one if you have the patience to sit quietly in a secluded spot at dusk or early in the morning. You're unlikely to chance upon one while out walking (they'll be aware of your presence and move on); you're much better off staying in one place and allowing them to come to you. Even if you don't see one, plenty of other birds (kingfishers, dippers, herons) and mammals (particularly bats on wooded stretches of rivers) will no doubt make an appearance.

family-orientated events (in recent years there was a creepy-crawlies 'roadshow' where children could touch various creatures) as well as the usual sheepdog trials and horticultural displays. The **Powburn Show** (2 miles north of the hamlet ◈ www.powburnshow.com; first Sat in Aug) features Cumberland and Westmorland Wrestling, food and craft stalls, pony jumping, livestock displays and so on.

▌▌ FOOD & DRINK

The **Muddy Boots Café** (✐ 01665 578120) sells simple sandwiches and cakes as well as walking books and a few local guides. The nearest place for hot food is the **Plough Inn** at Powburn (✐ 01665 578259), but you might want to venture a bit further east, to Eglingham's **Tankerville Arms** (page 241), to find really good pub fare.

Hedgeley Antiques & tea room
Hedgeley Service Station (A697), Powburn NE66 4HU ☏ 01665 578850

This is a great, affordable antiques emporium by the side of the A697 (formerly the Powburn Antique Shop). There's quite a lot to rummage through and some corners are better than others, but you'll generally find rustic wooden furniture (church pews, trunks, chest of drawers – that kind of thing), as well as linen, antique prints, secondhand books, china and oddments. Round the back by the petrol station is a friendly **tea room** (◌ closed Tue ♿) selling cakes and soups and which opens into another antiques shop mainly specialising in fabrics.

INGRAM HILLFORTS WALK

❋ OS Explorer map OL16; start: Bulby's Wood car park, ⚲ NU007163; 3 miles; difficulty: moderate hike with an initial strenuous climb; toilets in the car park; refreshments in Ingram (page 227)

This walk leads you to the most impressive hillfort in the area, as well as a few less obvious ones and offers views of ancient cultivation terraces. Some of the Hillforts Trail paths are not marked on the OS map but they are signed with waymarker posts and the tracks are clear.

Opposite Bulby's Wood car park (half a mile west of Ingram) a signed track leads steeply up Brough Law. Continue straight ahead to the most impressive settlement on this walk. **Brough Law hillfort** is a huge rampart of loose tumbledown rocks about 70 yards in diameter. With skylarks overhead, meadow pipits peeping from the grasses and far-reaching views into the valley, this is a wonderfully peaceful lookout spot.

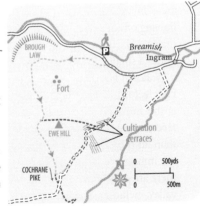

Continue in a southerly direction on a well-trodden grassy path across the plateau of Ewe Hill, ignoring the first Hillfort Trail path to the left. At the second waymarker post turn left and left again at the one after that. Walking down the east slope of Ewe Hill you'll see a mixed woodland bound by a wall. If instead you continue straight on you'll reach Cochrane Pike and its fort after a stiff hike up and down a steep sided valley.

When you reach a grassy track, turn left and head downhill. Look out for a fort on your right immediately next to the trail. The stones are grassed over but you can see the rounded shape of the settlement which is roughly 40 yards across.

Continue straight ahead, ignoring the waymarkers to the sides. Clearly defined cultivation terraces line the hillsides hereabouts. The path becomes a wide stony track which you follow back to the main road. Turn left and follow the road for a short way to the car park.

8 HARTHOPE VALLEY

Behold a letter from the mountains, for I am very snugly settled here, in a farmer's house, about six miles from Wooler, in the very centre of the Cheviot Hills, in one of the wildest and most romantic situations ... All the day we shoot, fish, walk, and ride; dine and sup upon fish struggling from the stream, and the most delicious heath-fed mutton, barn-door fowls, poys, milkcheese, etc

Sir Walter Scott in a letter to his friend, William Clerk, 26 August 1791

The house from which Scott penned the above letter was the remote farmstead at Langleeford by Harthope Burn which is regularly passed today by walkers exploring this glacial valley. Three of the highest peaks in the Cheviot range are within reach of the day hiker from here: The Cheviot, Hedgehope Hill and Comb Fell. Even those cycling along the valley bottom or pottering under trees by the river will find Harthope Valley as enchanting as Scott did over 200 years ago, with river birds and trout in abundance, sheep and grouse on the slopes and small waterfalls here and there.

Harthope Burn is wooded for much of its course and plenty of grassy areas invite a picnic and paddle. Those who can tolerate the icy waters flowing off the hillside will find bathing holes every so often including the magical Harthope Linn – a secluded plunge pool where the brave shower under a small fall overhung with mountain shrubs, trees and ferns.

Walks in Harthope Valley are plentiful. The path to the waterfall from Langleeford is described on page 230. Continuing beyond the waterfall is the most direct hike to **The Cheviot**. Another popular route is to **Hedgehope Hill** (the perfectly rounded massif you see poking up higher than all the other hills on the approach through the valley). You'll pass the impressive **Housey Crags** (a destination in themselves) from where there are great views of all the major summits peering down through the valley, including The Cheviot and Comb Fell.

The Cheviot

The most popular route to the top is that following Harthope Burn from Langleeford
(described opposite) but a more varied, longer & more strenuous alternative is via the
summits of Cold Law & Broadhope Hill accessed further downriver

If it weren't for the excellent Pennine Way footpath made of stone slabs, you'd really struggle to make your way across the table-flat squelchy quagmire that is the summit of Northumberland's highest mountain (2,674 feet). The gullies and peat bogs are so deep in places that to go off-piste means jumping from one island of coarse grass to another.

Perhaps I've just been unlucky, but pretty much every time I've been up to the top of The Cheviot, I find it sulking under a swirling smoke machine-like fog. If you happen to be here when The Cheviot is having a good day, you can see all the mountain ranges from Cumbria to the Lothians. Northeast of the stone monument, marking the highest point, are the fragmentary remains of a B-17 bomber that crashed into the mountain during World War II.

Despite the desolation, there's still something quite captivating about The Cheviot, partly because of its height and partly because it is located right in the middle of the Cheviot range with beautiful valleys and many other summits nearby. And, I suppose, there is a certain draw about a brooding hill like this that holds on to its cap of snow into summer.

⚐ TO THE CHEVIOT ON FOOT VIA HARTHOPE BURN

✳ OS Explorer map OL16; start: Langleeford, Harthope Valley ⚲ NT949220; 4½ miles to the
Cheviot & 8 miles for the round trip described here; difficulty: moderate route on grassland &
solid paths with some challenging climbs

Langleeford farmhouse is a popular starting point for the well-trodden footpath to Harthope Linn (and The Cheviot), for it lies at the end of the paved track into the valley.

If you continue on the farm track past Langleeford (don't cross the river but go through a kissing gate), you'll come to the inviting **Harthope Linn** in under two miles by following a path upriver. It's easy to navigate but feels longer because it's uphill the whole way.

From the waterfall to The Cheviot (a further 2½ miles), you will need a compass, map and good outdoor clothing. The stream bubbles in peaty hollows as it becomes narrower and quieter until Harthope Burn disappears altogether. Looking down the valley, you can see the yellow, lime and deep green slopes folding into each other, the North Sea in the distance and clouds sailing dangerously close to the hilltops. **The Cheviot** is reached after a stiff hike following a fence line to the Pennine Way (stone slabs lead the way to the summit at 2,674 feet). Return to Langleeford via **Scald Hill** – The Cheviot's shoulder.

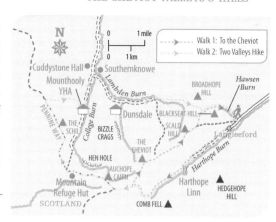

TWO VALLEYS HIKE VIA THE CHEVIOT

❊ OS Explorer map OL16; start: Langleeford, Harthope Valley ♀ NT952224; 16 miles; difficulty; moderate to difficult on account of the length, climb to the Cheviot & exposed hilltops; this is an overnight hike

Unless you're a super fit hill walker, you'll want to take two days to complete this strenuous circular route from Harthope Valley over The Cheviot to College Valley. I did it with a tent and camped out on The Cheviot (not recommended in poor weather, obviously), but a good option would be to stay overnight in the Mounthooly YHA at the foot of College Valley (page 276). Practicalities aside, this has to be one of the best long hikes in the area. It takes in two of the finest Cheviot valleys and provides many stupendous views of the endlessly folding Cheviot range where solitude and hardiness reign.

Set foot from Langleeford farmhouse off the main paved road through Harthope Valley and follow **Harthope Burn** upriver, passing the secluded waterfall, Harthope Linn. You'll cross the bolder-strewn river numerous times until the burn eventually sinks away under the peaty ground, not to be seen again.

With a fence line on your left, begin the final stiff ascent on to **The Cheviot**. At the top, turn right following the Pennine Way across the boggy summit on stone slabs. The highest point of The Cheviot (far from obvious on this table-flat hill) is marked by a prominent trig point on a plinth. Retrace your steps to the junction of two paths and continue along the Pennine Way in the other direction towards the Scottish border.

From **Auchope Cairn** all the way across **The Schil** enjoy the plunging views through College Valley below. Descending off The Schil, you soon come to a junction where you turn right for the downhill hike to the valley bottom along the edge of a conifer plantation. **Mounthooly YHA** sits by College Burn.

The return route begins on the east side of the river on a path that passes the remote holiday cottage of Dunsdale, which cowers beneath Bizzle Crags. Lambden Burn leads you away from College Valley and towards Harthope Valley, reached by hiking through ankle-tugging heather and up and over the saddle between **Broadhope** and **Blackseat hills**. Descend back to Langleeford along Hawsen Burn by way of a farm track.

* * *

9 HAPPY VALLEY

Some 2 miles south of Wooler; there's a rough parking area of sorts either end of Happy Valley: at Carey Burn Bridge & Coldgate Mill (reached by following Cheviot St from Wooler town centre to a ford); Middleton Hall has an official parking area but you'll need to make your way on foot to the river.

So the burning question will be: is Happy Valley as idyllic as it sounds? In an area with so many wooded glens and jazzy burns, Happy Valley has a lot of competition, but it is certainly a gem and easy to reach from Wooler. It's not on the scale of Harthope Valley (a continuation of Happy Valley) or Breamish Valley, but it has its own charms and can be walked in under an hour.

From Coldgate Mill, a footpath follows Coldgate Water upriver through woodland for a mile or so before the scenery opens into rough grazing pastures with gorse bushes and shrubs. Look out for hares and small birds. The final stretch to the junction with Harthope Burn is picturesque with heavily wooded slopes rising from the valley bottom and glimpses of the river which flows leisurely round shingle banks and boulders – and appears at its happiest.

FELL RACING

In June, runners make the climb over Black Braes to the summit of Windy Gyle during the annual **Windy Gyle Fell Race** – a nine-mile course with 1,500 feet of ascent. The current record holder completed the route in a breath-taking 57 minutes and (an all-important) 18 seconds; see www.northumberlandfellrunners.co.uk.

In comparison to the **Chevy Chase**, however, the Windy Gyle run is just a warm-up. The most arduous of all fell races in Northumberland is this 20-mile circuit from Wooler to the top of the highest peak in Northumberland (The Cheviot), involving 4,000 feet of ascent. Those up for the challenge should visit www.woolerrunningclub.co.uk.

10 WOOLER

🏠 **No 1. Hotel** (page 275), **▲ Highburn House Country Holiday Park** (page 276)

Promoted as the 'Gateway to the Cheviots', Wooler is indeed blessed with some very fine hill and river walks within just a few miles of its centre. If you are heading off into the Cheviot valleys or hiking the long-distance trail, St Cuthbert's Way, which passes through the town, this is your last opportunity to pick up supplies.

Wooler itself is a pleasant enough work a day market town built of stone and sits surrounded by green hills and fields. You'll find plenty of food shops, a couple of antiques emporiums, gift shops and cafés scattered along its principal street.

For **tourist information**, maps, hiking socks and walking books, head to the **Cheviot Centre** on Padgepool Place (page 212), which is located at the far western end of the High Street.

Every August Bank Holiday Monday sees the return of the **Glendale Show** (⬦ www.glendaleshow.com), held in farmland to the south of Wooler. It's one of the largest country shows in Northumberland where farmers display their best sheep and cattle, and musicians, local food producers, vintage vehicles enthusiasts and craftsmen and women put on a good family day out.

Walks from Wooler

To reach the start of some very fine hill walks, you need to venture several miles out of Wooler (I'm thinking particularly of Harthope and College valleys), but ramblers should not overlook the countryside closer to the town. **Wooler Common** and **Humbleton Burn** are reached within a mile of the town centre (signposted from Ramsey's Lane) and are ideal places for a short family walk or picnic. A longer hike could encompass **Humbleton Hill** and its Iron Age hillfort (tremendous views from up here). **Happy Valley** (two miles from Wooler; see above) is another child-friendly spot with a well-worn woodland trail by a merry little river. Waterfall lovers (and wild swimmers) should set foot for **Carey Burn Linn** – a short walk from its namesake bridge found on the road to Harthope Valley.

 FOOD & DRINK

The Good Life Shop High St, NE71 6BG ⬦ 01668 281700. Deli with everything you'll need for a picnic, including many local cheeses. Coffees to take away.

Milan Restaurant High St, NE71 6BY ✆ 01668 283692 ♿. Ask any local where the best restaurant in town is and they'll point you to this modern Italian set back off the High Street (go under the arch by the Black Bull). It's not cheap but the food's good.

11 KIRKNEWTON & YEAVERING BELL

Northumberland's largest Iron Age hillfort (pronounced 'Yevering') crowns the top of a double-peaked conical hill over 1,000 feet high near the entrance to College Valley (south side of the B6351 between Akeld & Kirknewton, ♀ NT928293). Apart from a superb view across the Cheviot tops in one direction and out to the North Sea in the other, you'll see scatterings of rocks and the signs of where over 100 roundhouses used to stand within the protective walls of the huge stone rampart. This perimeter wall would have once stood up to eight feet tall.

"Each herd is directed to the best grazing grounds by an old nanny who knows the hills well."

North of the B6351 in the field beyond the layby is the site of an Anglo-Saxon royal palace, **Gefrin** (the old name of Yeavering, derived from the Welsh for goat, 'gafr', which is nice because wild goats roam Yeavering Bell to this day.

If you continue northwards on the same road, you'll come to a picturesque church at **Kirknewton** dating from the 13th century. St Gregory's was mostly rebuilt in the latter half of the 19th century but its chancel is very old and it houses a 900-year-old stone relief of the Adoration of the Magi.

The annual **Kirknewton Country Show** is on the first Sunday in August.

WILD CHEVIOT GOATS

The shaggy, long-horned goats you may come across today in the Cheviots are descendants of the earliest primitive goats that were domesticated over thousands of years successively from the time of Neolithic farmers onwards. These scarce animals are not as timid as you might imagine but still have a wariness that is to be expected of a breed that has run wild in the hills for a very long time.

Occasionally walkers come across a kid that looks as if it's been abandoned. It hasn't of course and its mother will return soon enough.

Four herds are found in the national park: at Kielderhead NNR, Upper Coquetdale, and Yeavering Bell and Newton Tors near College Valley. Each herd is directed to the best grazing grounds by an old nanny who knows the hills well.

12 COLLEGE VALLEY

🏠 **College Valley Estates cottages** (page 275) ⚑ **Mounthooly Bunkhouse** (page 276)
Access from Westnewton (near Kirknewton on the B6351); permits for driving into the
valley are issued by Smithsgore (18–20 Glendale Rd, Wooler NE71 6DW ✆ 01668 281611)
on behalf of College Valley Estates; no permits are issued during the lambing season in
Apr–May; cost £10

This six-mile-long glacial valley is the most isolated and tranquil of all
the major valleys in the Cheviot range. Its seclusion is helped by the fact
that only 12 permits a day are issued for access by car (see above). Those
without a permit must leave their car in the designated parking area just
beyond Hethpool, and hike in. Sheep rule this road.

The paved riverside track into College Valley from Hethpool makes for a
wonderfully scenic cycle ride or drive through the valley, which is blocked
at the southern end by a wall of cloud-nudging summits protecting the
frontier with Scotland. You'll pass the odd plantation woodland and thick
patch of gorse; a few old shepherds' houses, now mostly converted into
holiday cottages, a bunkhouse (page 276), a load of sheep and an isolated
village hall about halfway through the valley.

Cuddystone Hall is a plain 1960s building with a nice big bell. It's
occasionally the scene of a night of dancing and celebration, this being
the most remote place to legally tie the knot in Northumberland – if
not England. If you get the chance to look inside (the door is sometimes
left open), the noticeboards display information about the planes that
crashed into the surrounding hills during World War II, and the famous
rescue of American airmen from the B-17 Flying Fortress (see box, page
236). Outside the hall is a **memorial** to those who lost their lives which
shows the locations of crash sites. If you hike to any of these places,
you'll find debris from the planes still lying *in situ*.

Exploring College Valley on foot

Some of the best Cheviot hill **walks** are reached from College Valley;
the only niggling thing for some hikers will be the long slog in on the
paved track running through the valley. You can, of course, hike from
Hethpool on St Cuthbert's Way then the Pennine Way, or various
other routes on the valley sides. If taking the road, when you reach
a wall of buxom hills at the southern end of the valley, the only way
onwards is up. Hiking along The Schil offers what Alfred Wainwright
described as an 'exquisite view' of the valley. I've described a less

SHEILA & THE FLYING FORTRESS

A snowstorm was battering the Cheviots on 14 December 1944 when nine US airmen were flying back to their base following an aborted bombing raid. They were flying low over the hills to avoid the plane icing up when they crashed into West Hill near the Braydon Crags. Two of the airmen were killed instantly and three managed to make their way to Mounthooly – now the bunkhouse at the head of College Valley.

Shepherds John Dagg and Frank Moscrop from Dunsdale and Southern Knowe cottages heard the plane come down. They went into the hills with John's border collie, Sheila,

which managed to sniff out the four other remaining survivors found huddled together in a peat gully.

The two shepherds each received a British Empire Medal. As for Sheila, she was awarded the animal equivalent of the Victoria Cross, the Dickin Medal, the first ever civilian dog to receive the medal.

The dying wish of the pilot of the B-17, who passed away in 2005 at his home in Fort Lauderdale, was that his ashes be scattered at the site of the plane crash where fragments of the wreckage still lie. The request was fulfilled by relatives later that year.

strenuous circuit taking in The Cheviot from Harthope Valley on page 231, as well as a couple of shorter walks at the entrance to the valley at Hethpool (pages 238–9).

Mounthooly YHA Bunkhouse (page 276) at the southern end of the valley is situated in a prime spot for exploring some of the most memorable hills and crags in the Cheviot range, including the Hen Hole, Bizzle Crags and the awesome whale-back Schil. A favourite view is from **Auchope Cairn** looking across to Scotland in one direction and down over the Hen Hole and the head of the valley in the other. Incidentally, if you were to get stuck up here in inclement weather, there's a basic refuge between The Schil and The Cheviot on the Pennine Way.

Hen Hole

This rocky, ice-sculpted chasm hides around the corner at the head of College Valley luring walkers into its deep cleft. It's well known to ravens, peregrine falcons and, in years gone by, golden eagles.

The demanding route criss-crosses College Burn the whole way to Auchope Cairn and requires hands and feet at times – and good lungs. Many an unsuspecting (and unprepared) hiker has scrambled too far through the chasm to turn back. The burn splashes from ledge to ledge for 1,500 feet until it reaches the valley floor, and at one point forms a trio of small waterfalls called the Three Sisters. A less strenuous route to The Cheviot is up and along The Schil (you can peer down the Hen Hole when you get to the mountain hut).

13 HETHPOOL

🏠 **College Valley Estates cottages** (page 276)

Hethpool is an eye-catching hamlet at the entrance to College Valley with a country house and a row of attractive cottages with roofs far longer than their walls are high. They were built in the Arts and Crafts style in the early 20th century.

Behind Hethpool House is a stand of mature oaks (no public access) called the **Collingwood Oaks**, which are named after Admiral Collingwood (see box, page 197) who is said to have walked around the countryside pushing acorns into the ground believing the trees would supply timber for the battleships of the future. Little did he know that metal would replace wood by the time his oaks matured. The Collingwood Oaks at Hethpool were actually planted by his wife while Collingwood was at sea. He was supposedly very pleased to hear about her project, but sadly Collingwood never saw these trees as he died in 1810 on his return to England. To mark the bicentenary of his death, a new oak woodland was planted near the road on the approach into Hethpool.

On the first Sunday in August you may see a small crowd gathering hereabouts for the annual **College Valley Show** which features terrier racing, sheepdog trials and folk music.

ADDERS

Britain's only venomous snake loves nothing more than a sunny clearing on a heather or bracken slope. An adder will quickly slip away into the vegetation if you get too close (usually before you've spotted it) and will move so fast that its distinctive black zig-zag appears as a thick straight line. Sometimes, they will coil and give you an angry hiss before making their exit. It's their way of saying 'back off' – and you should do just that. Anyone who is bitten should seek urgent medical help. Bites can be fatal to pets, though such occurrences are very rare. Few people would be stupid enough to approach an adder, but I did hear a tale of a soldier on the Otterburn Ranges who thought it would be funny to pee on a basking adder. Well, you can guess what happened.

Wanderings from Hethpool

Stunning views of College Valley are experienced on a number of walks from Hethpool. Of particular interest are the hillfort trails, of which there are quite a few around the entrance to the valley, including to Yeavering Bell (page 234) and the strenuous climb to the top of **Great Hetha** where you'll see the ramparts of a hillfort, as well as a stupendous view of the tops of many peaks. Also consider following St Cuthbert's Way along Elsdon Burn to **Ring Chesters** – another fort reached after a steep ascent (a slightly longer route this one). Less strenuous and under two miles long is the circuit to **Hethpool Linn** (see below).

Windy Gyle

The summit of Windy Gyle on the Scottish border tops 2,000 feet, making it one of the highest in the Cheviot range and for that reason one of the best known to hikers. For many Pennine Way walkers, crossing the peak is one of the most memorable moments on the entire long-distance path down the spine of England.

The windswept summit is one of the most remote corners in the Cheviots. All the major hills are in view: Shillhope Law, Hedgehope Hill, The Schil and The Cheviot. In the 15th and 16th centuries, wardens appointed by the king to control the lawless border country, used to meet in the Cocklawfoot/Windy Gyle area to settle disputes. These rendezvous sometimes ended in bloodshed, including one meeting in 1585 during which Lord Francis Russell, son-in-law of the English warden, John Forster, was murdered. Russell's Cairn, a Bronze Age burial cairn at the summit, is named in his memory. The many routes on foot to the summit include that from the River Coquet (page 224), along the Pennine Way, and from Cocklawfoot in Scotland.

✳ ✳ ✳

🚶 A LEISURELY STROLL TO HETHPOOL LINN

✳ OS Explorer map OL16; start: Hethpool, ♀ NT895282; 1½ miles; difficulty: easy route with just 1 short uphill section

Hethpool's waterfall is not a true cascade, but the rushing College Burn that pounds through a rocky chasm in a wooded glen is camera-pleasing stuff nonetheless, and this walk makes a very pleasant hour-long diversion.

Opposite Hethpool's row of cottages by a sharp bend in the road, a 'St Cuthbert's Way' (SCW) sign marks the start of this route. Head downhill and strike off left just after crossing the river, following the SCW sign. A stony track leads uphill on to open ground where a plantation forest has recently been felled. Ahead, you'll see a new woodland of mixed trees. For the time being, the views are uninterrupted. Go over a ladder stile by a gate (redundant when the stream is a trickle and easily crossed in one stride) and continue until you see another SCW sign leading you steeply downhill to the left following a high fence line. Entering woodland, you will hear the roar of the river in the deep ravine below. Ignore the SCW sign and follow instead the ordinary public footpath signs. You'll soon be at a footbridge above the river which offers the best river views on this walk. On crossing the bridge, the path swings to the left and you now continue upriver. When you reach a paddock, strike off left and cross a plank footbridge. Make your way over a hay meadow to meet the track you walked down on the outward journey. Turn right and return to the Hethpool cottages.

* * *

ROTHBURY & AROUND

From Hepple to Rothbury, luxuriant grasslands lie sheet-flat to the River Coquet which has carved a heavily ribboned course through the lowland meadows and created oxbow lakes under the gaze of the Simonside Hills. Beyond Rothbury – a prosperous town with a celebrated National Trust house nearby – the river curls around Brinkburn Priory before continuing on its journey to the sea at Warkworth.

14 ROTHBURY

🏠 **Alnham Farm & self-catering cottage** (page 275), **Hillcrest House** (page 275), **Orchard House** (page 275), **Tosson Tower Farm** (page 275) ▲ **Tomlinson's Café and Bunkhouse** (page 276)

Forested hills to the north and east shelter the capital of Coquetdale from the boisterous winds that punish the fell tops. To the south, beyond the River Coquet, green vales slope gently upwards until they come to an abrupt halt by the foot of the Simonside Hills. You can see why this market town makes an excellent base for walkers.

Rothbury itself is popular with visitors and has a couple of galleries and cafés and one of the most celebrated of all National Trust houses on its doorstep (Cragside), but mostly it's a busy rural town going about its business.

TWO SCENIC ROADS

Rothbury to Alnwick

A high road over the hills to the coast connects two of the most popular market towns in Northumberland. From Rothbury, the B6341 climbs steeply past Cragside and through Debdon Woods before reaching open heather moors. There are several pull-in places along the road from where you can take in the view of the Cheviot Hills. Don't miss Edlingham church and castle (page 249).

Rothbury to Breamish Valley

From Rothbury, follow the B6341 for a couple of miles to Thropton and then take an undulating road due north through the old-

world villages of Whittingham and Glanton to Powburn – the gateway to Ingram and the Breamish Valley. The roads around here climb quite high offering a tremendous view of the Cheviots rising above a timeless pastoral landscape: field upon field divided by hedgerows, old stone farm buildings, horses in paddocks, hares sprinting across pastures, foraging partridges and so on. This is a great bike ride. Early mornings are particularly memorable, especially in winter when the Cheviots are covered in snow and the lowlands look silvery green under a covering of frost.

The **town centre** holds much visual appeal: two rows of stone townhouses and traditional shops arranged either side of a green bank. A good number of **shops** around here go back several generations. They include a hardware shop and ironmongery established in 1888, a deli selling local produce, Otterburn Mill (an offshoot of the well-known clothes and country store in Redesdale; page 185), a bakery, a quaint toy shop that has been in the same family for 100 years (toy tractors seem to be their speciality), a traditional leather shoe shop, and a superb butcher. Many rural towns must have once been like this.

All Saints Church is a few paces away from the cross – dedicated to Lord Armstrong of nearby Cragside – on the triangular green, and it is worth visiting for its Anglo-Saxon font alone.

"All Saints Church is worth visiting for its Anglo-Saxon font alone."

The present-day church was largely rebuilt by the Victorians but the chancel still contains 13th-century masonry. It's the 1,200-year-old rectangular font pedestal that warrants a closer look (the bowl is 17th century). Considering its age, the stone carvings are remarkably bold and clear. On one side what looks like a tiger is carved walking through a forest, and on another, the haunting faces of the apostles looking up to Christ.

Housed in the Coquetdale Centre on Church Street is **Shepherds Walks** (✆ 01669 621044 ✐ www.shepherdswalks.co.uk ☺ daily ♿). The company is principally in the business of guided walks but they also sell pamphlets describing hiking routes all over Northumberland, maps and a comprehensive range of local guidebooks. Their hiking socks (Capricorn Mohair Socks) which are also stocked in many local shops in the region live up to their slogan: 'probably the best socks you will ever buy.'

Heading west along the upward-sloping High Street, you'll come to the **Congregational Art Gallery** that occupies an old church. Inside, there's a bright, contemporary art space displaying paintings, photographs and ceramics by highly regarded regional artists, and a large sofa by a fire where you can sit with a coffee and slice of cake (see below).

¶ FOOD & DRINK

Rothbury has plenty of cafés though none of them is particularly worth mentioning apart from the two places listed below. As for restaurants – the choice is really disappointing. You could try the **Turks Head pub** (✆ 01669 620434) on High Street (sunny back garden with children's play area), but for really good hearty food you're best heading out of town to somewhere like the **Tankerville Arms** at Eglingham (page 251) or **The Three Wheat Heads Inn** at Thropton (NE65 7LR ✆ 01669 620262), which has the added draw of a pub garden with a superb view of the Simonsides. **Picnickers** looking for supplies in Rothbury are well catered for thanks to a cluster of good local food shops around the centre. Sandwiches to take away and food for holiday cottages, barbeques, etc, are best sourced from **Tully's of Rothbury** (deli and pantry stocked with local produce), the **Rothbury Bakery** or **Rothbury Family Butchers**.

Congregational Art Gallery High St, NE65 7TL ✆ 01669 621900 ✐ www.thecongregational.org.uk ☺ Thu–Sun. Bright, contemporary café with a wood-burning stove and cosy settee in a converted church. Delicious cakes and good coffee.

Tomlinson's Café and Bunkhouse Bridge St, NE65 7SF ✆ 01669 621979 ✐ www.tomlinsonsrothbury.co.uk ♿ café only. Pleasant café adjoining the youth hostel and serving all-day breakfasts and good light lunches; evening meals on Fridays and Saturdays.

Walks from Rothbury

Breamish Valley, **Harwood Forest** and **Thrunton Woods** are a short drive from Rothbury, but there are also good walks right from the town centre. Two miles south along St Oswald's Way on the other side of the River Coquet from Rothbury are the well-known prehistoric rock carvings at **Lordenshaws** (see box, page 247). The views alone

BRIDGES ACROSS THE RIVER COQUET

Three striking multi-arched bridges span the Coquet from Rothbury to just beyond Brinkburn Priory. The oldest is in **Rothbury** town centre, parts of which are thought to be 15th century. East of Brinkburn, the mid 19th-century **Pauperhaugh Bridge** crosses the Coquet in five graceful arches. This is a good bridge from which to watch trout and salmon leaping over the rapids below in the autumn. Look out for goosanders and dippers from here to **Weldon Bridge** – the last crossing in the trio – which is best viewed from the riverside path. It dates to 1760 and has the added attraction of an inn (the Angler's Arms) with a dining area in an old train carriage. Follow St Oswald's Way along the south side of the river to gain the best views of Rothbury's bridges and riverside.

are worth the trek here. Keep on the same trail and you'll be into the Simonside Hills proper. It's a bit of a slog from Rothbury so you might want to drive (or get a taxi) as far as the Lordenshaws car park then put your boots on for a jaunt up into the hills.

Less punishing on the lungs is the gentle **riverside walk** from one end of the town to the other and on to beautiful Thrum Mill (eastern end of Rothbury). To access the **multi-use riverside path** (suitable for wheelchair users as far as the town centre), turn off the B6341 that enters Rothbury from the west. The turning is signposted and takes you to a car park where a clearly marked path descends to the River Coquet. Turning left will lead you to Rothbury town centre in half a mile. Look out for sand martins and kingfishers the whole way.

Another recommended **walk** outlined opposite climbs steeply from the town to the **Rothbury Terraces**.

Thrum Mill

A short stroll east from Rothbury along the River Coquet brings you to Thrum Mill. It's not so much the old flour mill (now converted into a house) that is of interest; more the dreamy river setting hidden from view by broadleaved trees. The Coquet is forced through a narrow stone gully and over rapids where anglers and herons fish by the water's edge, and the occasional kingfisher and dipper darts by; otters sometimes appear when it's quiet. I recently saw a young osprey catching a trout by the rapids – a very unusual sight for the location – but, in September when ospreys migrate, you never know where they might show up.

To reach Thrum Mill from Rothbury on foot, walk to the end of Bridge Street and take the footpath that leads to the riverbank (don't cross the bridge). Turn left and follow the path with the Coquet on your right for just under a mile. Cyclists or drivers should approach along the B6344 east out of town. There's a pull-in parking area by the river. Take care when walking along the road.

* * *

𝕔 A STIFF CLIMB ABOVE ROTHBURY

❀ OS Explorer map 332; start: Catholic church, Rothbury, ♀ NU053016; 4 miles; difficulty: don't be fooled into thinking that a walk from a town centre will be easy – this is a quite a demanding route with an initial steep climb & over some rough ground; refreshments: various cafés & pubs in Rothbury

So drawn are visitors to the view of the Simonsides and Coquetdale's floodplains to the south that most don't see the rugged heather moors to the rear of the town. To be fair, the Rothbury Terraces are well hidden by the town itself but the countryside up there is really worth seeking out. And even if you don't fancy the ascent, it's worth walking the first quarter mile from the town centre, just to enjoy the view of the river valley and Simonside Hills. I've outlined the route here but you'll need an Ordnance Survey map.

Head uphill away from the town centre and turn right up a lane by the Catholic church. It's a bit steep, but you gain good views after a few hundred yards. After another 500 yards or so, take a concealed path that runs alongside a house just after a cottage called Roding (stone steps and a handrail help you over the garden wall). Once past the quarry, there's a trail that takes you in a long loop under sandstone crags, across a heather plateau (sundews grow rampantly in localised areas up here) and through an old mixed woodland called Primrose Woods (a destination in itself) before descending steeply back to Rothbury town centre.

* * *

15 CRAGSIDE

Rothbury NE65 7PX ✐ 01669 620333 ☺ early Mar–early Nov, Tue–Sun during school holidays & bank holidays; gardens & woodland open until 19.00; in winter, open some weekends only; ♿ café but limited access to the house & paths; National Trust

> The electric light has been introduced into the house by the distinguished owner, who has utilised the power of a neighbouring burn to work the generating machine . . . Words are inadequate to describe the wonderful transformation which Lord Armstrong has made on the barren hillside as it existed prior to 1863. Every natural advantage has been utilised by the great magician.
>
> W W Tomlinson *Comprehensive Guide to Northumberland,* 1888

Tyneside industrialist and innovator, William Armstrong, was way ahead of his time when he set about filling his 19th-century country house on the outskirts of Rothbury with ingenious electrical gadgets. Cragside lays claim to being the first house in the world to be lit by electricity. Water was used to generate the electricity that lit Joseph Swan's novel filament lightbulbs; electrically powered gongs announcing dinner, buzzers to call servants and a fire alarm system were to follow. There's even a passenger lift for servants to transport coal through the house and an automatic meat spit in the kitchen.

Externally, Cragside is particularly eye-catching: part Gothic, part Tudor with many gables, tall chimney stacks, high-pitched roofs and timber additions. When viewed through a parting in the trees from the Debdon Burn, the house looks majestic crowded by so many lean conifers and thrust skywards like a Bavarian castle.

Armstrong (and his house) was famous in his lifetime and he hosted many dignitaries at Cragside, including the Prince of Wales and his family in August 1884 who came to inspect the intriguing new technologies. The **Drawing Room** was completed just in time for the royal visit. It's the grandest room in the house with a huge intricately carved marble fireplace, ornate plasterwork and a number of important paintings including a Turner watercolour. Reporting on the Royal Visit the *Newcastle Daily Journal* had this to say: 'The château itself was a blaze of light. From every window the bright rays of the electric lamps shone with the purest radiance.'

The rest of the house is by no means stately, but it's fascinating for other reasons and rich in Arts and Crafts detailing, including William Morris stained glass and wallpapers, and extensive oak furnishings.

Highlights for me are the **kitchen** with its lift and huge range, the **Turkish Baths** (especially the fine blue tile work in one plunge pool), and, of course, the **library** which was the first room in the world to be lit with Swan's lightbulbs.

The grounds

Some people visit Cragside just for the **gardens** and **woodland walks**. As its name suggests, the house is built into the craggy sandstone hillside and makes use of the rocks and varying heights to create romantic vistas. The wider landscape is very much part of Cragside's appeal and there are no walls shutting out the moors, burns and crags. The lakes are manmade and all the Scots pines, firs, redwoods, azaleas and rhododendrons were planted by Armstrong – well, technically by some 150 gardeners. They are said to have dug in seven million trees and bushes. Close to the house are formal terraces, picturesque bridges, an intricate bedding carpet, and the largest sandstone **rock garden** in Europe.

Narrow paths below the house wind through heathers and alpine plants and past a couple of cascades. A slender 1870s **footbridge** with elegant ironwork reaches across the Debdon Burn at some height offering a superb view of the industrialist's mansion through the trees. A short walk takes you to more **formal gardens** where hardy and tender plants from around the world bring an unexpected vibrant colour palate to the otherwise natural tones seen elsewhere on the estate. A beautiful **glasshouse** used to grow fruits must be seen. Note the turntables under each earthenware pot which enabled the fruits of fig, orange, grapefruit and apricot trees to evenly ripen (with the aid of an underground heating system).

"The house is built into the craggy sandstone hillside and makes use of the rocks and varying heights to create romantic vistas."

Armstrong's Victorian enthusiasm for efficiency, order and punctuality is not just reflected inside the house. The Gothic **clock tower** near the formal gardens helped regulate the hours of estate workers – all 300 of them at one time. It has two mechanisms: one to operate the clock and the other to chime a bell that sounded at meal times and at the start and end of every working day.

Within the wider grounds, there are 40 miles of waymarked **footpaths** as well as a scenic **carriage drive** that circumnavigates the whole estate via a couple of lakes.

Back at Tumbleton Lake by the visitor centre, there's a good **tea room** in a courtyard with all the usual National Trust offerings: scones, sandwiches and a handful of hot dishes made with seasonal produce. Around the peaceful lagoon are sought-after picnic tables.

16 BRINKBURN PRIORY

Near Longframlington (5 miles east of Rothbury) NE65 8AR ✆ 01665 570628 ⊙ Easter–end Sep (& shorter opening times in Oct); closed Mon & Tue; concerts most Sun afternoons ♿ English Heritage

At the bottom of a wooded track, the doorway to the priory church appears through a parting in the trees offering an enchanting first glimpse of Brinkburn. The 12th-century building, once inhabited by Augustinian monks, is otherwise completely hidden from view in a loop of the River Coquet. Late in the afternoon, sunlight pours through the stained-glass windows of the church bringing out the colour and patterns in the sandstone walls. You can hear the river, and thrushes singing outside, but on Sunday afternoons in summer, Brinkburn's string quartet or the local choir fills the priory. A **summer music concert** here is not to be missed.

"You can hear the river, and thrushes singing outside, but on Sunday afternoons in summer, Brinkburn's string quartet or the local choir fills the priory."

Architecturally, Brinkburn is celebrated for its Transitional style which blends Norman and Early English and dates from the end of the 12th century to the beginning of the 13th. A good example is the aforementioned entrance seen on the approach, which shows chevron detailing typical of the Norman style, and above, an arcade of three Gothic arches of the Early English style.

Inside the church – the only intact building in the monastic complex – there are no screens or obstructions to distract from the elegant tiers of lancet windows and towering pointed arches. Outside are a few remains of ruined priory buildings, but mostly your attention will be drawn to the **manor house** which was built out of the ruined monastic buildings and reconstructed in the 19th century. You can go inside, but it's in a terrible state. Some features remain undamaged including decorative plasterwork and the elegant floor-to-ceiling doors that open into the garden. Its very emptiness has a deeply evocative quality, however.

NORTHUMBERLAND'S SANDSTONE HILLS

Most visitors in Northumbria have heard of the Pennines and Cheviot Hills, but few people know of the sandstone hills sandwiched between the Cheviot foothills and the coastal plains that form a long arc from Berwick to Otterburn (roughly the area between the A697 and the A1).

The Simonside Hills near Rothbury are much walked; the rest is largely unheard of. Places like Bewick Moor, Hepburn Crags, Doddington Moor, Kyloe Woods and the Bowden Doors crags are appreciated only really by rock climbers, locals and archaeology enthusiasts. Unlike the rounded humps of the Cheviots, these hills are craggy and boulder-strewn and don't form quite such a pleasing panorama, but they do offer some of the most expansive views in the whole county: of the Cheviots on one side and the coast on the other. In a few places, you can see both on a clear day. Here, I've described the Simonside Hills and touched on some of the unsung crags, villages and moors further north between Rothbury and Doddington.

17 THE SIMONSIDE HILLS

A ramble along this whale-backed sandstone massif between Harwood Forest (on the outskirts of Elsdon) and Rothbury is a favourite with hill walkers from Northumberland and Tyneside. The views are magnificent:

PREHISTORIC ROCK ART

Northumberland is renowned for its numerous 5,000-year-old **cup-and-ring grooves and marks** carved into stone slabs. They are usually fist-size with a series of concentric circles formed around a central depression, and many are astonishingly well defined. Good examples are found at **Weetwood Moor** (east of Wooler), **Chatton Park Hill**, **Routin Lynn** and **Doddington Moor**. The most visited cup-and-ring marked stones in Northumberland are scattered in grassland close to **Lordenshaws** car park near Rothbury. They look particularly impressive when the sun is low in the sky and the lines really stand out. The remains of a medieval deer park wall, and ridge and furrow ripples in the fields indicate where medieval farmers ploughed the land.

Lordenshaws car park is four miles south of Rothbury and reached off an unclassified paved lane off the B6342.

MOUNTAIN BUMBLEBEES

Bombus monticola likes gorging on bilberry nectar in spring and heather in late summer, which makes Northumberland National Park a good place to see this distinctive bee with its black body, yellow mane and bright orange-red tail. It has declined massively in recent decades, but it's not too difficult to find in upland areas like the Simonside Hills.

miles of grasslands and forests stretching all the way to the North Sea, and the blue humps of the Cheviots in the distance. To the south, if the light is favourable, you can see Tyneside. I met a local walker up on Simonside who said you could once make out the red glow from Consett's furnaces in the days when the County Durham town manufactured steel.

What makes the Simonsides so distinctive, apart from the striking profile against the sky and famous prehistoric rock carvings at Lordenshaws, are its rocky outcrops. For the most part, however, the hills are covered in an expanse of heather with patches of bracken, cowberry, bilberry and the occasional peaty bowl and gully. Red grouse are easily startled in the heather and will take off with their characteristic 'go back, go back' call. In August, the Simonsides turn fuchsia when the heather flowers.

Walking in the Simonside Hills

You can traverse the Simonsides in a day – a hike made very manageable by the fact that once you reach the top of the escarpment, you stay at pretty much the same altitude the whole way (discounting the stiff climb to the summit of Simonside). A recommended **seven-mile linear route** starts from above the River Coquet at Hepple Whitefield Farm (by the unclassified road to Great Tosson, ♀ NY987996) and crosses the highest points on the Simonsides (Tosson Hill and Simonside) before descending to Lordenshaws. The route is pretty lonesome for the first few miles, but gets busier with hikers around Simonside. If you don't want to walk back the way you came, Coquetdale Taxis (page 214) will meet you at Lordenshaws car park if booked in advance.

The most popular linear route is from the cup-and-ring marked stones near the **Lordenshaws** (see box, page 247) car park to the top of **Simonside** and back down again (four miles). Many people also walk up through woodland from **Great Tosson** – a stone hamlet with old farm buildings and a crumbling pele tower at the foot of the escarpment.

18 EDLINGHAM

'Eadwulfingham' to give the hamlet its Anglo-Saxon name, lies equidistant between Rothbury and Alnwick (not to be confused with Eglingham further north). It's not so much the hilltop hamlet that is of interest; more its distinctive church and castle that are hidden somewhat from view at the end of a lane (reached from the B6341).

The stern-looking 14th-century tower of **St John the Baptist Church** provides a visual reminder of how dangerous the countryside around here once was. Invasions from the north were not uncommon and villagers and the priest may well have sheltered in the defensive-looking tower, which you'll notice lacks a belfry (you might as well open the door to attackers) and has slits instead of windows. It shares similarities with Ancroft's parish church, six miles from Berwick-upon-Tweed, which also has a rather squat, defensive tower dating to roughly the same period. The earliest masonry visible is Norman, seen in the south porch doorway (and its barrel-vaulted ceiling), nave and chancel arch.

Edlingham Castle stands in a striking position on a hillside close to the church with ragged moors and the viaduct of the defunct Alnwick–Cornhill railway as its backdrop. All that remains of the mid 12th-century house, which once had a moat and barbican, are its foundations, a few walls and part of its defensive tower, built in 1340. A severe chasm has formed in one of the walls, giving the structure a dramatic profile.

19 WHITTINGHAM

Are you going to Whittingham Fair?
Parsley, sage, rosemary and thyme.
Remember me to one who lives there,
For once she was a true love of mine.

Those who wander north of Thropton (which is west of Rothbury) on the quiet back lanes may chance upon this peaceful village on the edge of the national park. There's a traditional **summer show** held on the third Saturday in August, which was immortalised in the above ballad – at least it was until Simon and Garfunkel sang the now more famous Scarborough Fair version.

The village itself is very attractive with a good number of well-kept stone houses either side of a green bank studded with trees. The fountain at the top of the slope bears travellers in mind: 'May this pure fount perpetual streams supply to every thirsty soul that passeth by and may its crystal waters ever run unchanged by winter's frost, or summer's sun.'

Whittingham Tower, near the centre, is an impressive 14th-century fortified house constructed with huge sandstone blocks that was remodelled somewhat in the 19th century. Now a family home it was once a refuge for villagers during the centuries of cross-border fighting before it became an almshouse ('for the use and benefit of the deserving poor', as the inscription above the doorway informs us).

Following the River Aln westwards to Little Ryle, you'll see **St Bartholomew's Church** by the side of the road. The interior is notable for its surviving Early English architecture, but the most remarkable feature of the church is its tower, the lower part of which is Saxon.

20 OLD BEWICK

Most people whizz past Old Bewick on the A697 but for those taking a meandering route through the countryside or the high road to the coast, you might want to stop here. The hamlet itself is quaint enough with its old farm buildings and cottages, and there's a **hillfort** just behind the settlement, but it's the **Holy Trinity Church** tucked away up a lane half a mile north of Old Bewick that you should really see. Its hugely thick walls, slit windows and Romanesque chancel arch are clear giveaways as to its status as one of the oldest churches in Northumbria; it is Saxon in origin with enough of its structure surviving from the 11th century to describe it as Norman. One of the most interesting features is the carvings on the capitals of the chancel arch: the tree and two mean-looking heads at the top of each pillar may be a representation of the pre-Christian green man.

The ancient churchyard, enclosed by a burn and many firs and broadleaved trees, makes a wonderful sanctuary for animals and plants; snowdrops put on a dazzling display in February.

21 EGLINGHAM

Eglingham's stone houses stand either side of a sloping through-road. There's not a huge amount to see from a visitor's perspective, but what it lacks in attractions it makes up for with its pub which is one of the best for miles around (see opposite).

St Maurice Church has been much restored over the centuries, but it does have a Norman chancel arch. Its font dates to 1667 and bears the words 'wash and be clen' [sic]. One of the bells in the tower is called Anthony. It is apparently inscribed in German with the following words: 'Anthony is my name. I was made in the year 1489.'

¶¶ FOOD & DRINK

Tankerville Arms Eglingham NE66 2TX ✆ 01665 578444 ⊙ every day except Mon & Tue lunchtimes ♿. Downstairs this is a smart stone inn with low beams, wooden furniture, a fire and local ales; upstairs the rooms (B&B) are modern and decorated to a very good standard. The best thing about this cosy pub is the food, which is reasonably priced and extremely good (many locally sourced ingredients).

22 CHILLINGHAM CASTLE & PARK

Chillingham (2 miles south of Chatton) NE66 5NJ ✆ 01668 215359 ⌖ www.chillingham-castle.com ⊙ early Apr–end Oct, daily from 12.00, usually closed Sat; café

> Forgive any disorder by thinking and knowing that I rescued a roofless, floorless wreck of a castle, with a jungle having taken over the garden and grounds.
>
> Sir Humphry Wakefield Bt, 2002

Chillingham is one of the eeriest and most atmospheric castles you'll come across on your travels in Northumberland. It was besieged on numerous occasions during medieval times and many a captured Scot and Border Reiver were executed here. You certainly won't forget visiting the medieval fortress. A word of caution though: this is not like the castles at Alnwick or Bamburgh and you won't find polished cabinets displaying rare porcelain, dining rooms dripping in crystal and gold and immaculately laid-out rooms. I find it enthralling because it is not any of those things. Certainly, one of Chillingham Castle's greatest appeals is that you can touch a lot of what is on display and, in some rooms, even rummage through the owner's collections.

Many kings were entertained here, including Edward I who stopped off on his way north in 1298 to capture William Wallace (better known to Hollywood film enthusiasts as Braveheart). It wasn't until 1348 that Chillingham became a fully fortified castle. It's formed of four square-angled towers enclosing a central courtyard. The walls are embattled and the whole edifice looks pretty intimidating. You'll get the idea as soon as you step into the courtyard with its stern, grey walls, dark windows and ominous staircase leading to the Great Hall.

Cruel things have happened to prisoners held in the dungeons at Chillingham. 'If you were a Scot back in the 14th century and you were caught and brought to Chillingham Castle, it was a death sentence,' the curator, Bobby Fairbairn, told me. Still visible in the dungeon are lines carved by prisoners on the walls representing the number of days they had been in captivity. The recreated torture room contains skeletons in cages and various authentic medieval torture devices including an iron maiden and executioner's block. It's chilling stuff, and children (and adults) might find it harrowing, but you can just bypass that area of course.

Perhaps not surprisingly, Chillingham Castle is much frequented by ghost-hunters: many apparitions and strange goings-on have been reported by visitors and guests. 'I've experienced so many things that can't be explained – objects being thrown around the rooms and that,' says Bobby.

Many of the rooms are furnished in a medieval or Tudor style with wall tapestries, banners, armoury and the heads of various beasts hanging from the walls. You are unlikely to have seen antlers as big as those in the Minstrels' Hall: they once belonged to an elk that lived half a million years ago. When I visited the state rooms, it was winter time when the property is usually closed to visitors; Bobby pointed to the yellow drapes over the windows which I can only describe as looking full. 'If I drew those curtains, hundreds of bats would fall out,' he said. Time for a walk in the Italianate gardens.

Chillingham Park & cattle

Chillingham NE66 5NP ✆ 01668 215250 🖊 www.chillinghamwildcattle.com ☺ Easter–end Oct, closed all day Sat & Sun afternoons; tours on the hour

At the first appearance of any person, they set off in a full gallop; and, at the distance of two or three hundred yards, make a wheel round, and come boldly up again, tossing their heads in a menacing manner: On a sudden they make a full stop, at the distance of forty or fifty yards, looking wildly at the object of their surprise

Ralph Bailey describing a Chillingham bull in Thomas Bewick's *History of Quadrupeds*, 1792

The history of this ancient 365-acre parkland goes back to the founding of the Chillingham estate in the 13th century. When the wooded parkland was enclosed, its population of wild white cattle also became cut off; they have remained isolated from the outside world ever since.

Chillingham cattle are thought to be the last surviving native wild herd in Britain and are descended from the wild ox that used to inhabit the forests that covered much of the British Isles in prehistoric times. They certainly have a wild appearance with their unruly looking woolly coat and fierce horns.

The herd is currently around 100 animals strong but the population fluctuates from year to year. Over the hard winter of 1946 numbers plummeted to just 13 individuals. To prevent their near-extinction again, hay is provided during the winter; otherwise they are completely left to fend for themselves. 'They live and die by their own strengths as they have done for hundreds of years,' says Richard Marsh, the park warden.

"Chillingham cattle are thought to be the last surviving native wild herd in Britain ... they have a wild appearance with unruly looking woolly coats and fierce horns."

The best way of seeing the cattle is to join an hour-long tour with Richard through the parkland which encloses many ancient trees. You may see a bull fight, which is quite a spectacle. Because the animals are potentially dangerous, you can't visit the park without joining a tour. However, you can sometimes see the cattle from a permitted 6½-mile footpath (the Forest Walk) that runs around the perimeter of the parkland; take binoculars, and also look out for red squirrels.

SEVEN CASTLES

Close to Chillingham Castle and Park is a prominent earthwork where on a clear day you can see seven of Northumberland's castles: Warkworth, Alnwick, Dunstanburgh, Bamburgh, Lindisfarne, Ford and Chillingham. Known as Ros Castle (1 mile east of Hepburn, ♀ NU080253), this vantage point (above the Hepburn Crags) also provides an unparalleled panoramic vista of the Cheviots – catch them at first light for a truly memorable sight.

At about 3,000 years old and over 1,000 feet above sea level, **Ros Castle** is a double-ramparted earthwork which can be reached on foot from the Chillingham Park perimeter path (see above). If travelling by road, you'll need to zig-zag a little bit on the lanes east of the A697 (between Powburn and Wooler). You want the steeply ascending road between Hepburn and North Charlton (incidentally, this is a highly scenic route to the coast which goes over heather moorland). Before you reach the moors, there's a parking area from where you can walk to Ros Castle. Nearby and closer to the parking area is a hillfort.

Chillingham's church

Reached by stone stairs through the churchyard, St Peter's is usually overlooked by visitors entering the Chillingham estate to see its castle. Twelfth-century masonry survives in the nave but the most distinguished piece of stonework in the simple building is the mid 15th-century tomb of Sir Ralph Grey and his wife. Intricately carved alabaster saints and angels surround the tomb chest; on top lie the figures of the couple. During the Wars of the Roses, Grey had his son executed for supporting the wrong side though he escaped being hanged, drawn and quartered and instead suffered the somewhat better fate of being beheaded.

23 CHATTON & AROUND

🏠 **Chatton Park House** (page 275)

Admittedlly there's not a huge amount to see in Chatton, pleasant enough as it is, but the village does have an upmarket pub and restaurant (see below), and an esteemed art gallery at the eastern end of the main road. The **Chatton Gallery** (✆ 01668 215494 🖥 www.chatton-gallery.co.uk ⊙ Thu–Sun) showcases the paintings of the well-regarded landscape artist, Robert Turnbull, as well as other selected artists and sculptors.

The surrounding craggy hills are dotted with prehistoric sites, including **Chatton Park Hill** with its cup-and-ring marked stones. To find them, first locate the hill (a couple of miles northeast of Chatton) then look for the decorated stones inside the remains of a hillfort at the top.

🍴 FOOD & DRINK

The Percy Arms (Main Rd, NE66 5PS ✆ 01668 215244), at Chatton has reopened as an upmarket restaurant, pub and B&B. There's a luxurious finish to the 'country heritage' styled interior as seen at its sister inn, the **Northumberland Arms** at Felton, West Thirston (page 51). On the food front, expect a range of traditional British dishes (fish and chips, steaks, Sunday roast and so on), with plenty to satisfy carnivores.

White Swan Warenford (4 miles south of Belford) NE70 7HY ✆ 01668 213453. This 200-year-old, unpretentious inn off the A1 (once owned by the dukes of Northumberland, hence the family's motif about the place) is not well known outside of the local area but is very popular. I liked the fact that the provenance of the meat and fish is stated on the menu. Traditional meat dishes served with imaginative sauces and sides as well as vegetarian options. Book in advance.

24 ROUTIN LYNN:
PREHISTORIC ROCK ART & A WATERFALL

Between Doddington & Ford & just under 2 miles east of Kimmerston on an unclassified road to Lowick, ♀ NT982367

Although few visit this gem of a waterfall, possibly because of its obscure location, it deserves seeking out should you find yourself taking a cross-country route to Berwick-upon-Tweed or the coast. Its nearby prehistoric rock carvings are also well worth seeing.

If you fancy a walk to the waterfall, I recommend the route from Ford Moss Nature Reserve (page 260) via Goatscrag Hill, but, if you're short of time, the quickest way to Routin Lynn (sometimes called Roughting Linn) is to walk along a wooded farm track off the Lowick to Kimmerston road. After about 100 yards, follow a footpath on the left down to the secluded **waterfall**, which drops 50 feet over jagged rocks into a pool.

"Climb to the top of the craggy massif for a spectacular view of the Cheviots on one side and the North Sea on the other."

Return to the farm track and continue on your way to **Goatscrag Hill** following a fence line and passing a farm. Climb to the top of the craggy massif for a spectacular view of the Cheviots on one side and the North Sea on the other. A clear grassy track runs around the side of the hill whose south-facing rocky overhangs functioned in prehistoric times as a shelter and burial site. Take a closer look at the walls: what appear to be carvings of deer are etched into the sandstone.

SCENIC ROUTE TO THE COAST

If you are heading to the sea, I recommend the scenic B6349 which bypasses Chatton but does take you across a memorable bridge and over Belford Moor. **Weetwood Bridge** (a couple of miles east of Wooler on the B6348) spans the River Till and is one of the most elegant medieval bridges in Northumberland with a wide arch made of blushed sandstone. Its height above the water, rose masonry, splayed parapets, conical finals to its piers and view of the Cheviots are not easily forgotten, particularly when viewed *en route* to Wooler. There are also a few old metal lattice and stone bridges around here, including the early 19th-century **Fowberry Bridge**, set in woodland by **Fowberry Tower** (once a 15th-century towerhouse but now chiefly a late 18th-century manor).

More prehistoric rock carvings are found back at the crossroads (♀ NT983367). About 25 yards north of the road, and reached by a path through woods, is a huge stone slab in a clearing which is covered in **cup-and-ring** motifs of differing shapes. It is said to be the most decorated stone in Northumberland and the largest panel of prehistoric rock art in England.

25 DODDINGTON

At some point on your travels around Northumberland, you've probably come across **Doddington Ice Cream**. It's produced in the village of the same name, northeast of Wooler. Attractive as it is with its stone cottages and leafy surrounds, Doddington does not have a huge amount to warrant a special visit, unless you really like ice cream and prehistoric rock art (a winning combination in some people's books). Now, you need to hunt around a bit for the cup-and-ring marked stones on nearby Dod Law (see opposite); the ice cream, on the other hand, is easier to locate. Turn off the B6525 (signed for the Fenton Centre) and follow the road for no distance until you reach some farm buildings. Turn right and by the side of the lane you'll see a huge model cow (the real dairy herd grazes nearby fields – a rare sight elsewhere in Northumberland these days). Next to the cow is a refrigerator stocked with pots of ice cream for passing cyclists and walkers to enjoy on a summer's day (weekdays during office hours only). Help yourself and put your money in the honesty box.

"Next to the huge model cow is a refrigerator stocked with pots of ice cream for passing cyclists and walkers to enjoy on a summer's day."

Originally a traditional dairy farm, Doddington farm (✆ 01668 283010) began producing cheese in the 1980s and branched out into ice cream production in 2000 at a time when many dairy farms were closing. The family is proud of its heritage and product. Jackie told me: 'The ice creams sell themselves because they are quality products. There is nothing artificial in them; if it tastes of strawberries, that's because it is made with real fruit and nothing that is not natural.'

Northumbrian-inspired ices include Heather Honey made with produce from Chain Bridge Honey Farm in the Tweed Valley, Alnwick Rum Truffle and the legendary Newcastle Brown Ale.

NORTHUMBRIAN FOLK MUSIC TRADITIONS

Geoff Heslop, record producer who has recorded many of the most influential North East musicians over the last 40 years. He plays with his wife, Brenda, herself a songwriter, in their band, Ribbon Road (⊘ www.ribbonroadmusic.com).

The northeast of England is rich in music, and we are fortunate that this music is very much still alive with an increasing number of musicians performing and writing.

The history of music in the area probably begins for us in the Border Ballads, many of which were collected by Sir Walter Scott in the late 18th century. These songs tell the tales of great events and foul deeds from the region's bloody past. Many reflect the activities of the infamous Border Reiver families during the hundreds of years of troubles until around the mid 17th century. These were collected together in the volumes of the Child Ballads (those collected by Francis James Child in the 19th century). Many of these ballads are still sung today, including 'The Fair Flower of Northumberland', and 'Johnnie Armstrong' – which tells the story of one of the most notorious Border Reivers.

We have our own instrument, the Northumbrian smallpipes, which bellows-blown has a distinctive sweet tone. There's been a revival in the instrument since the mid 20th century, largely due to the increase in the number of pipe-makers; there are now a large number of players of all ages, both in the North East and throughout the world and many modern tunes are being written.

The two other contributors to the music of the area are the songs which came out of the industrial heritage of mining, shipbuilding and fishing and the music hall songs of the 19th century.

Many fine songs were written reflecting the often hard life of the workers and their families, but also the Geordie sense of humour in the face of it, such as 'Keep Your Feet Still Geordie Hinnie' and 'Cushie Butterfield'.

As for the **prehistoric rock art**, you'll need to first take a lane signed off the main B6525 at the south end of the village. It's signed for the golf course and is on the other side of the road from the turning for the church. A hundred yards ahead past a driveway with a cattle grid, you'll see a stile on your right into a field. Head uphill on to Dod Law. After about 150 yards, start looking for the decorated stones.

Doddington's **parish church** (originally 13th century but much altered since) is found in the far southwest corner of the village where it stands gazing over farmland to the Cheviot Hills. Note the little watch house which was built in the early 19th century to protect the dead from body-snatchers.

THE RIVERS TWEED & TILL

Tweed said to Till,
'What gars ye rin sae still?'
Till said to Tweed,
'Though ye rin wi' speed,
And I rin slaw,
Whar ye droon ae man,
I droon twa!'

Scotland's second-largest river, the Tweed, forms the border with England from Coldstream to Berwick-upon-Tweed. One of the best salmon and trout rivers in Britain, it is wooded for much of its length making it popular with anglers, canoeists and walkers. Along its banks are stone huts called shiels which were once extensively used by salmon fishermen; some have been converted to holiday cottages. There are several places worth stopping for, especially in and around Norham with its castle, old bridges and nearby honey farm.

The River Till (a tributary of the Tweed) flows north–south along the eastern edge of Northumberland National Park and eventually merges with the River Breamish. You'll find a cluster of quaint villages and historic sites along its northern reaches, notably Ford and Etal villages, Heatherslaw Mill and places associated with the Battle of Flodden in 1513 (now all part of the Joicey family's huge estate).

26 FORD

A sweeter little village than Ford could hardly be imagined outside of Arcadia.

W W Tomlinson *Comprehensive Guide to Northumberland*, 1888

Ford stays in the memory: its immaculate main street with an old fountain at one end (now a planter but wouldn't it be fabulous if it spouted water again?) is a picture of rural peace and has remained unchanged for well over 100 years. The Victorian-styled lanterns are not original, but let's not get too picky.

Few cars – and usually none at all – park on the street (apparently residents park at the back) so it really feels like you are stepping back in time. This could be the set of a BBC period drama; all it lacks is a carriage, and a bonnet for the lady behind the post office counter. The estate office told me: 'some visitors arrive at the village and it looks so perfect that they think it is private and they can't go in.' You can enter and parking is permitted on the main street, but do you dare pollute the view with your modern machinery?

Lady Waterford Hall (☏ 01890 820503, 07790 457580 ☉ mid Mar–end Oct, daily; by appointment during winter ♿) was a school until the 1950s. The building – and the rest of the village – was commissioned by Louisa Anne, Marchioness of Waterford, who became the sole owner of the Ford estate on her husband's death. She was an accomplished painter and spent 22 years creating the striking pre-Raphaelite-esque frescoes inside the hall. The paintings depict biblical stories but the figures are all local people who sat for Lady Waterford.

At the top of the street (the opposite end to the fountain) a ceramic relief of Queen Victoria bears down on the village from above the doorway of Jubilee Cottage. Turning left, you'll come to a curious cottage with a giant stone horseshoe over its doorway. It was once a blacksmith's but is

"At the top of the street a ceramic relief of Queen Victoria bears down on the village from above the doorway of Jubilee Cottage."

now an **antiques shop** (☏ 01890 820521). Further down the same lane, is a quaint **secondhand bookshop** (☏ 01890 820500, 01361 850692) squeezed into the two front rooms of the old estate Drawing Office.

St Michael's and All Angels Church stands by the side of Ford Castle facing the Cheviot Hills. The building goes back to medieval times but was restored in the mid 19th century. It has some curious features including the two faces either end of the arcades. The little man with a beard near the porch is medieval; his facing friend is Victorian. Outside, looking at the porch, you'll see more stone heads including two creepy faces to the right of the entranceway. At the back of the church (inside) are a few medieval memorial stones on the ground. One is said to show the Northumbrian bagpipes complete with a chanter and bellows but as much as I stared at the stone, I couldn't make it out (not helped by the table on top of it). Perhaps you'll have better luck. In the churchyard are a number of very old gravestones from the early 18th century and a tiny memorial stone dated 1641. In the sloping field is the ruin of a vicar's pele tower.

Opposite the church is the Old Dairy, now a café (page 260) and **architectural antiques emporium** (☉ Wed–Sun), selling an assortment of period furniture, fixtures, fireplaces, old garden tools, vintage jugs, maps and oddments.

Ford Castle is a staggering 13th-century fortified mansion with three surviving corner towers and imposing gateway and curtain wall. Unfortunately, it's not only closed to the public but is also mostly hidden by trees; the best views are from St Michael's churchyard. In the weeks before the Battle of Flodden in 1513 (see box, page 265), James IV of Scotland is said to have spent a few nights with Lady Heron in the fortress (her husband having been previously captured by the Scots). As the king took his leave, he set the place alight.

ᵀ❘ FOOD & DRINK

The Restoration Coffee Shop Old Dairy, TD15 2PX (opposite Ford Castle) ✆ 01890 820325, 01289 302658 ☉ Fri–Sun. Small café adjoining a great antiques store and serving posh coffees, teas, scones, sandwiches and cakes on vintage china. An outside marble champagne bar invites visitors to enjoy a glass of fizz while taking in the view of the Cheviots.

27 FORD MOSS NATURE RESERVE

Near Ford village, reached from the B6353, ♥ NT970375; Northumberland Wildlife Trust

Enclosed by a thick band of pine trees a mile east of Ford village is this rich lowland peat bog. Don't let those last two words put you off – it's a tranquil reserve inhabited by many birds and plants, and is a very pleasant place for a walk. The central area lies in a hollow (once a lake formed after the last ice age) and is covered by heather, thick sphagnum mosses, hare's-tail cottongrass and patches of cranberry and bog myrtle. The insectivorous round-leaved sundew grows here (see box, page 216).

The most prominent feature is a tall brick chimney that marks where a coal mine once operated. A path (part bridleway, part permissive footpath) runs around the perimeter of this basin. You can take a longer walk which encompasses **Goatscrag Hill** and **Routin Lynn** (page 255). A spectacular view, waterfall and prehistoric rock carvings await those who make the climb.

28 ETAL

Your first glimpse of Etal's single street, which connects the manor at one end with the castle at the other, is quite a surprise: the row of whitewashed stone cottages and thatched inn (the only thatched pub in Northumberland) looks more like Suffolk than Northumberland. The village was laid out in the mid 18th century (though some of the houses have since been rebuilt) and it draws a similar reaction as Ford because of its old-world character. These two villages must be some of the most photographed places in north Northumberland.

Just south of Etal and visible from the B-road, is a **cricket ground** where matches are held on weekends in summer. There's even a women's team that plays on Saturdays.

English Heritage cares for **Etal Castle** (✐ 01890 820332 ☉ 1 Apr– early Nov, daily) which is not exactly the most intact fortress in Northumberland but it still retains its gatehouse and keep. Inside, there's an interesting exhibition explaining the history of the Battle of Flodden fought in 1513 at nearby Branxton.

The castle stands above the **River Till** and the disembarkation point for the Heatherslaw Light Railway (page 262). A footpath runs north along the wooded riverbank, which is studded with old oak and willow trees and makes for a pleasant stroll. The old cornmill by the river is now the workshop of furniture makers, Taylor and Green of Etal.

Opposite Etal's main street on the other side of the B6354, **St Mary's Chapel** stands in the grounds of Etal Manor. The gated driveway gives the appearance that the parkland is private, but you are permitted to walk to the chapel. The building dates to the mid 19th century and was constructed in memory of Lord Frederick Fitz-Clarence, the one-time lord of the manor (and illegitimate son of the Duke of Clarence, later William IV). He is interred below a prominent tomb carved with a sword and foliated cross, which is reached via a small door to the left of the organ.

¶¶ FOOD & DRINK

For really good hot food and smart dining, the **Collingwood Arms** in Cornhill-on-Tweed is your best bet for miles around (page 264).

Lavender Tearooms TD12 4TN ✐ 01890 820777 ☉ daily, but closed Fri from Nov to Apr. Sweet café in the post office, selling sandwiches, scones and baked potatoes, coffees, etc. Outdoor seating when the weather's fine.

Heatherslaw Mill

Near Cornhill-on-Tweed TD12 4TJ ✐ 01890 820488 ⟁ www.ford-and-etal.co.uk ☉ Easter– end Oct school holidays, daily; café

Heatherslaw, between Ford and Etal is the only working water-powered cornmill in Northumberland (at one time there were 140 in the region).

Information boards inside explain that a mill has stood here since the 13th century, although the present structure dates to the 19th century. You'll also find out about the milling process and social history of the area and see the millstones and water wheel in action. The shop sells biscuits, cakes and bags of rye, wholemeal and spelt flour produced on site. The bakery opposite the cornmill was making Swiss rolls when I visited and the smell of chocolate was wafting along the riverside – it was enough to lure me off my bike.

Heatherslaw Light Railway

Near Cornhill-on-Tweed TD12 4TJ (between Ford & Etal) ✆ 01890 820317 ♦ www. heatherslawlightrailway.co.uk. ◌ Apr–end Oct & around Christmas, hourly service between 11.00 & 15.00

Small carriages clank along behind the 15-inch-gauge steam engine for the four-mile journey from Heatherslaw Mill to Etal village. It's very much aimed at families with children and costs just a few pounds. You can walk the return journey from Etal by way of a path running parallel to the B-road at the top of the village.

Hay Farm Heavy Horse Centre

Hay Farm (between Ford & Etal) TD12 4TR ✆ 01890 820601 ♦ www.hayfarmheavies.co.uk ◌ Tue–Sun; free admission but donations welcomed ♿

A short walk east from Heatherslaw Mill (under a mile) to see Hay Farm's Clydesdale horses is recommended for families and anyone who finds these friendly giants endearing (who doesn't?).

On demonstration days, horses are ridden in their finery and you'll hear about their traditional duties when they worked the land. At other times, visitors are welcome to get up close to the animals and see the displays of horse-drawn machinery. Built in the 18th century (with 19th-century additions), the farm's historic barns, stables, granary and engine house are an added attraction.

In the summer there is a dedicated heavy horse show, the **Festival of the Heavy Horse** (♦ www.heavyhorsefestival.co.uk), which makes for a great family day out. Watching the horses being ridden and pulling vintage machinery is quite a sight. It is also an opportunity to sample sample regional foods produced by local farms, and watch craftsmen and women demonstrating traditional skills (there's a wheelwright blacksmith, for example).

HEAVY HORSES IN NORTHUMBERLAND

See *Hay Farm Heavy Horse Centre*, opposite

'It's a horse with a purpose,' says Vivienne Cockburn from the Milfield Heavy Horse Association at Hay Farm near Etal. 'Clydesdales worked the land all over Northumberland and moved agriculture forward. They were used for everything: in forestry, haulage, shipping, agriculture and even by milkmen, but now they're a rare breed.' At Hay Farm, crops were threshed and then taken to nearby Heatherslaw Watermill – a job involving the use of some 17 Clydesdales that worked out of the farm. The introduction of the tractor changed all that and by the mid 1950s, these powerful work horses became redundant. Thousands of Clydesdales were destroyed all over Northumberland.

In 2011, Clydesdale horses returned to the Grade II-listed 18th-century farm predominantly for the enjoyment of local people and to preserve the connection of the breed with the area. 'It's very rewarding seeing children listening to grandparents talking of their memories of these gentle giants and passing on a bit of history,' says Viv.

Duddo Stones

1 mile northwest of Duddo village (between Norham & Ford), ♀ NT931437

This Bronze Age stone circle dates from around 2000BC and is prominently situated on top of a flat hill in an arable field. The five stones, which stand between five and ten feet tall, are pretty arresting (like giant fists thrust from the ground). They look most striking late in the afternoon when the sun picks out the grooves and ancient cup marks in the stones. Human remains were excavated from the central area in the late 19th century, suggesting the site had mythical or sacred value, as is common with stone circles elsewhere.

Duddo Farm permits access to the stone circle which is signposted from the village and takes about half an hour to reach.

29 BRANXTON

🏠 **Collingwood Arms** (page 275)

This unassuming hillside village is mostly of interest for its proximity to the Flodden battlefield (see box, page 265), but it does have a wonderful little church and one of the quirkiest visitor attractions in the region: the Cement Menagerie (page 264). On the side of the village green is a red telephone box that Branxton proudly claims is the smallest tourist information 'centre' in the world.

A short walk or drive west out of Branxton on your way to the Flodden Field battle site is the **Parish Church of St Paul**, situated on a breezy hill with views of undulating hills (if travelling from the village, go left when you reach a fork in the road). The oldest part is the chancel arch which dates from the 12th century. Wounded soldiers were brought here following the 1513 battle fought on the nearby hillside, and it's said that the body of James IV of Scotland, wrapped in the Royal Standard, lay here before being taken to London.

If you continue away from the church for a third of a mile up the road, there's a parking area from where a footpath leads steeply up Branxton Hill (site of the Battle of Flodden) to a memorial cross, overlooking the village and dedicated 'to the brave of both nations'.

The Cement Menagerie
Branxton village, opposite the telephone box & next to the fountain; free admission but please leave a donation to ensure its survival for the future pleasure of others

This is one of the most curious of museums – if you can call it that – in Northumberland and deserves to be better known. Between the shrubs, trees and water features in the back garden of an ordinary house in Branxton village are colourful life-sized animals made of cement. There's a giraffe, panda, deer and hippo; a man on a horse and another on a camel; and many small animals and birds hiding in bushes. It was built over several decades in the 20th century by a retired joiner for the enjoyment of his disabled son.

Since the death of its creator in 1981, the wonderful garden and its menagerie has been passed down through the family who, thankfully, have kept it open to the public.

FOOD & DRINK

Collingwood Arms Main St, Cornhill-on-Tweed TD12 4UH ☏ 01890 882424 ⚐. This old coaching inn above the River Tweed (note the words 'post horses' above the porch) is one of the best small hotels and restaurants in north Northumberland. The dining room is chic (muted colours, wooden floors, contemporary tableware), the service friendly and attentive, and the food a hit with those who appreciate traditional British dishes made with local ingredients (red meat from farms on the border, fish from Eyemouth, bakery items from Heatherslaw Mill and some vegetables from the kitchen garden); all puddings are made in-house. Lighter dishes and lunches are served in the brasserie and pretty rear garden. Also see *Accommodation* on page 275.

30 TWIZEL BRIDGE & CASTLE

Close to where the River Till breaks away from the Tweed (halfway between Cornhill-on-Tweed and Norham on the A698) is one of Northumberland's most striking medieval bridges.

Twizel has five arched ribs on its underside supporting a single-span that curves over the lazy River Till. In the days leading up to the Battle of Flodden in 1513, both the English and Scottish armies would have crossed this newly constructed bridge on their way to battle. Above the river and bridge, trees rise on a steep bank to meet Twizel Castle which peeps above the canopy. It's now a crumbling fortress draped in ivy but

BATTLE OF FLODDEN

The last medieval battle in England – and the most significant in Northumberland – was fought on a hillside just outside Branxton village, four miles southeast of Coldstream on the Scottish border.

The 1513 clash between the Scots and the English was sparked by Henry VIII's attack on France which put James IV of Scotland in the difficult position of renewing the 'auld alliance' between France and Scotland at the request of the Queen of France. And so a huge Scottish army left Edinburgh for northern England in mid-August, led by the king. They crossed the River Till over Twizel Bridge and took Norham after a siege lasting six days.

By the end of August, the Earl of Surrey, whom Henry VIII had left in charge of defending England, arrived in Newcastle and proceeded north with an army of equal size to the Scottish force – around 30,000 men.

The two sides came together on 9 September 1513, at Branxton Hill: standards flying, knights in armour and men with arrows, swords and long spears (pikes) at the

ready. The Scots had the more advantageous position at the top of the hill, bearing down on the English along Pallin's Burn, but they missed a prime opportunity to advance. In the end, the English archers were devastating in their precision and the Scots with their cumbersome pikes were slaughtered in their many thousands – perhaps 9,000 men. The battle lasted just a couple of hours, resulting in victory for the English army. By dusk, the King of Scotland, many noblemen and thousands of men on both sides lay strewn across the hillside.

Every year a few hundred horseriders make the journey from Coldstream to Branxton Hill to pay homage to the fallen soldiers of 1513. Led by the 'Coldstreamer' carrying the town's standard, it's quite a spectacle to see the riders galloping over the fields. The Coldstream Riders' Association (www. coldstreamcivicweek.com) organise the annual event in early August as well as a few other ride-outs in the same week, including to Norham.

still commands attention. It's made of the pinky grey sandstone you find quite a lot round here.

A stroll along the wooded banks of the Till makes a very pleasant diversion. I've described a circular route taking in the castle, bridge and Till (see below), but you could just take the **riverside path** that is reached through a gate by a parking area on the north side of the bridge.

❋ ❋ ❋

🚶 TWIZEL CASTLE & AN AMBLE ALONG THE TILL

✺ OS Explorer map 339; start: Twizel Bridge, 📍 NT885433; 2½ miles; difficulty: fairly easy route with an initial climb

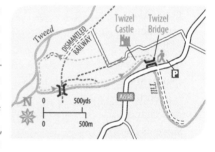

Though short, this walk involves a fairly steep ascent to the castle. The return is made via farmland and then along the wooded banks of the Till to meet Twizel Bridge.

From the parking area on the north side of Twizel Bridge, go through a gate and take a track steeply uphill to the medieval ruin of Twizel Castle. Once you've taken in the castle, strike across the field in a northwesterly direction and over a stile on to a quiet country lane. Turn left. The lane bends sharply to the right. After 150 yards, take a footpath on your left and cross the field in front and over the dismantled railway before descending to the River Tweed where you pick up the riverside path. Turn left and continue for no distance until you meet the Till. The final leg takes you under the stone legs of a viaduct and along the dreamy banks of the Till to meet the medieval Twizel Bridge. A short climb through trees leads back to the start of this walk by the gate and parking area.

❋ ❋ ❋

31 NORHAM

The ancient small border town of Norham is best known for its castle that rises above the River Tweed on a rocky eminence looking every bit as ragged and romantic as when William Turner painted the scene in the late 18th century. This fortress once kept a watchful eye on Scotland on the other side of the Tweed, and Norham town, nestled in a loop of the river half a mile to the west.

The history of Norham starts with the founding of a monastic centre in the 7th century. A church has stood here since at least AD830 though the present St Cuthbert's is of Norman origin. The town grew around the castle from the 12th century but pretty much everything you see today, except for the medieval layout, market cross and parts of the church, dates from the 19th century. When Beatrix Potter visited Norham she was not impressed, writing that 'every tenth house is a Public'. Today only two pubs remain in business.

Broad streets lead to a large **green** surrounded by stone houses where farmers and fishermen used to live. Round the corner on West Street a gun makers service the thriving country sport industry in these parts. Many of the houses are built of the

"Broad streets lead to a large green surrounded by stone houses where farmers and fishermen used to live."

same blushed sandstone used in the construction of the castle and other buildings in and around the Tweed valley. The stone **market cross** is quite an eye-catcher, the lower part of which dates to the medieval period (Norham was granted a licence for markets in 1293).

Even to the lay eye, **St Cuthbert's Church** has a strikingly long nave and chancel. The building has been much restored over the centuries since its construction in Norman times but there is stonework from the 12th century that survives, notably the chancel arches. Pevsner in his *Buildings of England* series describes the south arcade as 'truly majestic'.

On the outskirts of the town, Norham's **old train station** (on the A698, TD15 2LW) was lovingly restored and a small museum opened to the public on certain days but it was put up for sale in 2013 and it's not known if the new owners intend to allow access.

On the other side of the Tweed, reached by crossing Norham's stone arched bridge and turning right at the crossroads, is **Ladykirk Church** – a fine example of Scottish Gothic architecture in the village of the same name. It was built (on quite some scale) in the late 15th century on the order of James IV of Scotland after he saw a vision of the Virgin Mary on falling from his horse in the nearby river.

Norham Castle

TD15 2JY ✐ 0870 333 1181 ☺ Apr–end Sep, daily; English Heritage

In medieval times, the bishops of Durham ruled Norham, and the castle, which started life in 1121 as a timber building, was their northern stronghold. It was rebuilt in stone towards the end of the same century with a keep and curtain wall and thereafter underwent many changes and additions. Much of what remains today dates from the 16th century, though fragments of the early stone walls and arches survive. Situated as it is on the border with Scotland, it was besieged many times (13 to be more precise) from its construction until it succumbed to James IV of Scotland in the days before the Battle of Flodden in 1513. Since then it has been left to the elements and is now a ruin. Nevertheless, it's still an impressive fortress with a brute of a keep, moat (now dry), vaults and crumbling walls.

FOOD & DRINK

Norham has a couple of pubs, including the **Masons Arms Free House** on West Street (℘ 01289 382326), which serves real ales and food. The new owners have plans for a tea room and to install bike racks to make it attractive for touring cyclists passing through the village. Accommodation upstairs is to be refurbished. A 200-year-old butcher's shop, **Foreman & Son**, opposite the village green sells rare-breed meats and pies.

32 CHAIN BRIDGE HONEY FARM

Horncliffe, Berwick-upon-Tweed TD15 2XT ℘ 01289 382362 ⊘ www.chainbridgehoney. co.uk ⊙ Apr–end Oct, daily; weekdays only at other times; free admission; café (⊙ closed Nov–Easter)

Chain Bridge Honey is as ubiquitous in Northumberland as Craster kippers, Doddington Ice Cream and the Northumberland Cheese Company, and no doubt you will have already come across their pots of liquid gold in farm shops, B&Bs and delis across the North East. Fenwick's of Newcastle sells it and I've seen it on the shelves in London's Fortnum & Mason's.

"Chain Bridge Honey is as ubiquitous in Northumberland as Craster kippers, Doddington Ice Cream and the Northumberland Cheese Company ... the Flower Comb Honey has a particularly strong taste and scent."

You can buy (and try) all their different honeys and various beauty products from the friendly visitor centre at the farm. The Flower Comb Honey has a particularly strong taste and scent (I've never found a flower honey as good as this anywhere in England). In the shop you'll see a working hive with an observation glass panel where you can watch the honey bees doing their thing. An exhibition room next door tells you everything you want to know about bees and bee-keeping.

Vintage tractor enthusiasts may enjoy a display of vehicles on the farm, which includes an old double decker bus (now a quirky **café** selling sandwiches, teas and cakes). A memorabilia collection upstairs from the vintage tractors is full of an assortment of random objects from the 1940s onwards – from old radios to sweet jars.

33 UNION CHAIN BRIDGE

Connecting the Honey Farm with Paxton House, this magnificent 449-foot-long iron suspension bridge spans the Tweed. When it opened in 1820, hundreds turned up to watch its designer, Captain Samuel Brown, cross the bridge with horses pulling carts laden with an estimated 20 tons. Among those in the audience was the great Scottish engineer, Robert Stevenson (of lighthouses fame). A young Isambard Kingdom Brunel, accompanied by one of France's esteemed engineers, Charles Navier, visited a few years later. Clearly, this was a bridge causing quite a stir among the engineering giants of Europe – and rightly

"Connecting the Honey Farm with Paxton House, Union Chain Bridge, a magnificent 449-foot-long suspension bridge, spans the Tweed."

so: at the time it was the largest iron suspension bridge in the world. Captain Brown knew a thing or two about structures made with decking that are designed to move, from his time in the Royal Navy. His flexible chain links are said to have been based on a ship's rigging blocks.

To find out more about the bridge, see the exhibit at the Chain Bridge Honey Farm (see opposite).

34 PAXTON HOUSE

Near Berwick-upon-Tweed TD15 1SZ ℘ 01289 386291 ◌ www.paxtonhouse.co.uk ☺ Apr–Nov, daily; café ♿; café & partial access into house

On the Scottish side of the River Tweed – and reached quite marvellously by road from England by crossing the suspension bridge at Horncliffe – is this celebrated country house built in the Palladian style by James Adam in 1758. In 80 acres of landscaped parkland, it looks down through trees to the river below.

Much of the interior and its furnishings date to when the house was constructed, including the Chippendale furniture, French wallpapers and Rococo plasterwork. Many of the paintings and antiques were amassed during the first owner's Grand Tour of Europe.

The **picture gallery** is impressive for its collection of paintings, some of which are on loan from the National Galleries of Scotland. One canvas in the house which is of local interest depicts the nearby Union Chain Bridge spanning the Tweed with net fishermen in the foreground. Also memorable is the plasterwork in the **dining room** and the restored **Georgian kitchen**.

Seasonal highlights in the formal **gardens** are the daffodil displays in spring and flower borders in summer. Nearby, children can burn some energy on the zip wire in the **adventure playground**.

A pleasant downhill stroll through wooded grounds leads you to the banks of the Tweed where a tiny **museum** in an old boat house highlights the fishing heritage on the river. Traditional fishing using large nets is still practised today. The best thing about this for visitors is that some of the salmon and sea trout caught is sold in the café. On certain days in summer, visitors can help pull in the nets from the gravel shoreline in the time-honoured way.

SEND US YOUR SNAPS!

We'd love to follow your adventures using our Slow Travel Northumberland guide – why not send us your photos and stories via Twitter (@BradtGuides) and Instagram (@bradtguides) using the hashtag #northumberland. Alternatively, you can upload your photos directly to the gallery on the Northumberland destination page via our website (www.bradtguides.com).

ACCOMMODATION

Below I've listed a range of some of the special B&Bs, campsites, bunkhouses and small hotels I visited while researching this guide. They were selected on the basis of how comfortable and clean they were with a preference for interesting or historic buildings, 'green' credentials and use of local produce. I've selected a range of places to stay with most B&Bs, hotels and self-catering cottages falling within the average to above average price range (for a double room in one of the very good B&Bs included in this guide, you can expect to pay upwards of £80 for example). With the exception of a few hotels listed in Newcastle, I have not included any chain hotels. Where you see the ♿ symbol, the accommodation has step-free access into rooms and a wheelchair-accessible bathroom, but facilities vary so do check before booking. Also note that where you see the symbol next to holiday cottage companies, only certain properties have wheelchair access.

Go to 🖱 www.bradtguides.com/northumberlandsleeps for further details and my reviews of each place listed.

1 NEWCASTLE, GATESHEAD & THE TYNESIDE COAST

Jesmond (a residential suburb of Newcastle and connected to the city centre by the Metro) has one really good hotel (see below) and a number of mid-range and budget B&Bs strung along Osborne Road. Another affordable option, but in Newcastle's city centre is to hire a studio apartment with a kitchenette such as **Sleeperz Hotel** (15 Westgate Rd, NE1 1SE ☎ 0191 261 6171 🖱 www.sleeperz.com/Newcastle ♿) or **Roomzzz** (Clavering Pl, NE1 3NG ☎ 0203 504 5555 🖱 www.roomzzz.co.uk), both a stone's throw from Central Station.

A scattering of unremarkable hotels are found in the centre of Newcastle, particularly around Dean Street and on the quayside. A couple of the better ones on Newcastle's waterfront are listed below, as well as accommodation options at the coast.

Hotels

Hotel du Vin Allan House, City Rd, Newcastle NE1 2BE ☎ 0191 229 2200 🖱 www.hotelduvin.com ♿. Sister hotel to **Malmaison** (opposite the Millennium Bridge ☎ 0844 693 0658 🖱 www.malmaison.com ♿).

Jesmond Dene House Jesmond Dene Rd, Newcastle NE2 2EY ✆ 0191 212 3000
🖰 www.jesmonddenehouse.co.uk ♿

B&Bs
Martineau House 57 Front St, Tynemouth NE30 4BX ✆ 0191 257 9038
🖰 www.martineau-house.co.uk
Number 61 61 Front St, Tynemouth NE30 4BT ✆ 0191 257 3687 🖰 www.no61.co.uk

Self-catering
Southcliff Apartments 4 Southcliff, Whitley Bay NE26 2PB ✆ 0191 251 3121
🖰 www.southcliffapartments.co.uk

2 THE NORTHUMBERLAND COAST
B&Bs
The Anchorage 35 Woolmarket, Berwick-upon-Tweed TD15 1DH ✆ 01289 302424
🖰 www.theanchorageat35.co.uk
Courtyard Gardens 10 Prudhoe St, Alnwick NE66 1UW ✆ 01665 603393
🖰 www.courtyardgarden-alnwick.com
Greycroft Croft Pl, Alnwick NE66 1XU ✆ 01665 602127 🖰 www.greycroft.co.uk
Northumbrian Arms The Peth, West Thirston, Felton NE65 9EE ✆ 01670 787370
🖰 www.northumberlandarms-felton.co.uk
The Red Lion 22 Northumberland St, Alnmouth NE66 2RJ ✆ 01665 830584
🖰 www.redlionalnmouth.com
Roxbro House 5 Castle Terrace, Warkworth NE65 0UP ✆ 01665 711416
🖰 www.roxbrohouse.co.uk
St Cuthbert's House 192 Main St, Seahouses NE68 7UB ✆ 01665 720456
🖰 www.stcuthbertshouse.com ♿

Self-catering
Reputable holiday cottage companies in the area include **Grace Darling Holidays**
(✆ 01665 721332 🖰 www.gracedarlingholidays.com ♿), **Coastal Retreats**
Northumberland (✆ 0191 285 1272 🖰 www.coastalretreats.co.uk ♿), and **Outchester**
and Ross Farm Cottages, near Waren Mill (✆ 01668 213336 🖰 www.rosscottages.co.uk
♿). Also consider the cottages on **Springhill Farm** near Seahouses (opposite).
Hunting Hall Beal (near Lindisfarne) TD15 2TP ✆ 01289 388652 🖰 www.huntinghall.co.uk
(see advert in the third colour section)
Lindisfarne Bay Cottages West of Fenwick on the shores of Lindisfarne National Nature
Reserve (NNR) ✆ 07565 891795 🖰 www.lindisfarnebaycottages.co.uk ♿

Campsites, wigwams & bunkhouses

Considering how many beautiful bays are cut into Northumberland's shores, you'd think that somewhere there would be a secluded independent campsite with a divine view of the sea, but there's not really and camping in the sensitive dunes is strictly forbidden. If you're a member of the Camping and Caravanning Club there are a few options within easy reach of a beach including **Annstead Farm** (Beadnell NE67 5BT ✆ 01665 720387 🖥 www.annstead.co.uk). Non-members wishing to camp hereabouts should try **Beadnell Bay Camping and Caravanning Club Site** (Beadnell NE67 5BX ✆ 01665 720586 🖥 www.campingandcaravanningclub.co.uk/beadnellbay).

The Barn at Beal Beal Farm (close to Lindisfarne) TD15 2PB ✆ 01289 540044 🖥 www.barnatbeal.com

Joiners Shop Bunkhouse Chathill NE67 5ES ✆ 01665 589245 🖥 www.bunkhousenorthumberland.co.uk

Pot-a-Doodle Do Wigwam Village Scremerston, south of Berwick ✆ 01289 307107 🖥 www.northumbrianwigwams.com

Proctor's Stead Dunstan, near Craster NE66 3TF ✆ 01665 576613 🖥 www.proctorsstead.co.uk
Springhill Farm West of Seahouses NE68 7UR ✆ 01665 721820 🖥 www.springhill-farm.co.uk
Tewart Arms Cottage Camping & Caravan Site Near Chathill NE67 5JP ✆ 01665 589286

3 THE TYNE VALLEY & NORTH PENNINE FRINGES
Hotels
Angel Inn Main St, Corbridge NE45 5LA ✆ 01434 632119 🖥 www.theangelofcorbridge.com
Langley Castle Near Hexham NE47 5LU ✆ 01434 688888 🖥 www.langleycastle.com ♿

B&Bs
Ashcroft Guesthouse Lanty's Lonnen, Haltwhistle NE49 0DA ✆ 01434 320213 🖥 www.ashcroftguesthouse.co.uk
Fairshaw Rigg Lowgate, near Hexham NE46 2NW ✆ 01434 602630 🖥 www.fairshawrigg.co.uk
High Keenley Fell Allendale NE47 9NU ✆ 01434 618344, 07765 001005 🖥 www.highkeenleyfarm.co.uk ♿

Self-catering
Grindon Farm North Rd, near Haydon Bridge NE47 6NQ ✆ 01434 684273 🖥 www.grindonfarm.co.uk ♿
High Broadwood Hall Cottages Allendale NE47 9AF ✆ 01434 683458 🖥 www.highbroadwoodhallcottages.co.uk ♿

Campsites & youth hostels
Ninebanks YHA Mohope, West Allen Valley NE47 8DQ ✆ 01434 345288
🖰 www.ninebanks.org.uk
Rye Hill Farm Slaley, near Hexham, NE47 0AH ✆ 01434 673259 🖰 www.ryehillfarm.co.uk

4 HADRIAN'S WALL COUNTRY
Also consider accommodation options listed for *Chapter 3* (page 273).

B&Bs
Carraw B&B Carraw Farm, Humshaugh NE46 4DB ✆ 01434 689857 🖰 www.carraw.co.uk
🚻

Chapelburn House Gilsland CA8 2LY ✆ 016977 46595 🖰 www.chapelburn.com
Willowford Farm Gilsland CA8 7AA ✆ 016977 47962 🖰 www.willowford.co.uk 🚻

Campsites & youth hostels
There are a few campsites and bunkhouses within a few miles or less of Hadrian's Wall,
including **Winshields Farm** (NE47 7AN ✆ 01434 344243 🖰 www.winshields.co.uk),
Hadrian's Wall Camping (NE49 9PG, near Melkridge ✆ 01434 320495, 07947 003518
🖰 www.hadrianswallcampsite.co.uk), and **Herding Hill Farm** (Shield Hill, NE49 9NW
✆ 01434 320175 🖰 www.herdinghillfarm.co.uk). The **Once Brewed YHA** (Military Rd,
near Bardon Mill NE47 7AN ✆ 0845 371 9753 🖰 www.yha.org.uk) is close to the Wall but
it's not a great youth hostel in terms of comfort.

5 KIELDER TO MORPETH
Hotel
Battlesteads Hotel & Restaurant Wark NE48 3LS ✆ 01434 230209
🖰 www.battlesteads.com 🚻

B&Bs
Boat Farm Bellingham NE48 2AR ✆ 01434 220989 🖰 www.boatfarm.co.uk. Also has two
self-catering cottages.
Pheasant Inn Stannersburn, Kielder NE48 1DD ✆ 01434 240382 🖰 www.thepheasantinn.com
Shieldhall Wallington NE61 4AQ ✆ 01830 540387 🖰 www.shieldhallguesthouse.co.uk

Self-catering
The Hytte Bingfield (5 miles north of Corbridge) NE46 4HR ✆ 01434 672321
🖰 www.thehytte.com 🚻
Kielder Water Lodges Leaplish ✆ 01434 251000 🖰 www.nwl.co.uk/kielder 🚻.

The **Calvert Trust** near the Bull Crag Peninsula (page 169) also let out lodges which have been designed with those less mobile in mind including an exclusive treehouse hut, **Sky Den** (page 170).

Southlands Farm Cottages Gunnerton, south of Wark NE48 4EA ✆ 01434 681464
🖱 www.southlandsfarmcottages.co.uk

Campsites, wigwams & bunkhouses

Backcountry campers will be pleased to know that there are several places in remote parts of Kielder where you can pitch up for a night. For details of these wild spots (and bothies open to walkers), see page 170.

Demesne Farm Bellingham NE48 2BS ✆ 01434 220258 🖱 www.demesnefarmcampsite.co.uk
Kielder Campsite NE48 1EJ ✆ 01434 250291 🖱 www.kieldercampsite.co.uk
Boe Rigg Campsite & Bunkhouse Charlton, a couple of miles east of Bellingham NE48 1PE ✆ 01434 240970
Tarset Tor Bunkhouse Greystones, Lanehead, Tarset NE48 1NT ✆ 01434 240980
🖱 www.tarset-tor.co.uk
Wild Northumbrian Thorneyburn, Tarset NE48 1NA ✆ 01434 240902
🖱 www.wildnorthumbrian.co.uk

6 THE HILLS

Hotels

Collingwood Arms Main St, Cornhill-on-Tweed TD12 4UH ✆ 01890 882424
🖱 www.collingwoodarms.com ♿
No 1. Hotel 1 High St, Wooler NE71 6LD ✆ 01668 283089 🖱 www.no1highstreetwooler.co.uk

B&Bs

Alnham Farm & self-catering cottage Alnham, near Rothbury NE66 4TJ ✆ 01669 630210 🖱 www.alnhamfarm.co.uk
Chatton Park House Chatton NE66 5RA ✆ 01668 215507 🖱 www.chattonpark.com
Hillcrest House High St, Rothbury NE65 7TL ✆ 01669 621944 🖱 www.hillcrestbandb.co.uk
Ingram House Ingram, Breamish Valley NE66 4LT ✆ 01665 578906 🖱 www.ingram-house.com
Orchard House High St, Rothbury NE65 7TL ✆ 01669 620684
🖱 www.orchardhouserothbury.com
Tosson Tower Farm Great Tosson, near Rothbury NE65 7NW ✆ 01669 620228
🖱 www.tossontowerfarm.com

Self-catering

Cheviot Holiday Cottages Ingram NE66 4LT ✆ 01665 578236
⬙ www.cheviotholidaycottages.co.uk ♿
College Valley Estates cottages Hethpool, College Valley ✆ 016977 46777, 07974
797724 ⬙ www.college-valley.co.uk

Bunkhouses & camping barns

Barrowburn Camping Barn, Cottage and B&B Barrowburn, near Alwinton (Upper
Coquetdale) NE65 7BP ✆ 01669 621176 ⬙ www.barrowburn.com
Mounthooly Bunkhouse College Valley, Kirknewton NE71 6TX ✆ 01668 216358
⬙ www.college-valley.co.uk/Mounthooly.htm
Tomlinson's Café and Bunkhouse Bridge St, Rothbury NE65 7SF ✆ 01669 621979
⬙ www.tomlinsonsrothbury.co.uk

Wild camping & campsites

Camping in the hills is not permitted, but you are unlikely to be bothered if you're walking
with a bivvy bag or backpacking tent and stay above the tree line (1,500 feet or higher) and
out of farmland and Forestry Commission woodlands. There are very few official campsites
in the Cheviots except for a couple of caravan sites at Wooler, including **Highburn House
Country Holiday Park** (Wooler NE71 6EE ✆ 01668 281344 ⬙ www.highburn-house.
co.uk). You'll find more options in the Kielder and Bellingham area (page 275).

SEND US YOUR SNAPS!

We'd love to follow your adventures using our Slow Travel Northumberland guide – why not
send us your photos and stories via Twitter (@BradtGuides) and Instagram (@bradtguides)
using the hashtag #northumberland. Alternatively, you can upload your photos directly to the
gallery on the Northumberland destination page via our website (⬙ www.bradtguides.com).

INDEX

Entries in **bold** refer to major entries.